# AFRICA
# SOUTH OF THE SAHARA

# AFRICA
## SOUTH OF THE SAHARA

# A Resource and Curriculum Guide

Project Africa.

## Barry K. Beyer

Assistant Professor of History and Director
of Project Africa
Carnegie-Mellon University

# PREFACE

Americans used to refer to Africa as "the dark continent." To most it still is. In spite of the advances made in communications and education over the past generations, there is no other area of the world about which Americans know so little--and so inaccurately.

This is especially true of that part of Africa that lies south of the Sahara. Ask American high school students what this region is like. The typical reply will be that it is a hot, primitive, savage land where wild animals prowl the jungles, stalking and being stalked by black savages armed only with spears or poison darts. To most of them Africa south of the Sahara is a land of mystery, filled with witchdoctors, drums, straw huts and rich deposits of precious gems.

Ask American adults what this land is like. The most common reply will be that it is a large nation, covered by dense steamy jungles inhabited by black natives best noted for their ignorance, backwardness and savagery. To some it is a land of pagan barbarism, of superstition and vilence. To others it is only an untapped frontier rich in the resources needed by the modern world.

Even scholars with special interests in Africa south of the Sahara are hard put to generalize accurately about this vast and complex region. Scholarship in the subject is weak, spotty, specialized—and new, for the most part. The dynamics of change which mark the region contribute to the confusion, creating information gaps with such rapidity that much of what is written about the subject is sadly out of date before it comes off press.

It is not surprising, therefore, that the image most Americans have about Africa is characterized by ignorance, misinformation, confusion and even suspicion.

Nowhere is this more evident than in our schools. In most, the study of Africa south of the Sahara has been conspicuous by its absence. In the few where it is studied, the approach has been most superficial, consisting usually of a country-by-country sweep that does little more than catalog capitals, resources, major products, chief political leaders and selected geographic features. Rare, indeed, has been the school whose graduates have come to know this region and its peoples as they really are.

That is, until recently. Today there is vigorous interest in Africa south of the Sahara in educational circles as well as in other segments of public and private endeavor. Schools in increasing numbers are becoming much concerned about introducing into their curricula serious, up-to-date, in-depth studies of this region and its peoples. In fact, many schools are now initiating such studies.

Other educational agencies are also at work. Over a dozen social studies curriculum projects of national importance have been commissioned since 1967 to develop worthwhile programs of study as well as appropriate, new instructional materials on this region. Yet none of these have materials presently available, nor is it likely that any will appear in the immediate future.

Nevertheless, classroom teachers in many schools are faced with the necessity of "doing something" on Africa now—of teaching a unit or even a course, at best next year or next semester, but in many cases starting tomorrow. And they are not prepared to do so.

This guide is designed precisely for those who find themselves in this position. It is based on research conducted by Project Africa, a social studies curriculum research and development project at Carnegie-Mellon University. This project was created with the assistance and support of the U.S. Office of Education to design, develop and evaluate new instructional programs and materials for use in teaching about Africa south of the Sahara. The wide range of imaginative new materials it is developing are expected to be available by mid-1970 or 1971. Project Africa also attempted to identify what American students knew about this region and to locate commercially prepared materials that would be useful in teaching about it. A report on the results of this research was placed in the public domain during the Fall of 1968.

This *Resource and Curriculum Guide* is a much expanded and considerably revised version of that original Project Africa report. It consists of two parts. The first contains data and ideas that may serve as useful guidelines for the design of instructional programs on Africa south of the Sahara at virtually any grade level. It includes a detailed analysis of why a study of this region should be included in our social studies curriculum today and how it best may serve the goals of education for effective citizenship in a democratic society that exists in an ever-shrinking world. It also includes an analysis and summary of what American children think about Africa and what the experts recommend in the way of teaching about this region. It concludes with a statement of guidelines to follow in preparing a unit or course of study in keeping with the preceding information. Appended to these guidelines are several suggested instruments for the teacher to use in pre-testing his own students.

Part II is a guide to resources that can be used in planning for and conducting a classroom study of Africa. Most of this section is devoted to listing and describing briefly each of the more than 500 commercially prepared written, audio and visual media and materials available as of February 1969 for use in teaching about Africa. Suggestions for selecting and evaluating these are also included, as is a description of the flaws and weaknesses to which they are most prone. A special section singles out those which the author regards as having the greatest potential for classroom use. Lists of the addresses of publishers whose materials are cited herein and of the addresses of sources for other materials on Africa—including African diplomatic missions and tourist and information services in the United States and American organizations interested in Africa—conclude this section of the guide.

It is not the intent of this guide to describe *the* best way to organize the classroom study of Africa south of the Sahara. Given the diverse nature of the American school population and a variety of local educational needs and interests, there can be no single program that will meet the specific requirements of all. It *is* the intent of this guide to provide educators with information that will enable them to develop up-to-date, realistic, accurate programs of study on Africa south of the Sahara expressly suited to the needs, abilities and desires of their own student populations.

Selecting and adapting from the ideas and materials outlined here is, of course, the prerogative and the responsibility of the teacher or curriculum builder himself. However, it is our hope that this guide will be a useful reservoir for those faced with the need to teach something now about Africa; and that it will enable their students to engage in a meaningful study of Africa south of the Sahara, its history, peoples and culture.

I would like to express my deep appreciation to Professor E. Perry Hicks of the School of Education of the State University of New York at Buffalo, to Mrs. Barbara Hawk and Sven E. Hammer of the Department of History of Carnegie-Mellon University, and to Joseph Cirrincione of the School of Education of The Ohio State University for the contributions they have made to the preparation of this guide. A special and most sincere note of thanks goes to Miss Rita Pastorelli for her tireless efforts in typing and retyping the manuscript through its many revisions. Peter Stillman provided valuable assistance in preparing the final manuscript for publication and his efforts and support are very much appreciated. Most of all, my deepest gratitude goes to my wife Judy and our sons Steve and Gary for their assistance and support in this effort and especially for their understanding and tolerance of the confusion and long hours that attended the final stages of this effort. Without their help this guide could not have been prepared.

*Carnegie-Mellon University*                                          *Barry K. Beyer*
*February 1969*

# CONTENTS

# AFRICA
# SOUTH OF THE SAHARA

# PART I

# Teaching About
# Africa South of the Sahara

## TEACHING ABOUT AFRICA: WHY?

Our planet Earth is immense. Its huge land masses stand in marked contrast—and sometimes amazing similarity—to each other. Each is inhabited by a multitude of peoples having a rich diversity of cultures. All of these people and each of these land masses play an important part in this world. Being informed about them is the mark of an intelligent, effective citizen.

But becoming informed about so immense and diverse an area is not easy. One cannot come to grips with the world on the basis of an overall survey of the globe or its population as a whole. Rather, what is required is a much more detailed study of the specific parts of which it is comprised. Only by studying the various parts of the world can the whole world be adequately understood.

### Why Africa South of the Sahara?

One part of the world is Africa south of the Sahara. This is, of course, not a precisely defined geographical or cultural delimitation but merely a designation of convenience. Certainly it is true that Africa exists as a single continent. It is true, too, that the peoples both north and south of the Sahara have a history of economic and cultural contact going back at least 5000 years. Despite the formidable barrier of this desert, the links between these people have never been completely severed.

However, Africa is too large and too diverse to be understood with any degree of accuracy by a continent-wide survey. Such a survey, especially in the brief time available to it in our schools, would tend to obstruct rather than facilitate the development of useful insights about its lands and peoples. Given the great territorial extent, numerous cultural groups and other diverse features of this land mass, meaningful limits must be assumed. One such limit is the immense Sahara Desert, which stretches across this continent.

To the north lie a tier of nations predominantly Arab and Berber in population, culture and affiliation. In modern times their links with other Arab nations in the Middle East have proved stronger than those they possess with the nations south of the Sahara. They have always been part of a non-African world—Phoenecian, Greek, Roman, Arab, Turkish— in a sense that no sub-Saharan areas have been, at least until modern times. It is, indeed, virtually impossible to understand the history and culture of northern African in isolation from the parallel history and culture of the lands of the Middle East and Mediterranean Basin.

To the south of the Sahara are nations which must be regarded as different culturally, ethnographically and historically from those of the north. Africa south of the Sahara is obviously no clearly homogeneous culture unit. Yet it does possess at least two clearly definable traditions which mark it off from northern Africa and from the rest of the world as well. "Black Africa" is an amalgam of hundreds of more or less diverse peoples living between the Sudan and the southern tip of the continent. These peoples possess their own languages, forms of political and social organization, and life styles. But they are all "Black Africans" and, as such, distinct. "White Africa," the settler region of south and east-central Africa, is also clearly different from those parts of the continent inhabited by indigenous peoples, and, for that matter, from anywhere else in the world. They, too, have languages, customs, political and social institutions and a history of their own. Both black and white sub-Saharan Africa are closely interrelated. Together these comprise a unique region.

Thus, singling out Africa south of the Sahara as an object of special study is not as arbitrary as it might first appear. It is based on sound historical and cultural as well as pedagogical principles. It is, in fact, comparable to studying the United States as a single unit separate from the entire North American continent. A study of Africa south of the Sahara, like a study of the United States, or of southeast Asia, or any other unique region, can contribute to a better understanding of the earth and its peoples as a whole.

### Why Study Africa?

Determining why Africa* should be studied in a social studies program is the essential first step in planning for instruction. For this determines the more specific objectives to be set for the learning experiences which will constitute this study. And these, in turn, influence the organization of the course, the specific content to be included, and the instructional strategies and media to be employed. Only after a rationale and objectives have been delimited can a worthwhile study of Africa be planned.

---

*Africa* is used throughout the remaining pages of PART I to refer only to that part of Africa that is south of the Sahara.

It has been fashionable at times for schools to include the study of Africa, Asia, or other regions merely because they exist. These are worth knowing, the argument goes, for themselves alone; they are interesting, have contributed significantly to human achievement on this planet, and represent significant proportions of humanity. Ergo, educated citizens need to know something about them.[1]

This, however, is hardly a sufficient reason for studying anything; if this were the sole yardstick for determining what is to be included in a curriculum, everything that ever existed would be studied. In a changing world where what we know doubles every ten years or so, and where the time available for classroom learning is relatively short, more precise and delimiting selection criteria are needed.

To be practical about it, Africa is no different from any other body of content which could be studied in any classroom. Decisions about which content to put into a curriculum cannot be made without reference to the total educational program in which it is to be included. No body of content should be studied merely as an end in itself but should be viewed instead as a vehicle for accomplishing some objective more important than mere mastery of the subject matter itself. Content is used best to help students move *from* one place in terms of what they know and can do *toward* another.

If Africa's inclusion in a social studies curriculum cannot be viewed only as an end in itself. Then it must be seen as part of a larger whole, as one stage of a larger, ongoing process. It may be a topic within a unit or a unit within a course or even a course within a broader sequence of courses. Regardless of its place, it must always be viewed for what it really is—one of a number of bodies of content, each of which serves to accomplish certain unique objectives while leading students closer to the attainment of overall course and sequence objectives.

In planning a study of Africa, then, one must first determine why it should be a subject of study in an already overcrowded curriculum. How will the study of this region and its peoples help students to be better citizens? How will it help accomplish the objectives of the school's social studies programs? These are vital questions to be answered before any further planning or teaching can be attempted.

There are many reasons why the study of Africa can and should be included in a social studies curriculum today. The prime objective of every school in the United States—indeed, in any society—is to develop "good citizens." "Good citizenship" in a democratic society implies active and informed participation in that society. To do this well requires certain knowledge, skills and values. One kind of knowledge deemed most useful to good citizens is that about other peoples and cultures. Few schools, indeed, do not claim as a major educational objective learning about foreign peoples, how and why they live as they do, what they think or value and why, and what their problems are and why.

Some schools have included the study of Africa in such a program for many years. However, the way in which this study has been conducted reflects only a limited and frustratingly vague perception of the value of such study. It also reflects to a large degree the temper of the times in which the study was first introduced.

For instance, prior to 1950 most educators seem to have believed that the best reason for studying Africa and its peoples was that they were different—generally speaking, an exotic and primitive lot. Thus the study of this region, especially in elementary schools, came to be primarily a descriptive survey of strange peoples (pygmies or Watutsi) who live in strange ways in strange lands and climates. Today in many schools this still appears to be a major reason for studying Africa.[2]

During the late 1950's and especially around 1960 educators advanced another reason for studying about Africa. This was the claim, in essence, that it was in the interest of the United States to have a citizenry well informed about these peoples because it now had economic, military, and foreign aid commitments and interests throughout this region.[3] Africa, it was argued, was a significant part of the world and important in and of itself. For one thing, it was the second largest continent in the world. Its 300,000,000 people (few authorities agree on the exact figure) were important by sheer weight of numbers. It supplied much of the world's gold, most of its diamonds, and a considerable number of other valuable resources. Recent research suggested that it was the birthplace of man himself. In many ways it was and still is considered a frontier—and a strange and fascinating one at that.[4]

This view also held that Africa and its peoples ought to be studied too, for the role they were coming to play in world affairs. Its peoples had in just one decade attained independent status in a complicated twentieth century, subject to all the problems attendant upon such changes. They were demanding and securing a voice on the world stage.[5] Many saw Africa as a strategic battleground in the Cold War and believed its nations held the balance between peace and war.[6] If the United States was to survive in a world divided into rival political, military, and ideological camps, the argument went, its citizens must know more about Africa, a principal arena in the competition between these camps. Since Africa's newly independent nations constituted the largest single bloc of votes in the United Nations and thus could tip the balance of power at any time, a sympathetic understanding of its peoples and nations was imperative.[7] Africa's problems were the world's problems.

It is not surprising, therefore, that studies based on this rationale, especially at the secondary level, tended to emphasize Africa as a rich source of valuable mineral and forest products (world geography) and as an arena in which the destinies of imperial Europe were played out after 1500 (world history). It was studied most frequently in American history or problems of democracy courses as a source of problems that affected the world's international relations and United States foreign policy in the post World War II era. The course of study was basically descriptive.

Studies of Africa such as these rarely rise above the most superficial level. Generally they consist primarily of cataloguing and memorizing names and other facts—capital cities, important resources, the names of rivers and seaports, lists of important dates, and the names of leading political figures. As such they can hardly be a legitimate component of any educationally worthwhile social studies curriculum today.

Studying about other cultures and peoples, but especially about Africa, can and should serve purposes much more significant than "becoming informed." If anything, that should be only the first and most rudimentary goal of such study, for this new knowledge can be used to accomplish much more useful objectives:

### To reduce ethnocentrism and eliminate cultural biases and prejudices

One objective which the study of Africa can accomplish is an awareness of the realities of life in a multi-ethnic, multi-cultural world leading to an understanding of, and respect and tolerance for, other peoples and ways of life.[8]

4

Many scholars have commented on the value of this objective. Most people have what P.D. Hey has called "a dogmatic belief in the ascendency of one's own style of life."[9] This often leads them to make erroneous decisions in matters of public policy regarding people about whom they know very little. Too many people harbor deep-rooted, ethnocentric biases and prejudices born of ignorance, myth, or misinformation. And they act in accord with these biases. This is a most dangerous situation today.

The United States has been and is today deeply involved in Africa. It maintains there stations of strategic importance to both our space and defense programs. Thousands of American citizens live and work in this land. Events there can directly affect us. But the initiative has now shifted. Major decisions affecting the United States in Africa are now in African rather than American hands.

Knowing more about African nations and peoples is therefore extremely important today. This knowledge is needed to help develop tolerance and respect to promote friendly international relations, destroy mistaken notions that might lead to erroneous decisions in the future, and to help us understand the major forces at work in the world today—including those of urbanization, ideological conflicts and rising populations. It is also needed to extend students' experience so they can "think intelligently and without prejudice about other peoples."[10]

This is especially revelant in regard to Africa. About no other area of the world do both black and white Americans possess so little accurate information or have such deep-rooted false impressions and biases. No other peoples have been as maligned or dehumanized in the American mind as have black Africans. If American students of today are to be constructive citizens in the future, able to make intelligent, informed decisions free from misinformation and ethnocentric bias, they must know more and more accurately about Africa.[11] This takes on even greater importance when it is realized that almost one-tenth of the American people are direct descendants of black Africans.

Moreover, many educators believe that the futures of the United States and Africa are somehow linked together. Africa is a market for American investment capital, agriculture and industrial goods, and technical and educational services, and is a source of resources which Americans find useful or valuable. Yet, it has significant problems and needs expert help and financial support to solve them.[12] The United States must provide this assistance, if not because of humanitarian interest then at least because, as one author has noted, "We cannot rise without helping the African peoples to rise with us."[13]

Regardless of the specific evidence cited by those who support this idea, it must be obvious that there is considerable need to enlarge our perspective of other people; the study of Africa provides the opportunity to do this where it is needed the most.

### To lead to better understandings of our own culture

The study of information about a foreign culture can also facilitate a better awareness and understanding of our own way of life. It can provide an avenue by which students may come to grips with American culture, "to see ourselves as others see us," to gain a clearer perception of our roles in society in order to become more effective participants. The obvious implication is that by studying other cultures one can better perceive his own.[14]

5

Knowledge about Africa is crucial to the accomplishment of this and its related goals. By studying Africa one can examine alternative ways for ordering life and solving problems; this in turn can help set in perspective the way we order our lives and solve our problems. By understanding Africa we can better understand ourselves, our own way of life, and our relations to those who share it with us.

But the study of Africa can be a vehicle to accomplish other equally worthwhile goals in this area, too. The cultural and ancestoral roots of many Americans lie there. Many of these peoples have a deep desire to know more about their heritage and the ways it has contributed to the culture of America today. Some educators and scholars feel that an in-depth study of Africa would go far toward helping them develop a more positive self-image and achieve a sense of human dignity of which they have so long been deprived.[15]

At the same time this study would benefit white Americans, for it would help to replace their biases with knowledge, understanding and finally respect for black people as intelligent, creative, achieving human beings who share the same problems and aspirations that they do. The results of such study, it is frequently maintained, can only lead to better relations between blacks and whites, to a more realistic appreciation of one's own cultural heritage, and to an awakening of American culture to new possibilities for future development.

### To develop useful social science concepts

Selected concepts and generalizations from the social sciences rather than a catalog of factual data should be the prime knowledge objectives of any social studies learning experience. Data that is true today may not be true tomorrow. Moreover, the current knowledge explosion makes it impossible to learn all that is now known. The most useful learning, therefore, must stress that knowledge which is transferable and which will provide organizational structures around which one can assemble relevant data to give meaning to new situations.

It is more valuable to know, for example, the implications for many nations of being tied closely to a one-product economy than it is to be able to recite the number of tons of cocoa beans exported last year by a specific nation. It is certainly more meaningful in coming to grips with our world to know that a people's way of life is shaped largely by its culture, its level of technology, its contacts with other peoples and the nature of its habitat than it is to know that a certain people's dietary staple is blood from their cattle.

The study of Africa can be a most useful vehicle by which to develop generalizations and concepts such as these. It can, for example, be used to develop the nature and role of the "frame of reference" concept in making sense of human experience. Such study can help students realize that it is not possible to judge fairly the products, institutions or behaviors of other cultures in terms of our own values; and to recognize that intelligent decisions require unprejudiced and informed judgments and attitudes.[16]

By using techniques of comparative analysis the study of information about Africa can provide insight into such fundamental concepts as social change, economic development, sanctions, decision-making, role and status. It can provide an understanding of the nature of culture itself, its basic patterns and the process of culture change, just as it can contribute to an understanding of the fundamental similarities in human experience and institutions. It

6

may also provide opportunities for students to validate institutions, ideologies and structures based on American culture. Study of African family, legal, economic, and social systems can refine basic analytical concepts such as role, status, function, family and so on.[17] And these can then be used to make sense of other cultures—even our own; they will also be useful in interpreting and manipulating fundamental trends, processes and features of life today and in the future.

## To facilitate the study of controversial issues

Study of a local situation that is highly emotion-laden or infused with intense personal commitments or biases may be forbidden in the classroom. Or because it is not susceptible of simplified or dispassionate, objective treatment it may be avoided. But the same issue in a foreign setting is frequently much more open to rational and unrestricted analysis. The study of Africa offers an ideal vehicle for examining just such issues.

African nations and people have experienced and still do experience certain problems quite similar to some of those faced by Americans—problems of urban development, inter-group relations, governmental reforms, education, economic development, to list just a few. Study of these in their African settings may be undertaken with a minimum of personal in-volvement; there is thus the possibility that the essence of the problem and its alternative solutions may be much more readily identified and analyzed rationally. Such study may then yield insights that can be transferred to similar local problems and conditions and lead to much more rational perceptions than would otherwise be possible.

## To develop skills of intellectual inquiry

Finally, the study of other cultures is frequently used to help students refine their skills of learning how to learn by inquiry—an objective which is being increasingly emphasized in social studies instruction today. Since the world is characterized more by change than any-thing else, students need to develop those skills that will enable them to cope with change—skills of hypothesizing, validating hypotheses and generalizing. Subsumed under these skills are those of identifying, interpreting and organizing information, making comparisons, and detecting biases, unstated assumptions and unwarranted conclusions. Studying a variety of peoples and cultures other than one's own provides an excellent way to develop these skills, particularly those of comparison, analysis and synthesis. And as future changes occur these sharpened skills will be sorely needed.

Of all the content on other world cultures, that on Africa is best suited to facilitate this. Opportunities for honest student inquiry are unlimited here. There are significant knowledge gaps about this region; much of what is claimed as knowledge represents little more than speculation or conjecture. Even what is accepted as true today may not be several years hence. Scholarly research regularly turns up new data about this region and its peoples. Sometimes this adds to what is already known. Very often it challenges what is thought to be true. Not only does it help answer questions that already exist, but it also raises new ques-tions. As a body of knowledge it is by no means cut-and-dried. It is, rather, very fluid and dynamic, continually enlarging and changing.

Because of this, study of Africa offers unlimited opportunities for helping students sharpen their skills of intellectual inquiry. The numerous gaps in our knowledge of Africa's history, culture and life in general provide excellent opportunities for students to improve their learning skills. They may engage in historical, geographical or anthropological inquiries which involve collecting and interpreting relevant data, evaluating, analyzing, and synthesizing it into tentative explanations. This more than anything else will help them understand the complexities of knowledge and by so doing will illustrate the pitfalls of searching for the single solution to a problem or a single cause or result of a specific event. It will also help them learn how to learn.

## Summary

The study of Africa, then, can and should serve some purpose other than mere description. Africa should be included in a social studies curriculum because it is important in itself and to Americans. But, more importantly, it should be included because information about it can be used to help accomplish the broader goals of legitimate education today—including those of eradicating dogmatic ethnocentrism, helping students better understand themselves and their own culture, developing basic analytical social science concepts, clarifying controversial issues and refining the skills of intellectual inquiry.

There are, of course, other purposes which the study of Africa may well serve, too. These may vary considerably with each school or grade level, because instructional objectives are shaped in part by the ability and interest levels of the students for whom the instruction is intended as well as by the nature of the overall local educational program. Regardless what these objectives may finally be, however, they must be closely identified *before* any further plans can be made for teaching. For what and how one teaches is directly shaped by the objectives selected for instruction.

# TEACHING ABOUT AFRICA: WHAT AND HOW?

Selecting objectives, although the first step in planning for classroom instruction on Africa, cannot be done without some attention to other equally important facets of teaching about this region. Decisions about content and how best to organize its study are very closely related to decisions about objectives, and, in fact, are largely shaped by them. Making these decisions is the responsibility of the individual teacher or curriculum builder.

But teachers can turn to at least two sources for assistance in identifying, selecting, and organizing objectives and content for instruction about Africa. One is the accumulated advice of experts—what qualified scholars and educators declare ought to be taught. The other is the students themselves—what they already know or believe to be true.

## What the Students Say

Most American students know a great deal about Africa. Unfortunately, most of their knowledge amounts to nothing more than myth, superstition and hearsay, and is often the result of making hasty generalizations on the basis of very limited experience.

Identifying precisely what students do believe to be true about Africa, however, is a most useful step in determining what content to include in its study and how to organize it. Once this has been done a unit or course may be planned that reinforces what the students know with accuracy and that hits head-on what they think is true but really isn't.

Just what is it that American students know or think about Africa?

American elementary school students in the mid-1950's saw Africa in the following terms:

> Africans are black people who live in the Congo and are called natives. They don't wear clothes. They fish and hunt animals with spears and kill them, too. At the end of the hunt they feast and dance. There are lions and tigers in Africa.... African people love jewelry and wear long things in their ears. They sell ivory to the white man and get salt in exchange which they eat like candy. They live in huts and sleep on the floor. The white man taught them to read.[18]

There is no evidence that elementary school students today have views that are any different.

In fact, the evidence is that what they know a few years later is quite similar—and even more stereotyped. An October 1967 survey of 3259 seventh and twelfth graders in schools throughout the United States revealed that they viewed Africa as:

> ...a primitive, backward, underdeveloped land with no history—a hot, strange land of jungles and deserts, populated with wild animals, such as elephants, tigers, and snakes and by black naked savages, cannibals and pygmies. Missionaries and witch doctors vie for control of the natives, who live in villages, are prone to superstition and disease and hunt with spears and poison darts when not sitting in front of their huts beating on drums.[19]

This is hardly an accurate picture of the present African scene. Indeed, it is not an accurate picture of the African scene past or present!

The findings of this survey are quite relevant for educators who plan to teach about Africa. One instrument used to collect data was a perception test consisting essentially of a large world map and a deck of small cards. On each card was written a word or phrase. Some could best be used to describe Africa; some best described other regions of the world; and still others were quite neutral. There were, in all, ninety such terms:

## Terms

| | | | |
|---|---|---|---|
| *Strange | Palm Trees | Forests | Friend |
| Department Store | Trade | Freedom | Temples |
| *Villages | Daktari | *Deserts | *Tribe |
| Disease | Socialism | Hindu | Illiterate |
| Enemy | *Superstition | Bonanza | Mountains |
| *Snakes | Dictatorship | *Poison Darts | *Pygmies |
| Brave | Cowardly | Cities | Sculpture |
| Art | *Wild Animals | Oil | Underdeveloped |
| *Mineral Wealth | Folk Songs | *Drums | Grasslands |
| Houses | Plantations | Muslim | *Witch Doctors |
| Clean | *Tigers | Weak | Television |
| *Huts | Christian | Railroad | Dance |
| Automobiles | White | *Savages | Malnutrition |
| *Missionaries | Glorious Past | Schools | Powerful |
| Civilized | *Spears | Dirty | Religion |
| *Hot | Democracy | Cold | *Cannibals |
| Farms | Beautiful | Backward | Rich |
| Industry | *Black | Well-Educated | *Primitive |
| *Naked | Overpopulated | Fishing | Violence |
| Music | Lakes | Racial Problems | Cattle |
| Churches | Capitalism | *Elephants | Neutrality |
| No History | *Jungles | Buddhist | |
| Peace | Poor | *Natives | |

None of the students who took this survey were aware that it was designed to discover how they perceived Africa. Thus, the responses could not have been loaded in that direction. And the possibility of any item being arbitrarily associated with any of the seven regions on the map was only 1 in 7, or about 14 per cent. Yet thirty of the ninety terms were associated with Africa by more than 25 per cent of all the students. The following table lists these words and indicates what percentage of seventh graders and seniors associated them with Africa:

### Terms Associated with Africa

| By Seventh Graders | | By Twelfth Graders | |
|---|---|---|---|
| Wild Animals | 87.25 | Witch Doctors | 92.78 |
| Daktari | 85.32 | Wild Animals | 91.40 |
| Elephants | 84.32 | Drums | 91.00 |

---

*These words represented what the authors of the survey believed, on the basis of pre-tests and other research, were the typical American student's stereotype of Africa.

## Terms Associated with Africa (Continued)

| By Seventh Graders | | By Twelfth Graders | |
|---|---|---|---|
| Witch Doctors | 84.66 | Daktari | 90.69 |
| Jungles | 79.64 | Black | 89.45 |
| Tigers | 79.38 | Spears | 89.72 |
| Spears | 79.17 | Tribe | 88.19 |
| Tribe | 78.36 | Savages | 88.08 |
| Natives | 77.98 | Elephants | 86.65 |
| Poison Darts | 77.57 | Natives | 86.49 |
| Drums | 77.33 | Cannibals | 84.90 |
| Black | 76.94 | Pygmies | 84.11 |
| Savages | 75.90 | Poison Darts | 82.06 |
| Cannibals | 69.14 | Naked | 78.21 |
| Naked | 67.96 | Tigers | 77.66 |
| Pygmies | 64.94 | Jungles | 76.12 |
| Huts | 59.00 | Huts | 69.41 |
| Snakes | 55.36 | Primitive | 69.03 |
| Villages | 49.40 | Superstition | 68.82 |
| Superstition | 48.47 | Snakes | 56.35 |
| Disease | 46.46 | Missionaries | 52.50 |
| Primitive | 45.99 | Strange | 44.20 |
| Hot | 42.02 | Backward | 43.61 |
| Strange | 40.58 | Illiterate | 42.41 |
| Deserts | 35.80 | Villages | 41.39 |
| Dirty | 35.21 | Hot | 39.02 |
| Underdeveloped | 33.62 | Disease | 39.00 |
| Missionaries | 33.57 | No History | 38.15 |
| No History | 26.90 | Underdeveloped | 32.09 |
| Poor | 26.22 | Deserts | 29.27 |
| Backward | 25.06 | | |

After five years of schooling twelfth graders had a more stereotyped view of Africa! It was almost identical to that of the seventh graders. And it was just as inaccurate.

This suggests that not only do American students have distorted views of Africa and its peoples but that between seventh and twelfth grade they are learning *more misinformation* and learning it well. This hypothesis is further reinforced by other findings of this survey.

These students were also administered a multiple choice survey of knowledge about Africa. It was designed to measure what they know about six aspects of its geography and culture. These were:

*Physical Geography:* size, climates, landforms, major rivers, animal life, map locations.

*History Prior to European Penetration:* ancient civilizations; Sudanic forest and other early kingdoms; conditions at the time of European penetration.

*History of Europe in Africa:* exploration, the slave trade, colonialism, imperialism and independence.

*Indigenous society:* ethnic groups, language, religion, music, and the plastic arts.

*Economic development:* resources, products, infrastructure, and problems and present levels of development.

*Current affairs:* political leaders, major nations, foreign and domestic policies of various nations, and current events.

This survey consisted of 60 items. By guessing, students could have scored almost 15 correct answers. However, the mean number of correct responses by seventh graders was only 18.78 and by twelfth graders 25.11. Although twelfth graders knew more than seventh graders, neither mean was much above the level of chance.

Analysis of these results indicates that when students enter the seventh grade they have a very limited and superficial knowledge of Africa. Twelfth graders generally know more, but not much. Students at both grade levels knew most about economic development (the mean number of correct responses was 4.7 out of a possible 10) and physical geography (6.4 out of a possible 16). They knew less about society and culture, European imperialism and current affairs. Both knew almost nothing about Africa before European penetration.

These surveys also revealed that both knowledge and the tendency to stereotype were least strong in the West; both seem more evident in urban and suburban than in rural schools. Rural, mid-western seventh graders had the least pronounced stereotypes, while the most stereotyped images were held by suburban twelfth graders in the northeast.

Moreover, certain misconceptions about Africa were strongly held among both groups of students. Questions in which over 45 per cent of the students selected the same incorrect response were taken to indicate these misconceptions. They are listed here by giving the stem of the item, the response chosen by most of the students and in parentheses the correct response. For example, item 29 on the survey read:

> Timbuctu was important for:
> A   its diamond mines.
> B   its cool, refreshing climate.
> C   its university.
> D   its refinery.

Most students chose A rather than C. Therefore, this is listed below as: "Timbuctu was important for its diamond mines" (rather than for its university). The major misconceptions identified by this survey and the percentage of students holding each were:

| *Major Misconceptions* | *Seventh* | *Twelfth* |
|---|---|---|
| 1. Large wild animals—such as lions, elephants, and giraffes—would more likely be found deep in the African jungles (rather than roaming through African parks and game reserves). | 56.67% | — |
| 2. Most of Africa south of the Sahara is covered by jungles (rather than by grasslands). | 55.12% | 56.05% |

| Major Misconceptions | Seventh | Twelfth |
|---|---|---|
| 3. Traditional religions of Africa south of the Sahara stress a belief in the necessity of human sacrifice to please the gods when they are angry (rather than a belief in a Supreme Force or Being who created the universe). | 50.48% | 63.35% |
| 4. Timbuctu was important for its diamond mines (rather than for its university). | 48.45% | 63.48% |
| 5. When European explorers first came to Africa they found no towns or cities, only small villages of huts (rather than many strong kingdoms). | 46.67% | 55.54% |
| 6. In dollar value, the most important exports of Africa south of the Sahara are mineral products (rather than agricultural products). | 43.45% | 74.31% |
| 7. A chief product of the Congo (Kinshasa) is petroleum (rather than copper). | – | 51.89% |

In essence, this suggests that those students who are best informed about Africa are also most likely to be the most *misinformed* about it. On the total multiple choice instrument twelfth grade students scored better than seventh graders. Yet, of the five identical misconceptions held by both groups, every one was supported by a greater percentage of twelfth graders than of seventh graders. This seems to reinforce the results of the perception test, in which a greater percentage of seniors reported a particular stereotyped image than did seventh graders. It appears that in the secondary school years students are developing more misconceptions about Africa than they are learning accurate, up-to-date knowledge.

This is partially confirmed by other, though less precise, attempts to identify what American students know about Africa. A number of scholars on the basis of their own observations and experiences have identified certain stereotypes which they feel are held by many.[20] An analysis of their writings suggests that the following are the most commonly held:

1. Africa is a single nation.
2. Africa is covered either by a dense mass of steamy, hot, tropical jungle or by hot, sandy desert.
3. Africa has an unbearably hot, humid climate.
4. Africa is filled with wild animals.
5. The nations of Africa are rich in mineral deposits.
6. All Africans are alike—black, pagan, and ignorant.
7. Europeans in Africa came either as selfless missionaries or selfish searchers for slaves, gold or diamonds.
8. There are serious racial problems everywhere in Africa.
9. Africa is savage, barbaric and primitive—a land of superstition and violence.
10. Recreation in Africa consists primarily of tribal rites, dancing, feasts and drumming.
11. Africans create only grass skirts and drum music.
12. The major African occupations are hunting, fishing, and trading.

13. There is no industrialization in Africa.
14. All Africans live in small tribes and in huts.
15. There are no cities in Africa, only small villages.
16. Africa had no history before the arrival of Europeans.
17. Africa was isolated from civilization prior to its opening by the West.
18. African states are unified in their efforts and aspirations today.

Awareness of what today's students know or believe to be true about Africa can be useful in a number of ways to those planning instruction about this region.

First, it is obvious that students have very definite ideas about what Africa is like *before* they recieve any formal instruction about it. Most of these ideas are quite wrong but they exist nonetheless. They begin to develop early in life. Furthermore, they are brought by these students to their formal study of this region in school. Teachers must be aware of this, of the nature of these impressions, and of the knowledge that supports them, if classroom learning is to be effective.

Any teacher planning to deal with Africa ought to know as precisely as possible just how his students perceive Africa before instruction starts. For, if they hold erroneous impressions, then much of the teaching might well be directed toward destroying these once and for all. Additional effort might be directed toward reinforcing what they already know that is accurate. Teachers can then build on this to broaden and up date students' knowledge of this region and its peoples. If students aren't helped to unlearn the errors and myths to which they cling, all other study will be for naught.

Second, it appears that what students know and learn about Africa is more the result of out-of-school experience than of classroom instruction. Taking into account that schools until recently have taught very little or very superficially about the region, this is hardly surprising. For example, it is no wonder that students see Africa as a land without a history of its own; the surveys cited above clearly demonstrate that they know virtually nothing about this region prior to the arrival of the Europeans. Students simply have never heard of Zimbabwe, Benin or Kush or of Sonni Ali, Osei Tutu or Mansa Musa.

Students have numerous opportunities to secure misinformation or only partial information about this region, however. One such source is their parents. It is no wonder these students reflect the image they do when one considers how and what their parents and even grandparents learned about Africa:

> To our great grandfathers, Africa was little more than occasional tales of Livingston, slave raids and elephant ivory. To our grandfathers it was a vague awareness of brave missionaries and big game hunts. To our fathers, it was Tarzan stories and Humphrey Bogart movies.[21]

Other sources are even more significant. As Leonard Kenworthy has noted:

> The image of Africa in the minds of almost everyone has been blurred by the accounts of missionaries, by the excess of books on animals and safaris, by the stress in films and popular magazines on the bizarre and grotesque, and by the inaccuracies of textbooks written by authors who have little intimate, first-hand knowledge of that part of the world.[22]

Certainly the popular media do circulate a rather unbalanced picture of Africa. Much of how one perceives Africa may come primarily from movies, television and pulp literature. Thus, while students may never have heard of Africa's Sudanic kingdoms, they probably have heard of Tarzan, Jungle Jim, and King Solomon's mines. If a student has seen numerous drawings or animated cartoons of missionaries in the cooking pot with savages dancing around the fire, but has never seen a photograph of an African farmer or fisherman, he will not have a balanced image of the region. Gross distortions such as this may be entertaining but they don't do justice to Africa.

It should be pointed out, however, that the current content of some popular media presents a somewhat more accurate view than it has in the past. *Daktari* and *Cowboy in Africa* may very well still "o'er unhabitable downs, place elephants for want of towns," but at least people travel by jeep and plane rather than by swinging vine, and the Africans communicate in languages rather than by grunts and beating on hollow logs.

Teachers need to be aware that students learn about Africa from sources other than classroom study and that these sources have greater impact on them than does formal instruction. Students attend social studies class less than 180 of their 5000 waking hours each year. A one-week survey of Africa (or even one ten times as long) is not going to offset whatever erroneous impressions they develop as a result of out-of-class experiences.

To have any kind of useful impact at all, instruction about Africa must be in some depth and offered in different ways over several years. This will not, of course, change the image of Africa presented in the media. But at the very least it should help students see this image for what it is—an unbalanced distortion built up through centuries of ignorance and viewed through the culture-bound prejudices of Western eyes. At most it could even lead students to a more balanced perception of Africa based on accurate, up-to-date information and knowledge.

Finally, there is every reason to believe that most educators who have had no formal study of or no extended first-hand experience in Africa probably have a stereotyped image of Africa similar to that of their students. This means two things for teachers. First, they must be deliberately alert to avoid permitting their own cultural biases from coloring the way in which they direct learning about Africa. They must, for example, guard against allowing words which have come to represent erroneous stereotypes—primitive, native, backward, for example—slip into their teaching; they must avoid making invidious comparisons; and they must avoid any aura of paternalism in dealing with Africa.

Second, those teachers assigned to teach about Africa who have little knowledge of this region should take immediate steps to become better informed. This can be accomplished through summer school study at a local university or participation in special in-service workshops or NDEA institutes on Africa. For the teacher who is unable to take advantage of these avenues, individual reading and study are the best answer; an excellent point of departure is F. Seth Singleton and John Shingler's extremely readable, accurate and up-to-date *Africa in Perspective.**

---

*See a detailed description of this on p. 49 of Part II of this guide.

## What the Experts Say

A second source of information that may prove useful in planning a study of Africa is the accumulated suggestions of scholars and educationists knowledgeable about this subject. Unfortunately, however, only of few of them have addressed themselves in print to what ought to be taught about Africa in our schools.

This is due in considerable measure to a long-standing attitude of disinterest in the study of Africa in our elementary and secondary schools, an attitude that is shaped by two somewhat contradictory views. One is that Africa is a strange, exotic place full of wild, jungle animals, giants and pygmies, and that not even these things are worth a passing glance. The other is that there is *nothing* there worth studying at all:

> Africa is a land with little or no history. South of the Sahara the indigenous peoples cannot look back on any golden age, on any truly great civilization. Of the twenty-one outstanding cultures in world history listed by the English historian Toynbee, none is Negro. It has been truly said that 'Africa south of the Sahara has always been poor and powerless. The political and cultural emptiness of the African past is the key to any understanding of the continent's present problems.' ...The African produced no alphabets, no adequate system of numerals, no calendar or exact measurements, no currency, plough, or wheel. He built few towns and created nothing that could endure. Worst of all, he was a creature of fear and superstition helpless in the grip of magic and witchcraft.[23]
>
> The truth, of course, is that all of the most exciting and rewarding developments in Africa, even those of which the sole beneficiary is the native population, are the fruit of the brain, the conscience and the imagination of the European.[24]

Many scholars today would sharply disagree with the impressions created by statements such as these, if not with their very substance. For them, Africa is a land of considerable history, of "glorious" empires and civilizations whose peoples have made major contributions to the culture and history of the entire world. Such a division of scholarly opinion poses a serious dilemma for those planning instructional programs about Africa.

Several efforts have been made in recent years to assist teachers in resolving this dilemma. In 1965 Leonard Kenworthy published an outline which suggests twenty major topics on which an elementary or secondary grade study of Africa should focus; within each topic he further suggested specific facts or general knowledge that he believed a well-informed student should know about Africa at the conclusion of its study.

James W. King, a geographer, has also described in some detail certain geographic concepts or generalizations which should be stressed in a study of this region—including those related to landforms, climates, vegetation and soils, and wild game; suggestions are also offered regarding ideas of fundamental importance about African peoples, history, and economic and political development. In 1964, a University of Wisconsin historian, Philip D. Curtin, authored a pamphlet designed to acquaint teachers with interpretations and writings of significance about African history. The suggestions of all three of these scholars warrant careful scrutiny by those planning any classroom instruction about the region and its peoples.[25]

Although many others knowledgeable about Africa have definite ideas about how it should be studied and what ought to be included in such a study, these ideas have not been developed in any detail in the literature. Instead, there are only a few suggestions scattered widely throughout their writings. To a large degree they reinforce or supplement the suggestions put forward by the trio cited above. Taken together, what all of these scholars and educators recommend as major knowledge objectives in any up-to-date study of Africa may be briefly summarized as follows:

1. Africa is a land of great diversity—in peoples, cultures, geography and other aspects of life.
2. Africa presently is in the throes of rapid, far-reaching change; one of the most pressing problems there today is the breakdown of the traditional way of doing things.[26]
3. There is a very recent sense of history in Africa.
4. The history and geography of each African region are very closely interrelated.
5. There is constant competition for land between animal life and an increasing population.
6. Many of the problems that Africans face are also facing the United States, e.g., urbanization, education, social change.
7. Most inhabitants of tropical Africa live in perpetual poverty, hunger, disease and ignorance; the implications of these for future progress are enormous.
8. Africans have developed a passion for education.
9. Africa ia a good illustration of how different people perceive and react to their environments differently.
10. Africa is playing an increasingly significant role in the world today. Although it is one of the most illiterate, diseased, fragmented and underdeveloped of all the continents, it also has the world's largest underpopulated habitable areas and a wide variety and significant quantity of important natural resources.

Agreement is not complete on all topics suggested for inclusion in the study of Africa, however. While one African official, for example, suggests that Americans should be helped to realize the extent to which the Sahara serves as a barrier between North Africa and the nations in western Africa, an American scholar implies that this is a gross error and misconception.[27] Such direct contradictions, fortunately, seem more the exception than the rule.

Quite obviously, *what* and *how* one teaches about Africa depend to a large degree on the objectives he seeks to accomplish. If the aim is to study America's role in world affairs, Africa may be studied primarily in terms of its position as a third power bloc in international affairs. If, on the other hand, the aim is to examine a variety of cultures in various stages of development, then selected cultural groups in Africa might be chosen for study. Only when these objectives have been defined is it possible to organize or structure an effective study of Africa. The literature contains descriptions of several possible approaches to the study of African cultures.

Professor William B. Conroy feels that the study of non-Western peoples ought to be organized on the basis of cultural rather than physical regions because the traditional continental approach might lead the students to make erroneous generalizations about all peoples on the continent.[28] Within this framework, some educators have emphasized area studies in order to stress the unique features of each culture. Others favor a cross-cultural approach in order to focus, by comparison and contrast, on kinds of human behavior.[29] There is, however, little detailed discussion of either of these approaches in the literature, although one author did point out that a danger inherent in the comparative approach is an invidious "we-they" attitude.[30]

No one single way of organizing a study of Africa, or any non-Western culture for that matter, seems to predominate. In fact, at least five different structures have been suggested in some detail. William Clark Trow, for example, suggests that the study of a culture be built around the following questions:

1. How do they live? (anthropology)
2. What have they done? (history)
3. Where do they live? (geography)
4. What is their nature? (psychology)
5. How do they make a living? (economics)
6. How do they live together? (sociology)
7. How are they governed? (political science)
8. How do they express themselves esthetically? (the arts)
9. How do they take care of themselves? (health, education, welfare)[31]

Others such as Kenworthy and Stanley Miller suggest structures built around geography as the setting; the people and how they live, including their value systems, family structure and social organization; the creative arts; patterns of political and economic development; and selected current problems.[32] A third type of structure focuses on:

1. family structure
2. land tenure systems
3. child-rearing habits
4. assumptions underlying religious beliefs
5. physical environment[33]

Another approach has been to emphasize change in a variety of areas including intra-family relations, government, educational systems, the nature of economic activity, the broader social system, and the intellectual and esthetic aspects of society. A variation of this is to devote an approximately equal amount of time to:

1. the traditional culture in all its economic, social, political and technical aspects, in order to show the validity of the culture for its environment.
2. The impact of the West and the nature of change occasioned by industrialization and urbanization.
3. Selected problems of social change and/or political growth and/or economic development occasioned by the changing environment in which the culture exists.[34]

Although these approaches appear somewhat varied, they have much in common. Generally they focus on the geographic setting of the culture and on the people themselves—

their value systems, folklore, customs, and social structure, their economic activities and political system and problems or features unique to their own way of life. Many suggest giving considerable attention to the nature and impact of social change by contrasting the traditional with evolving cultural institutions. All seem to be highly selective in what they choose to include in their study of any individual culture.

In spite of there being no apparent general consensus as to how best to organize the study of a non-Western culture, agreement does exist on a number of considerations that ought to influence such a study. Most apparently feel that an essential aim should be to examine differences in cultures in such a way that our students can come to realize that people can act unlike us and still not be inferior or wrong; that people are affected in how they act by the kind of place in which they live, the mores of their culture, their history and the location of their country; and that because of these factors and others it is entirely reasonable and possible for them to act as they do.[35] In stating such a view regarding the study of Africa, Joseph Harris has declared:

> Students should be taught to understand African culture and history as dynamic entities with a past, present and future based on their own environment, goals and needs.[36]

Many scholars and educators who have written on this subject seem to agree with James McAree who noted in 1966, "The only fruitful way of studying the non-West is from the inside...."[37] A foreign culture cannot accurately be examined or evaluated through the values and assumptions of another culture. As anthropologist Paul Bohannan has written, "There is no more complete way to misunderstand a foreign civilization than to see it in terms of one's own civilization."[38] Thus, the following suggestions have been made:

1. Students must have "first-hand contact" with the culture being studied. Literature, folklore, art, music, and philosophy embody in concrete forms the values and ways of life of a culture and should be major items in its study.[39]
2. Opportunities for valid comparisons should be built into the course.
3. The contemporary period should be emphasized; the main object of study should be people as they now are.
4. The study should be as sympathetic as possible. Similarities of peoples should be emphasized in keeping with the Confucian observation that "the nature of men is always the same; it is their habits that separate them."[40]
5. The interdisciplinary approach should be used, since no single discipline can paint an adequate or complete picture of a culture.
6. The role of history should be to develop empathy, to awaken an interest in why the culture is as it is, and to "command a sense of respect for the power of the past."[41]

While there are a variety of ways in which the study of Africa can be organized, a number of pitfalls seem to plague instruction about it and other cultures as well. These should be avoided at all cost. Gilbert Wilson listed some of the more mistakes as:

1. Giving the impression that because Africans are of a different race than most Americans they are inferior.

2. Teaching complex ideas with too little knowledge.
3. Emphasizing facts for their own sake.
4. Assuming that students are not interested in other peoples.
5. Teaching "too much about too many places in too short a time with inadequate materials."[42]

Other authors suggest there are additional mistakes and pitfalls to be avoided as well:

6. Treating a region only as it relates to the United States.
7. Dating the history of a people from their first contact with Europe or the United States.
8. Emphasizing political history to the exclusion of other aspects.
9. Covering!
10. Generalizing too broadly.
11. Overemphasizing or exaggerating the unusual or exotic as typical.
12. Overemphasizing chronology and the distant past for itself alone.[43]

Another important aspect of classroom instruction about Africa concerns the materials to be used. However, little attention has been directed to date to the qualities requisite for effective materials. Where these have been touched on, only written materials have been discussed. Several authors suggest that a variety of written materials aside from texts can be used profitably. The range should include newspaper and magazine articles, interpretative and analytical reports, essays or articles, documents and other primary source materials, and literature—novels, autobiographies, poems and the like.[44] The entire gamut of audio and visual media should also be utilized. Moreover, regardless of the types of media used, they must be "readable," inexpensive, and based on modern scholarship.

**Summary**

Analysis of what students know about Africa prior to beginning its study can provide clues to the objectives, content and structures that could be woven into a useful study of this region and its peoples. Examination of the pertinent comments of qualified scholars and educationists may provide suggestions about these, too, as well as about possible ways in which such a study might be organized. Certain pitfalls to be avoided may be gleaned from both of these sources.

Reliance on only one of these sources will obviously not be enough to plan the most worthwhile study of Africa. The literature on teaching about this region is relatively meager in quantity and spotty in quality. Much more needs to be written. On the other hand, reference only to what the students know or think they know about Africa does not indicate what they *ought* to know. But sources must be consulted if a study of Africa is to be effective and worthwhile.

20

# TEACHING ABOUT AFRICA: GUIDELINES FOR PLANNING

The study of Africa in our schools should not be a haphazard affair. Even though there has been an inadequate amount of published attention to date regarding what specifically ought to be taught about Africa in our schools, there do exist some useful suggestions on these points. When these are examined in the light of what students know or think is true about Africa and the possible ways its study might well fit into a social studies program, some specific guidelines for planning instruction about this region do emerge.

## Guidelines for Planning the Study of Africa*

### Objectives

The primary objectives of a study of this region and its peoples should be (1) to acquire information and insights that will make contemporary and evolving Africa intelligible; and (2) to facilitate the development of knowledge, skill and affective objectives of the course and sequence of courses of which its study is a part. These latter should include the development of valid generalizations about the how's and why's of human behavior, of concepts that will be useful tools in organizing future information in a meaningful way, of the intellectual skills of inquiry, and of attitudes and values supportive of these objectives.

Such a study must be planned in relation to the objectives set for the study of each other region or peoples included in the same course or sequence. If, for example, one overall objective of the sequence or course is to know that *all people* have to deal with similar basic problems, such as providing food, clothing, shelter, security, and opportunities for self-expression, then the study of Africa must be designed to lead to the understanding that its peoples all deal with these kinds of problems. If another overall course objective is to know that any people's way of living is shaped by its perception of the environment, its culture, and its level of technology, then the study of Africa must develop this understanding about its peoples.

Emphasis on such objectives does not mean that facts are unimportant—that they should be ignored altogether. But it does mean that the study of this region must do more than inform students about another region of the world. If it were to accomplish only that, it would amount to little more than a travelog or catalog of facts, dates, places, and products.

The study of Africa should aim to help students develop concepts and generalizations that will be useful in explaining future experience—such concepts as power, decision-making, role, sanctions, scarcity, for example. By acquainting students with the people of Africa, their value systems, aspirations, and creative endeavors, such a study will enable them to grasp the principles that motivate and characterize human behavior in general. And it will help develop an understanding of the nature, roots, and implications of the basic problems and issues that

---

*Some of the suggestions included here originally appeared in the author's article "Uncovering Africa," in *Social Education,* May 1968. pp. 440-444.

confronted all individuals, groups and nations in the past, confront them today, and will confront them in the future.

Furthermore, the skills of distinguishing fact from opinion, making inferences from data, making analytical comparisons, hypothesizing, validating hypotheses and generalizing can be readily developed in the process of conducting this study. So, too, can attitudes such as empathy, a respect for evidence, objectivity and suspended judgement, and tolerance. All of these appear essential for coping successfully with today's world.

The study of Africa, then, must be considered as a means for accomplishing a multitude of learning objectives as well as an object of learning itself. Awareness of this is fundamental to the development of an educationally worthwhile program of study about this region in the social studies curriculum. *Planning for teaching must commence with learning objectives—not just content alone.*

### Content

Content is important, of course, especially as a vehicle for accomplishing the objectives of the entire learning experience. For the curriculum builder the selection of appropriate content is a major task. Clearly, the content needed to fulfill the objectives above must be such that it eliminates the stereotypes and incorrect impressions that now exist about Africa and its peoples, provides information that will make Africa and Africans of today and tomorrow intelligible, and serves as an avenue to the achievement of the broader objectives of the entire learning experience. In order to do this:

1. The study of Africa must be selective. It must avoid being a sweeping survey of the entire region. A common dictionary definition of the verb "to cover" is "to hide or obscure from view or knowledge." Any attempt to cover all of Africa will do just that; students will most likely emerge from such an exercise less knowledgeable than when they started.

   At the same time, the dangers of hopscotching across the continent by studying in some detail just one region, one tribe, or one colonial administration, must also be recognized. So, too, must the dangers of overemphasizing the study of the exotic or unusual. A study of Pygmies in the elementary grades without any attention to other peoples of Africa, for example, has given many students the lasting impression that *all* Africans are unusually short, black people barely subsisting in tropical rainforests. Sweeping generalizations based on scant evidence should be avoided.

   Africa should be viewed as a world within itself consisting of a multiplicity of features. Instead of studying only one example of a particular feature, several should be studied in depth. Students should then generalize about these, noting commonalities and differences, exploring how and why these exist, and examining current changes and trends which affect them. In this way they will be able to develop valid understandings about this region and its peoples that can then be considered tentative hypotheses and used as tools to investigate other world regions in the quest for valid generalizations about people and their cultures.

2. The primary emphasis should be on contemporary Africa—what it is today and what it is becoming. This is not to say that the study of the region's past or of the political,

social, economic, and geographical forces which have been at work over the centuries should be entirely omitted. Far from it.

Considerable attention must be paid to Africa prior to the arrival of Europeans. The major cultural inventions or accomplishments of the Africans—such as the development of highly centralized political systems, elaborate religious systems and long-distance trade—should be emphasized. So should the problems involved in delimiting their details. The lack of written records is a serious handicap to the study of this period; yet the research of anthropologists, archeologists and other social scientists provides valuable clues to reconstructing knowledge about it.

Other events and forces should be examined, too—especially the rise of political kingdoms and empires, the Moslem penetration, the slave trade, European penetration and the consequent rise of nationalism that culminated in independence and nation-building. Knowledge of these is absolutely essential to an understanding of the route by which Africans came to be where they are, as they are, today. Yet care must be taken not to overemphasize these events for themselves alone, nor to get bogged down in a detailed chronological narrative of the past.

3. Africa must be studied from the inside, in its own terms. No culture or region can be accurately understood or analyzed through the values and assumptions of another culture.

A study of this region must provide the learner first-hand contact with it. The art, literature, music, and folklore of a people should be the prime media of such study because these reflect their fundamental mores, values and beliefs—the very essence of their culture. This study, furthermore, should be as sympathetic as possible; it should emphasize the similarities in the nature of men as well as the differences in their habits. It should not make invidious comparisons. Neither should it examine Africa only as it relates to American history or development.

4. The major focus of the study of this region should be on people. Too many studies of world regions or cultures overemphasize physical and/or institutional features and pay scant attention to the most fundamental element in any area—human beings. A worthwhile study of any region must essentially be an examination of the people in it; certainly current and future world problems and trends cannot be made intelligible without considerable understanding of the people who figure in the events that reflect these problems and trends.

Instead of generalizing about Africans as a vague group or of studying a single group such as the Bushmen, Tutsi or Pygmies, emphasis should be placed on an examination of several different tribes and ethnic groups which *in toto* represent the major features of African culture. Attention must be given to those of European, Asiatic and mixed descent as well as to peoples commonly considered more typically African. Those selected for study should exemplify different but quite prevalent kinship patterns, economic systems, political systems, types of social organization, and habitats; the study should involve students in identifying the basic features of African culture, in generalizing about what Africans have in common, in exploring how and why they came to be the way they are today, and in examining the current changes now underway and the impact of these changes on individuals.

Not all of this can be done in any one unit or course at any single grade level. Instead, it may be most useful in the early elementary grades to focus primarily on eliminating stereotypes about the peoples of Africa by studying what they are like, and how and where they live today. Later elementary grade and junior high school study can reinforce and broaden the ideas developed in the initial study; and the secondary grades could then emphasize more sophisticated aspects of Africa, such as its historical, political and economic growth and development, and contemporary problems.

## Structure

The study of Africa can be organized variously. The traditional secondary school approach is to examine the land, then the people, and finally their history, economic development and current problems. Elementary grade studies usually focus on the habitat of a people and then on a small family, group or community; this is usually intended to illustrate what life is like in the region, nation, occupational group or climate region under consideration. These are useful approaches.

But other structures can be used, too. A study of Africa whose primary objective is to dispel erroneous stereotypes might well categorize these under the headings of geography, history, and so on. Then the teacher can design learning activities that will shatter erroneous notions and substitute accurate impressions. If students apparently think all Africans are either under four feet or over seven feet in height and live in grass huts in the jungle, then likely subjects for study would be the Hausa of northern Nigeria, or the Masai of East Africa, or the Bantu of South Africa—preferably all three. If it is evident that little is known about Africa before the European penetration, then a study of the exploits of Stanley, Livingston and their compatriots should be replaced by a study of Africa's ancient kingdoms such as Ghana, Mali, Songhai, Kush, Axum and Zimbabwe.

A more sophisticated structure permits the accomplishment of this objective while providing students an opportunity to develop their skills of intellectual inquiry. In such a structure the students are put through activities or units that require them to identify a problem for investigation, develop possible solutions, gather and analyze data relevant to their hypotheses, and draw conclusions about their inquiry. An entire course or unit might be organin this way:

| | |
|---|---|
| POSING A PROBLEM FOR STUDY | *Introductory unit:* Students articulate what they think Africa is like* and then examine a set of pictures of modern Africa that challenges their stereotypes. From this can emerge a problem: "How can this be?" |
| HYPOTHESIZING | Having stated a problem, tentative solutions are needed. Students might suggest that the materials are "loaded" or inaccurate; perhaps they will suggest that certain things have |

---

*One way to do this would be to have the students report what the word "Africa" suggests to them. Several instruments for doing this in a more elaborate way may be found in the Appendix to Part I.

happened to alter Africa today. A statement of what these things are could serve as a hypothesis for further study.

| | |
|---|---|
| GATHERING AND ANALYZING DATA | *Major units:* Several weeks could be devoted to gathering from books, films, records and other media data relevant to the hypothesis advanced in the introduction. Students could hear formal presentations, engage in small-group discussion and do independent research to gather, analyze, interpret and evaluate this data. |
| CONCLUDING | *Concluding unit:* Here the students can bring together the results of their inquiry and can determine how correct their hypotheses are. Students might do this by writing reports, creating a series of pictures that would more accurately portray life in Africa, or making radio or TV programs. The intellectual activity of pulling the data together into a meaningful whole can take many forms. |

Weekly units could also be organized along these same lines of inquiry. For example, students may have hypothesized that all Africans are foragers who live in grass huts. To examine this they might be put in touch with data about a variety of peoples of Africa. A week's inquiry unit on the Hausa might be as follows:

| | |
|---|---|
| POSING A PROBLEM FOR INVESTIGA-TION | *Introduction (1 day):* Students could examine pictures of Hausa wearing western and traditional dress engaged in a variety of activities and postulate their major characteristics as a group. They might say they are Moslem, farmers, merchants, illiterate, etc. |
| GATHERING AND ANALYZING DATA | *Research (3 days):* They could then study some folktales, filmstrips, movies, travelers' diaries, anthropological studies or even Nigerian newspapers to see if their hypotheses are correct. |
| CONCLUDING | *Conclusion (1 day):* The students could evaluate their hypothesis by writing a report on what the Hausa are like. This would serve as a foil against which they could study another group of Africans such as the Amhara, Ganda, or Afrikaners. |

## Methods

The instructional strategies to be employed in a study of Africa designed in accordance with these guidelines should be multidisciplinary and inquiry-oriented. The tools and analytical concepts of all of the social and behavioral sciences must be employed to make this region and its peoples come alive with meaning and relevance.

Teaching for conceptual objectives rather than for mere memorization of facts implies the use of inquiry teaching strategies. Concepts, generalizations and skills cannot be given to anyone. They are, rather, the product of active and repeated intellectual interaction with content or data. The search for meaning and significance requires that this content be used—manipulated, pulled apart, examined and reassembled in new ways. And this is something that the learner, not the teacher, does. Students must engage in the techniques of inquiry in order to learn them. They must practice hypothesizing, separating fact from opinion, detecting biases, identifying relationships, making comparisons, extrapolating, and performing the numerous other intellectual operations which constitute inquiry.

Above all, the learner must have opportunities to generalize, to make his experiences mean something. It is essential that he be required to wrap up his inquiry in order to relate what he has learned to his previous knowledge and to provide a springboard for further learning. Those generalizations that are developed must be considered merely as tentative conclusions, subject to their further testing as tools to investigate other world regions in the quest for a better understanding of people, cultures, and change.

Solid grounding in these techniques will lead not only to the development of more meaningful conceptual knowledge but also to knowledge that is retained longer, has greater transferability and is more relevant to the learner.

## Materials

In order for a study of Africa to be effective, learning materials must be varied, readily accessible, based on the best available scholarship, and at least partially structured.

The most essential feature of these materials is that they present information, data or evidence *without* interpreting it or explaining its significance; these tasks must be left to the learner. Interpretive accounts may occasionally be useful for checking conclusions, initiating the study of a problem, or as a device for developing a wariness of the written word as the absolute truth; but unannotated descriptions, narratives, and presentations in the form of original sources, documents, diaries, letters, journals, statistics, and similar materials are the primary requisite for the type of study suggested here.

Probably the most important criterion for selecting written materials—assuming their scholarship, currency, and relevance—is that they be readable. They must also be of a level of difficulty commensurate with the abilities of the learners, and they must be legible. Reproduction of documents or first-hand accounts in their original style, language or print is not essential to effective learning unless somehow these affect their meaning or use; where such reproduction interferes with effective learning, these materials should be rewritten in a style and vocabulary more easily understood by those who will use them.

Written materials must not be the only instructional medium used, however. Filmstrips, slides, 16 mm films, 8 mm film loops, tapes, records, overhead transparencies, maps of all types, still pictures, art objects—all of these must be used in studying this region. Only by these means will the students become immersed in the subject. The multi-media approach to the study of Africa is essential in order to provide variety, to individualize instruction, to secure a closer approximation of reality, and to involve students more actively in the learning process.[45]

Furthermore, these audio and visual media must be used as an integral part of the learning experience, not merely as supplementary or enrichment activities or as rewards for good behavior. They should serve as the major media for instruction; they can be applied to good advantage in large groups or normal class situations; and some are admirably suited for independent and small group study. A range of these materials should be used. Some should be employed to initiate inquiry, others to present data for analysis, and still others to provide foils for final evaluation. This is important for three reasons. First, it adds variety essential to motivating and maintaining student interest. Second, it gets the students involved—it makes it possible for them to develop empathy with the subject being studied—and this, after all, is a primary objective of teaching about Africa or any other region.

Finally, certain media are best suited for certain tasks and not for others; for example, transparencies with overlays are best suited for identifying and analyzing potential relationships among things which can be depicted graphically, while films are most useful in presenting information in which movement or sequence is crucial. With these media too there should be little or no accompanying interpretive narration, commentary or captions. The responsibility of giving meaning to data belongs to the learner.

These materials should also be internally structured to varying degrees. Filmstrips cannot be a random selection of pictures if a specific knowledge objective is being sought; written materials should not consist of unrelated information if students are to develop a specific generalization. Material must be carefully sequenced, for by means of the internal structure of the materials the teacher or curriculum designer can provide the guidance needed by the learner inexperienced in inquiry. Obviously, those more experienced will be able to deal successfully with materials that are only loosely structured, if at all.

Many social studies teachers apparently share a belief that there are no instructional materials now available that can be used as suggested here. Fortunately, this is not true. In fact, a number of existing collections of primary sources, uncaptioned filmstrips, single-concept films, slide-record sets, overhead projections, tapes and records can be used with a minimum of adaptations for inquiry learning about Africa. Of course, many more traditional materials—paperback texts, captioned filmstrips and narrated films—can also be useful. In some instances, it may even be desirable to create materials especially suited to a local program of study.

## Summary

Many factors must be considered in using these guidelines. Among the most important of these are the interests and abilities of the students for whom the study is being planned. Generally, elementary school students have the curiosity and drive to want to know considerably more about Africans—and other peoples—than any traditional "Peoples of the Forest" study permits.

Often, students enrolled in secondary school courses where Africa is most likely to be studied are not there by choice. In many schools it is common for slower students to be assigned such courses as world geography, while the college-bound are channeled into the study of European history. This must be taken into account in planning a study of Africa, particularly as it applies to designing motivational activities, selecting content, and structuring specific learning activities.

Another factor should be considered, too. This is the very nature of Africa south of the Sahara. It consists of over three dozen independent nation-states in which live some eight hundred distinct ethnic groups, each speaking a tongue and observing a set of customs and laws of its own. The various facets of its political, economic, cultural, and social development and life are almost unlimited. Yet, the time available in most schools for the study of this region may vary from only two to a dozen weeks. Thus, it is obvious that classroom study of this region cannot and should not attempt to cover everything known about it.

Nor should it be taught with an atmosphere of absolute finality. A great deal is as yet unknown about this region and its peoples, and even that which is accepted as true today may have to be discarded in the face of future findings. Teaching must therefore be in somewhat tentative terms. It should strongly suggest the limitations of our knowledge. It should be open-ended and suggestive; a spirit of inquiry—of questioning and of critical investigation—should be reflected and fostered.

The guidelines suggested here focus on people, contemporary culture, and individual and group problems relevant to life in the latter part of the twentieth century. They suggest an inquiry-oriented, multi-disciplinary, in-depth study of topics selected because of their intrinsic worth as knowledge as well as their utility in serving as a vehicle for the development of the broader cognitive and affective objectives of the total program of which the study of Africa is but one part.

Certainly there is more than one way in which the study of Africa can be structured to accomplish the objectives of the social studies. These guidelines represent only one approach. Nevertheless, perhaps they—and the other ideas found elsewhere in this guide—will be of use to those currently faced with the task of planning a program of study about this region and its peoples for inclusion in their social studies curricula.

# APPENDIX TO PART I

Included here are two surveys which may be used to determine how students perceive Africa and what they know about it *before* they start studying about it. Spirit masters of these may be duplicated on any type of automatic copier.

Results may be tabulated by the teacher, by several students under his direction, or by the entire class. Once the students' image of Africa has been identified, or their degree of knowledge determined, a program of study can be devised to develop a more accurate image, to correct false information and to build a more balanced understanding of Africa.

Administration of these surveys *after* Africa has been studied may serve as a very useful evaluation of the degree to which the objectives of course were realized.

Answers to

AFRICA SOUTH OF THE SAHARA

| Geography | Economic Development | Society and Arts | History | People |
|---|---|---|---|---|
| 1. 2 | 16. 1 | 26. 3 | 36. 3 | 51. 3 |
| 2. 3 | 17. 3 | 27. 2 | 37. 4 | 52. 1 |
| 3. 3 | 18. 1 | 28. 1 | 38. 1 | 53. 4 |
| 4. 4 | 19. 2 | 29. 4 | 39. 3 | 54. 6 |
| 5. 1 | 20. 4 | 30. 4 | 40. 1 | 55. 5 |
| 6. 3 | 21. 2 | 31. 1 | 41. 1 | |
| 7. 1 | 22. 1 | 32. 4 | 42. 3 | |
| 8. 2 | 23. 3 | 33. 2 | 43. 1 | |
| 9. 4 | 24. 4 | 34. 3 | 44. 2 | Terms |
| 10. 2 | 25. 1 | 35. 2 | 45. 3 | |
| 11. 1 | | | 46. 2 | 56. 4 |
| 12. 4 | | | 47. 4 | 57. 3 |
| 13. 3 | | | 48. 1 | 58. 6 |
| 14. 1 | | | 49. 4 | 59. 1 |
| 15. 2 | | | 50. 3 | 60. 5 |

# ANSWER SHEET
## AFRICA SOUTH OF THE SAHARA

Name _____    Date _____

Class Period _____

| | | | | |
|---|---|---|---|---|
| 1. ____ | 16. ____ | 26. ____ | 36. ____ | 51. ____ |
| 2. ____ | 17. ____ | 27. ____ | 37. ____ | 52. ____ |
| 3. ____ | 18. ____ | 28. ____ | 38. ____ | 53. ____ |
| 4. ____ | 19. ____ | 29. ____ | 39. ____ | 54. ____ |
| 5. ____ | 20. ____ | 30. ____ | 40. ____ | 55. ____ |
| 6. ____ | 21. ____ | 31. ____ | 41. ____ | |
| 7. ____ | 22. ____ | 32. ____ | 42. ____ | |
| 8. ____ | 23. ____ | 33. ____ | 43. ____ | |
| 9. ____ | 24. ____ | 34. ____ | 44. ____ | |
| 10. ____ | 25. ____ | 35. ____ | 45. ____ | |
| 11. ____ | | | 46. ____ | 56. ____ |
| 12. ____ | | | 47. ____ | 57. ____ |
| 13. ____ | | | 48. ____ | 58. ____ |
| 14. ____ | | | 49. ____ | 59. ____ |
| 15. ____ | | | 50. ____ | 60. ____ |

# WORLD REGIONS PERCEPTION SURVEY

DIRECTIONS: Place a check (√) in the space under the region or regions which you believe can best be described today by each of the following terms or phrases. (The same term may be used to describe more than one region):

| Terms | A<br>Africa South<br>of the Sahara | B<br>Asia | C<br>Europe | D<br>Middle<br>East | E<br>North<br>America | F<br>Russia | G<br>South<br>America |
|---|---|---|---|---|---|---|---|
| 1. Strange | | | | | | | |
| 2. Department Store | | | | | | | |
| 3. Villages | | | | | | | |
| 4. Disease | | | | | | | |
| 5. Enemy | | | | | | | |
| 6. Snakes | | | | | | | |
| 7. Brave | | | | | | | |
| 8. Art | | | | | | | |
| 9. Mineral Wealth | | | | | | | |
| 10. Houses | | | | | | | |
| 11. Clean | | | | | | | |
| 12. Huts | | | | | | | |
| 13. Automobiles | | | | | | | |
| 14. Missionaries | | | | | | | |
| 15. Civilized | | | | | | | |
| 16. Hot | | | | | | | |
| 17. Farms | | | | | | | |
| 18. Industry | | | | | | | |
| 19. Naked | | | | | | | |
| 20. Music | | | | | | | |
| 21. Churches | | | | | | | |
| 22. No History | | | | | | | |
| 23. Peace | | | | | | | |
| 24. Palm Trees | | | | | | | |
| 25. Trade | | | | | | | |
| 26. Daktari | | | | | | | |
| 27. Socialism | | | | | | | |
| 28. Superstition | | | | | | | |
| 29. Dictatorship | | | | | | | |
| 30. Cowardly | | | | | | | |
| 31. Wild Animals | | | | | | | |
| 32. Folk Songs | | | | | | | |
| 33. Plantations | | | | | | | |
| 34. Tigers | | | | | | | |
| 35. Christian | | | | | | | |
| 36. White | | | | | | | |
| 37. Glorious Past | | | | | | | |
| 38. Spears | | | | | | | |
| 39. Democracy | | | | | | | |
| 40. Beautiful | | | | | | | |

| Terms | A<br>Africa South<br>of the Sahara | B<br>Asia | C<br>Europe | D<br>Middle<br>East | E<br>North<br>America | F<br>Russia | G<br>South<br>America |
|---|---|---|---|---|---|---|---|
| 41. Black | | | | | | | |
| 42. Overpopulated | | | | | | | |
| 43. Lakes | | | | | | | |
| 44. Capitalism | | | | | | | |
| 45. Jungles | | | | | | | |
| 46. Poor | | | | | | | |
| 47. Forests | | | | | | | |
| 48. Freedom | | | | | | | |
| 49. Deserts | | | | | | | |
| 50. Hindu | | | | | | | |
| 51. Bonanza | | | | | | | |
| 52. Poison Darts | | | | | | | |
| 53. Cities | | | | | | | |
| 54. Oil | | | | | | | |
| 55. Drums | | | | | | | |
| 56. Muslim | | | | | | | |
| 57. Weak | | | | | | | |
| 58. Railroad | | | | | | | |
| 59. Savages | | | | | | | |
| 60. Schools | | | | | | | |
| 61. Dirty | | | | | | | |
| 62. Cold | | | | | | | |
| 63. Backward | | | | | | | |
| 64. Well-Educated | | | | | | | |
| 65. Fishing | | | | | | | |
| 66. Racial Problems | | | | | | | |
| 67. Elephants | | | | | | | |
| 68. Buddhist | | | | | | | |
| 69. Natives | | | | | | | |
| 70. Friend | | | | | | | |
| 71. Temples | | | | | | | |
| 72. Tribe | | | | | | | |
| 73. Illiterate | | | | | | | |
| 74. Mountains | | | | | | | |
| 75. Pygmies | | | | | | | |
| 76. Sculpture | | | | | | | |
| 77. Underdeveloped | | | | | | | |
| 78. Grasslands | | | | | | | |
| 79. Witch Doctors | | | | | | | |
| 80. Television | | | | | | | |
| 81. Dance | | | | | | | |
| 82. Malnutrition | | | | | | | |
| 83. Powerful | | | | | | | |
| 84. Religion | | | | | | | |
| 85. Cannibals | | | | | | | |
| 86. Rich | | | | | | | |
| 87. Primitive | | | | | | | |
| 88. Violence | | | | | | | |
| 89. Cattle | | | | | | | |
| 90. Neutrality | | | | | | | |

# AFRICA SOUTH OF THE SAHARA

## A SURVEY

DIRECTIONS: Write in the space provided on the answer sheet the number of the word or phrase that best completes or answers each of the following statements or questions:

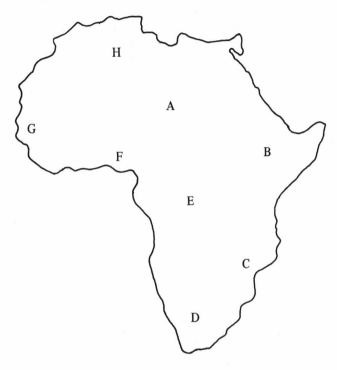

*Questions 1–9 refer to the map*

1. The Congo River flows through area
   1. B
   2. E
   3. D
   4. G

2. The equator passes through
   1. H
   2. A
   3. E
   4. D

3. Senegal is closest to
   1. H
   2. D
   3. G
   4. B

4. Afrikaners live closest to which of the following?
   1. A
   2. G
   3. E
   4. D

5. Which of the following is in the Sahara Desert?
   1. A
   2. G
   3. B
   4. D

6. Which of the following areas has the *highest* elevation?
   1. G
   2. F
   3. B
   4. D

7. The most heavily populated part of Africa south of the Sahara is located around
   1. F
   2. D
   3. A
   4. C

8. Which of the following areas has the *least* annual rainfall?
   1. F
   2. D
   3. G
   4. E

9. In flying from point G to point C, which of the following would you be *least* likely to fly over?
   1. grassy plains
   2. mountains
   3. rainforest
   4. desert

10. Africa is
    1. the same size as the United States.
    2. more than three times the size of the United States.
    3. half the size of the United States.
    4. almost twice the size of the United States.

11. Which of the following is located in East Africa?
    1. Tanzania
    2. Ghana
    3. Liberia
    4. Botswana

12. Africa's West coast touches the
    1. Indian Ocean.
    2. Mediterranean Sea.
    3. Arabian Sea.
    4. Atlantic Ocean.

13. Most of the land in Africa south of the Sahara is covered by
    1. swamps.
    2. jungles.
    3. grasslands.
    4. deserts.

14. Large animals such as elephants, leopards and giraffes can be found
    1. mainly in African game preserves and national parks.
    2. scattered throughout most of Africa.
    3. deep in Africa's jungles.
    4. only in the remotest parts of Africa.

15. A "Harmattan" is
    1. an African holiday.
    2. a monsoon rain from the Indian Ocean.
    3. A broad expanse of desert.
    4. a dust-laden wind blowing off the Sahara.

16. Most of Africa's natural resources
    1. are still undeveloped.
    2. are not worth much.
    3. can never be used.
    4. have been used up.

17. A major product of the Congo (Kinshasa) is
    1. oil.
    2. gold.
    3. copper.
    4. peanuts.

18. Most people in Africa south of the Sahara earn their living from
    1. farming.
    2. hunting.
    3. working in factories.
    4. fishing.

19. Which of the following pairs matches a product with the area where it is produced?
    1. copper–Niger
    2. rubber–Liberia
    3. petroleum–Tanzania
    4. tea–Ghana

20. In terms of dollar value, the most important exports of Africa south of the Sahara are
    1. mineral products.
    2. personal services.
    3. manufactured goods.
    4. agricultural products.

21. A major manufactured product of East Africa is
    1. automobiles.
    2. textiles.
    3. washing machines.
    4. radios.

22. A major problem facing African farmers is
    1. the reliance on one main crop.
    2. the shortness of the growing season.
    3. their laziness.
    4. their unwillingness to sell their crops.

23. A major obstacle to economic development in many African states is the
    1. destruction caused by World War II.
    2. tendency of Africans to hoard their money.
    3. lack of basic education.
    4. unwillingness of Africans to leave their homes to find work.

24. Which of the following African states is the most economically developed?
    1. Liberia
    2. Ethiopia
    3. Nigeria
    4. Republic of South Africa

25. The average yearly income of Africans is about
    1. $100.
    2. $500.
    3. $1000.
    4. $2500.

26. The number of people living in Africa south of the Sahara is approximately
    1. 3,500,000 persons
    2. 42,000,000 persons
    3. 220,000,000 persons
    4. 1,500,000,000 persons.

27. Which of the following are considered part of the Bantu peoples?
    1. Bushmen
    2. Zulus
    3. Ethiopians
    4. Afrikaners

28. Whites, although a minority of the population, control
    1. Rhodesia.
    2. Guinea.
    3. Kenya.
    4. Cameroon.

29. Arab culture has most influenced
    1. Nigeria.
    2. Ethiopia.
    3. Lesotho.
    4. Zanzibar.

30. Racial problems have been most evident in
    1. Ghana.
    2. Zambia.
    3. Liberia.
    4. the Republic of South Africa.

31. A conflict involving the Mau Mau occurred in
    1. Kenya.
    2. Nigeria.
    3. Angola.
    4. the Ivory Coast.

32. In general, most Africans
    1. are incapable of inventing anything good on their own.
    2. copy foreign things for their own use without altering them.
    3. need much guidance to adapt foreign ways.
    4. change foreign ideas to fit their own purposes.

33. Traditional religions of Africa south of the Sahara stress a belief
    1. in Heaven as reward and Hell as punishment.
    2. in a Supreme Force or Being who created the universe.
    3. in the Ten Commandments.
    4. in the necessity of human sacrifice to please the gods when they are hungry.

34. Examples of traditional sculpture in Africa south of the Sahara include all of the following *except*
    1. bronze heads.
    2. ceremonial masks.
    3. marble statues.
    4. wooden figures.

35. The traditional music of Africa south of the Sahara is usually
    1. quiet and sad.
    2. about everyday life.
    3. sung by women.
    4. written down by tribal scribes.

36. Fossil remains of the earliest man have been found in
    1. North Africa.
    2. West Africa.
    3. East Africa.
    4. South Africa.

37. When European explorers first came to Africa
    1. the Africans worshipped them.
    2. they established the first governments Africans had ever had.
    3. they found small villages but no large cities.
    4. they found many African kingdoms.

38. Which of the following was created as a home for freed American slaves?
    1. Liberia
    2. Nigeria
    3. Kenya
    4. Rhodesia

39. Kilwa, Sofala and Mogadischio were most famous as
    1. African kings.
    2. Portuguese explorers of Africa.
    3. trading cities in East Africa.
    4. African tribal gods.

40. Henry Stanley, Mungo Park and John Speke
   1. were explorers.
   2. came from the United States.
   3. died in Africa.
   4. served as Christian missionaries.

41. Timbuctu was most famous for its
   1. university.
   2. diamond mines.
   3. cool climate.
   4. sailing ships.

42. Which of the following was once the center of a major empire in East Africa?
   1. Lagos
   2. Cambodia
   3. Zimbabwe
   4. Masai

43. The slave trade to the Americas
   1. affected East Africa more than the rest of Africa.
   2. led to increased tribal warfare in Africa.
   3. was conducted mainly by Arab shieks.
   4. brought economic prosperity to most Africans.

44. Africa was divided into colonial empires by European nations at a meeting held in 1884-85 in
   1. Berlin.
   2. New York City.
   3. London.
   4. Paris.

45. Patrice Lumumba, Joseph Kasavubu and Moise Tshombe were political leaders of
   1. Ghana.
   2. Kenya.
   3. Congo (Kinshasa).
   4. Nigeria.

46. Which of the following occurred before all the others?
   1. European discovery of the source of the Nile
   2. The Great Trek
   3. Invasion of Abyssinia by Italy
   4. Rhodesia's declaration of Independence

47. The greatest number of countries in Africa south of the Sahara became independent
   1. between 1800 and 1885.
   2. between 1885 and 1915.
   3. between 1915 and 1955.
   4. after 1955.

48. Which of the following is ruled by an emperor?
   1. Ethiopia
   2. Rhodesia
   3. Sierra Leone
   4. Ghana

49. The Boers were
   1. native traders in western Africa.
   2. European soldiers who fought in Africa in World II.
   3. Arab merchants in East Africa.
   4. descendents of Dutch farmers in southern Africa.

50. Our knowledge of early Africa is limited because
   1. we cannot decipher Africa's early writing.
   2. Europeans destroyed all the African records when they conquered Africa.
   3. there are few written records by Africans except for the past 200 years.
   4. Africans have never kept written records.

(Questions 51-55)  Write in each space provided on your answer sheet the number of the country in column B with which each person listed in column A is most closely associated.

| Column A | Column B |
|---|---|
| 51. Kwame Nkrumah | 1. Ethiopia |
| 52. Haile Selassie | 2. Rhodesia |
| 53. Sekou Touré | 3. Ghana |
| 54. Julius Nyere | 4. Guinea |
| 55. Chinua Achebe | 5. Nigeria |
|  | 6. Tanzania |
|  | 7. The Congo (Kinshasa) |

(Questions 56-60)  Write in each space provided on your answer sheet the number of the phrase in column B that best defines each term in column A.

| Column A | Column B |
|---|---|
| 56. Swahili | 1. An African word meaning "freedom." |
| 57. Apartheid | 2. A mountain range in eastern Africa. |
| 58. Sudan | 3. A policy of complete separation of the races. |
| 59. Uhuru | 4. A language spoken throughout East Africa. |
| 60. Kimberley | 5. A great diamond mine in South Africa. |
|  | 6. The area in West Africa between the Sahara and the coastal rainforests. |
|  | 7. An ancient city in Southwest Africa. |

## FOOTNOTES

[1] George H. T. Kimble and Ronald Steel, *Tropical Africa Today.* St. Louis: Webster Division of McGraw-Hill Book Company, 1966, p. 2; Leonard S. Kenworthy, *Studying Africa in Elementary and Secondary Schools.* New York: Bureau of Publications, Teachers College, Columbia University, 1965 (second edition), p. 1; David Hapgood, *Today's World in Focus: Africa.* Boston: Ginn & Company, 1965, p. 3.

[2] Edward W. Brice, "Studying Africa," *Childhood Education,* December 1961, p. 156.

[3] Wendell P. Jones, "What Teachers Should Know About Emerging Africa," *NEA Journal,* May 1963, pp. 38-41; Kenneth C. Snyder, "The Role and Importance of Africa South of the Sahara: A Challenge to American Education," *High School Journal,* November 1963, pp. 46-59.

[4] John Gunther, *Inside Africa.* New York: Harper & Brothers, 1955, p. 4; Brice, *op. cit.,* p. 156.

[5] Paul T. Welty, *Man's Cultural Heritage.* Philadelphia: J. B. Lippincott Company, 1956, p. 592.

[6] Gerald Leinwand, *The Pageant of World History.* Boston: Allyn & Bacon, Inc., 1966, p. 558.

[7] Ward Morehouse, "Asia and Africa in Today's World," *Teachers College Record,* Vol. 63, 1961-62, p. 552; Fred L. Hadsel, "The United States and Africa," *Social Education,* March 1960, pp. 112-114, 116.

[8] Harold Long and Robert N. King, *Improving the Teaching of World Affairs.* Washington, National Council for the Social Studies, Bulletin #35, 1964, p. 1.

[9] P. D. Hey, "International Understanding: Philosophic, Religious and Moral Assumptions Illustrated from South Africa," *Yearbook of Education,* 1964, p. 83.

[10] Brice, *op. cit.,* p. 157.

[11] Long and King, *op. cit.,* p. 20.

[12] Emil Lengyel, *Africa in Ferment.* New York: Oxford Book Company, 1963 (revised edition). Preface.

[13] Oliver J. Caldwell, "Africa and American Education," *American Association of Colleges for Teacher Education Yearbook,* 1961, p. 82.

[14] Seymour Fersh, "Introduction to Culture Regions of the World," in *Understanding India.* New York: The Macmillan Company, 1966, p. viii; Long and King, *op. cit.,* p. viii.

[15] Kimble and Steel, *op. cit.,* p. 2.

[16] Brice, *op. cit.,* p. 157.

[17] Howard Mehlinger, "Area Studies and the Secondary Schools," *Educational Record,* Spring 1966, p. 245.

[18] Marguerite Cartwright, "The Africa Unit," *The Social Studies,* November 1953, p. 265.

[19] E. Perry Hicks and Barry K. Beyer, "Images of Africa" in *Social Education,* December 1968, p. 780; the summary of the findings of this survey is taken from this article (pp. 779-784); and Barry K. Beyer and E. Perry Hicks, *Images of Africa: A Report on What American Secondary School Students Know and Believe About Africa South of the Sahara.* Pittsburgh: Project Africa, Carnegie-Mellon University, 1968, 36 pp.

[20] See Giles T. Brown, "What Americans Must Learn About Africa," *Overview,* November 1961, pp. 44-45; George E. Haynes, "Americans Look at Africa," *The Journal of Negro Education,* Volume 27, No. 1 (Winter, 1958), pp. 94-100; John Mather, "Africa–Its Images and Realities," *Minnesota Journal of Education.* February 1963, pp. 11-12; James W. King, "Africa," in John W. Morris, ed., *Methods of Geographic Instruction.* Waltham, Mass.: Blaisdell Publishing Company, 1968, p. 238; Cartwright, *op. cit.,* p. 264-268; Kenworthy, *op. cit.,* pp. 8-10; Leinwand, *op. cit.,* pp. 557-561.

[21] Waldemar A. Nielsen, *Africa.* New York: Altheneum, 1966, pp. 5-6.

[22] *Op. cit.,* p. 8.

[23] T. Walter Wallbank, *Contemporary Africa: Continent in Transition.* Princeton: D. Van Nostrand Company, Inc., 1956 (revised edition), pp. 14-15.

[24] Cornelis W. deKiewiet, "Africa in Today's World," in Howard Anderson, ed., *Approaches to an Understanding of World Affairs,* 25th Yearbook of the NCSS, 1954, p. 291.

[25] Kenworthy, *op. cit.,* pp. 12-21; King, *op. cit.,* pp. 237-244; Philip D. Curtin, *African History.* Washington: Service Center for the Teachers of History, 1964, 55 pp.

[26] Caldwell, *op. cit.,* p. 76

[27] W. L. Tsitsiwu, "Suggestions for Teaching About Africa," *Social Education,* March 1960, p. 116; King, *op. cit.,* p. 239.

[28] William B. Conroy, "The Cultural Region–Framework for Teaching World Geography," *The Social Studies,* February 1966, pp. 71, 74.

[29] Long and King, *op. cit.,* p. 11.

[30] James McAree, "A Select Bibliography of Paperback Books on Africa for Secondary School Use," *The Social Studies,* December 1966, p. 305.

[31] William Clark Trow, "An Area-Study Social Studies Curriculum," *Social Education,* March 1965, p. 143.

[32] Stanley N. Miller, "The World Cultures Course," *Social Education,* February 1962, pp. 69-70.

[33] Long and King, *op. cit.,* p. 2.

[34] David S. Eldredge and Clark Moore, "An Approach to Afro-Asian Studies," *Educational Leadership,* May 1962, p. 502; Mehlinger, *op. cit.,* p. 250.

[35] Gilbert Wilson, "Teaching About Africa in the Elementary School," *Journal of Education,* Boston University School of Education, October 1961, p. 6.

[36] Joseph E. Harris, "Bring in Africa," *The New England Social Studies Bulletin,* Fall 1965, pp. 19-21.

[37] McAree, *op. cit.,* p. 305; Miller, *op. cit.,* p. 70.

[38] Paul Bohannan, *Social Anthropology.* New York: Holt, Rinehart and Winston, 1963, p. 9.

[39] George M. Beckmann, "Curricular Methods of Introducing Foreign Area Studies," *Educational Record,* Spring 1966, p. 277.

[40] Fersh, *op. cit.,* p. vii.

[41] Stanley Spector, "The Coordination of High School and Undergraduate Studies in Non-Western Languages and Cultures," *Educational Record,* Spring 1966, p. 261.

[42] Wilson, *op. cit.,* p. 7.

[43] For example, see Brown, *op. cit.,* p. 45; Hadsel, *op. cit.,* p. 112; Bohannan, *op. cit.,* p. 9.

[44] Robert F. Byrnes, "Teaching Materials for Foreign Area Instruction," *Phi Delta Kappan,* December 1965, pp. 223-227.

[45] Specific suggestions for using multi-media for inquiry teaching about Africa may be found in E. Perry Hicks's, "Inductive Teaching and the Overhead Projector," in *Media and Methods,* May 1968, pp. 34-36; Barry K. Beyer and E. Perry Hicks, "Meet the Single Concept Film," in *Media and Methods,* February 1967, pp. 40-42.

# PART II
# MATERIALS
## for Teaching About
## Africa South of the Sahara

## INTRODUCTION

Teachers have long been reluctant to include the study of Africa south of the Sahara in their programs of study because of a common belief that there was a serious shortage of suitable instructional materials. At one time, only a few years ago, perhaps such a shortage did indeed exist. Today, however, it does not.

There is now available an abundance of instructional materials designed for use in teaching about this region and its peoples in our schools. Over 500 of these are described in this guide. With several exceptions, all those specifically designed for classroom instruction are included here, the vast majority consisting of filmstrips, slides, 8mm film loops, tapes, records, study prints, programmed materials and selected types of written materials. Where no reasonably comprehensive bibliographies of other materials exist, such as is the case for African novels and other types of literature, descriptions of these are also included. However, when adequate bibliographies of some materials already exist, this is noted and no further reference is made to them here.

The purpose of this part of the guide is to facilitate the identification of materials that may be potentially useful in classroom instruction about Africa south of the Sahara. It consists of four parts. The first lists materials that will be directly useful to teachers or curriculum developers seeking guidance about how to organize and conduct instruction about this region and its peoples. These should be consulted in conjunction with Part I of this guide.

The second part of this section is an annotated bibliography of all commercially produced materials available as of Spring, 1969. They have been classified by regions, nations, and types of media to make identification easier. A quick reference guide to this classification system follows this introduction.

This annotated bibliography is followed by a list of materials that should be considered by schools which are seeking to start a collection of resource materials for use in teaching about this region but which have only limited funds available for their acquisition. Reference to this list will provide guidance to what are some of the best materials of their kind now available.

Finally, there is a list of the addresses of publishers whose materials are described in this volume. Educators interested in examining these materials should write directly to the publishers. A list of African diplomatic missions, African information and tourist services, and selected American organizations whose primary interests lie in this region of the world concludes Part II.

# QUICK REFERENCE GUIDE TO MATERIALS

# MATERIALS FOR THE TEACHER

Planning for instruction on any topic requires some knowledge about general social studies curriculum and teaching, as well as about the specific content to be taught. For this reason the materials cited here have been divided into two major groups. The first includes materials related to social studies teaching strategies and techniques in general. No adequate program of study—on Africa south of the Sahara or any topic in the social studies curriculum—can be developed without practical knowledge of the latest research and writing in the field. The materials included here represent those that will be most useful to teachers desirous of developing an effective, stimulating study of this region and its peoples.

The second group of materials is related directly to teaching about Africa south of the Sahara. These include guides to content, techniques of instruction, and materials. Although placed according to their primary focus in one of these categories, all contain some information relevant to the other categories. Consequently, teachers involved in planning or teaching units or courses about this region and its peoples should consult *all* of these materials.

# CURRICULUM AND TEACHING

## RATIONALE

Bruner, Jerome, *The Process of Education.* New York: Vintage Books, 1960. Paper. $1.95

The final draft of the report of a 1959 conference on science teaching which articulates the basic rationale of contemporary curriculum change in all academic subjects. Chapters on structure, readiness for learning, intuitive and analytic thinking, motivation and teaching aids. Index. 97 pp.

Fenton, Edwin, *The New Social Studies.* New York: Holt, Rinehart and Winston, Inc., 1967. Paper. $1.95.

A statement of a rationale for innovation in the social studies curriculum based on a survey of curriculum development in the social studies and on the experiences of the author. Chapters on objectives and evaluation, teaching strategies, materials, pupil deployment and teacher preparation. Index. 144 pp.

Holt, John, *How Children Fail.* New York: Dell Publishing Company, 1964. Paper. $1.75.

An analysis of techniques devised by children to meet or appear to meet the demands of adults, especially in the formal classroom situation; emphasizes learning (or non-learning) strategies, the nature of learning and the impact on both of these of failure or fear of failure. Written in the form of memos and notes. No index. 181 pp.

## OBJECTIVES

Bloom, Benjamin et al., *Taxonomy of Educational Objectives—Handbook I: Cognitive Domain.* New York: David McKay Company, Inc., 1956. Paper. $2.50.

A discussion of educational objectives and curriculum development followed by a detailed analysis of the various levels of the cognitive domain of learning, complete with illustrative objectives and test items. Appendix has shortened version of taxonomy. 207 pp.

Krathwohl, David et al., *Taxonomy of Educational Objectives—Handbook II: Affective Domain.* New York: David McKay Company, Inc., 1956. Paper. $2.50

A description of the affective continuum and its relation to the cognitive domain, a discussion of curriculum evaluation and research, and a detailed outline of the classification of affective objectives with examples of educational objectives and test items. Appendix contains condensed versions of both affective and cognitive domains. Bibliography. 196 pp.

*Mager, Robert, *Preparing Instructional Objectives.* Palo Alto: Fearon Publishers, 1962. Paper. $1.75.

A programmed text designed to help one understand how to specify instructional objectives in behavioral terms. It focuses on the form of usefully stated objectives in all areas, not on the selection of the objectives. 62 pp.

## STRATEGIES AND STRUCTURE

Allen, Rodney et al., eds., *Inquiry in the Social Studies.* Washington: National Council for the Social Studies, 1968. Paper. $2.25.

A collection of short essays and articles gleaned from the professional literature and other sources on various aspects of inquiry, especially on questions, structure, and modes of inquiry. Includes several models for inquiry as well as transcripts of classroom discussion and model learning materials. 114 pp.

*Beyer, Barry, *Using Inquiry in the Classroom— Guidelines for Teaching.* Athens, Ohio: Cooperative Center for Social Science Education, 1968. Paper. $1.00.

An analysis of the nature of inquiry and an outline of a derived teaching strategy. Emphasizes the planning of lessons and units structured along the lines of this strategy. Discusses also the role of the teacher and implications of the use of this strategy in the classroom. 18 pp.

Beyer, Barry K., *Inquiry in the Classroom—Guidelines for Teaching.* Columbus: Charles E. Merrill Books, Inc., 1969. Paper.

A handbook for teachers interested in planning and teaching inquiry-oriented lessons; describes the nature of intellectual inquiry and its component operations; describes a teaching strategy

based on these; provides examples of daily lessons and units constructed on this strategy. 128 pp.

Fair, Jean and Fannie R. Shaftel, *Effective Thinking in the Social Studies.* Washington: National Council for the Social Studies, 1967. Paper. $4.00.

This 37th yearbook of the NCSS contains chapters by Hilda Taba on thinking, by Millard Clements on inquiry as related to various disciplines, by Charlotte Crabtree on reflective thinking and by Dana Kurfman on evaluating inquiry. 275 pp.

Hunt, M. P. and Lawrence Metcalf, *Teaching High School Social Studies.* New York: Harper & Row, Publishers, 1968. Second Edition. Hardcover. $10.50.

A revised edition of the classic social studies methods text on teaching for reflective thinking. Pp. 65-274 focus on the teaching of concepts, generalizations, and value analysis as well as on techniques for motivation, discussion and evaluation. Index. 463 pp.

Massialas, Byron and C. Benjamin Cox, *Inquiry in Social Studies.* New York: McGraw-Hill Book Company, 1966. Hardcover. $6.95.

An analysis of the use of inquiry in the social studies classroom focusing on the theoretical rationale as well as on materials, participation techniques, and evaluation procedures. Index. 353 pp.

Massialas, Byron and Jack Zevin, *Creative Encounters in the Classroom.* New York: John Wiley and Sons, Inc., 1967. Paper. $2.50.

A discussion of the nature of inquiry with transcripts of classroom discussion involving analysis and discovery in the areas of geography, non-western studies, history and values. Index. 274 pp.

---

*Items thus marked will be of greatest use in structuring unit and daily lesson plans in accordance with the preceding guidelines.

Raths, Louis et al., *Teaching for Thinking: Theory and Application.* Columbus, Ohio: Charles E. Merrill Books, Inc., 1967. Hardcover. $7.25.

An attempt to delineate a theory of instruction for teaching children how to think and to provide examples of learning experiences teachers can use to help students learn how to compare, observe, summarize, classify, interpret. 348 pp.

*Sanders, Norris, *Classroom Questions–What Kinds?* New York: Harper & Row, Publishers, 1966. Paper. $2.50.

An outline of types of questions designed to elicit thinking, translation of data, interpreta-

tion, analysis, synthesis, and evaluation; includes sample questions and self-test items. Index. 176 pp.

*Taba, Hilda, *Teacher's Handbook for Elementary Social Studies.* Palo Alto: Addison-Wesley Publishing Company, 1967. (Introductory Edition). Paper. $1.95.

A rationale for curriculum development that is relevant to any content area at any level. Provides a structure for organizing any study and specific guidelines for designing teaching strategies in the cognitive domain. Key questions analyzed and suggested. No index. 150 pp.

# TEACHING ABOUT AFRICA SOUTH OF THE SAHARA

## GUIDES TO CONTENT

Banfield, Beryle, *Africa In the Curriculum.* New York: Edward W. Blyden Press, Inc., 1968. Paper. $3.50.

A teaching guide for elementary school instruction designed to develop a "positive self-image" in Afro-American students; includes information on ancient empires, resistance heroes, independence leaders, the coming of independence, social institutions, traditional literature and the arts, and a section on teaching suggestions that attempts to relate study of Africa to study of science, language arts, math, music, as well as social studies; a short list of materials; bibliography for the teacher. No index. 124 pp.

*Bohannan, Paul, *Africa and Africans.* Garden City: The Natural History Press, 1964. Paper. $1.25.

A scholarly introduction to Africa south of the Sahara—its people and history. Half of the book emphasizes the people and their arts, family organization, politics, labor systems, and religion. The remainder emphasizes African history to 1900. Index. 260 pp.

*Brown, Ina Corinne, *Understanding Other Cultures.* Englewood Cliffs: Prentice-Hall, Inc., 1963. Paper. $1.95.

An analysis of the concept of culture organized around discussion of family and economic institutions, the arts, life, manners, values, religion, and change; examples from a wide variety of cultural groups used to illustrate general principles; selected bibliography. No index. 184 pp.

Curtin, Philip D., *African History.* Washington: Service Center for Teachers of History of the American Historical Association, 1964. Paper. $.75.

A brief survey of African historiography with comments on selected historical works, new sources of data, and ways to organize the study of African history; also discussion of selected problems of African history such as the Bantu migration, myths, the slave trade, the scramble for empire. No index. 55 pp.

Kenworthy, Leonard, *Africa–A Teaching Guide.* Chicago: F. E. Compton & Company, 1962. Paper. 25¢.

A brief guide for teaching about Africa; includes concepts to emphasize, a suggested outline to follow, pertinent facts about Africa, maps, and some suggested activities. 12 pp.

Kenworthy, Leonard S., *Kenya–A Background Paper.* Brooklyn: World Affairs Materials Center, 1961. Paper. 50¢.

A mimeographed description of the geography, peoples, homes, food, economic activity, health conditions, education, religion, government, and leaders of Kenya; special pages on the Mau Mau, important dates, landscape and recreation; bibliography of teaching materials. 25 pp.

Kenworthy, Leonard S., *Nigeria—A Background Paper.* Brooklyn: World Affairs Materials Center, 1959. Paper. 50¢.

A mimeographed outline of basic data on Nigeria including land, resources, people, homes, food, clothes, economic activities, cities, religion, recreation, education, arts and crafts, history, government, leaders, bibliography of books and other instructional materials. 22 pp.

Kenworthy, Leonard S., *Tanganyika—A Background Paper.* Brooklyn: World Affairs Materials Center, 1961. Paper. 50¢.

A mimeographed outline describing the geography, history, peoples, social conditions, economic conditions, education, and government of Tanganyika; bibliography of teaching materials. 20 pp.

King, James W., "Africa," in John W. Morris, ed., *Methods of Geographic Instruction.* Waltham, Mass.: Blaisdell Publishing Company, 1968. Hardcover. $7.50.

A description of geographic concepts and generalizations that the author believes ought to be included in a study of Africa; includes lists of common misconceptions; some concern with African history, economy, political development.

Lystad, Robert A., "Sub-Saharan Africa," in Shirley Engle, ed., *New Perspectives in World History,* (34th Yearbook of the NCSS). Washington: National Council for the Social Studies, 1964. Paper. $5.00.

23 pp. survey of African historiography and pre-history with outlines of pre-colonial, colonial and independent Africa history. No index.

Moore, Clark D. and Ann Dunbar, *Africa Yesterday and Today.* New York: Bantam Books, Inc., 1968. Paper. 95¢.

A collection of edited excerpts from scholarly writings (Kimble, Hance, Ottenberg, Fage, etc.) and other sources focusing on the structure of traditional Africa, early African history, various colonial systems, Africa since World War II, and the future of Africa. Index. 394 pp.

*Oliver, Roland and J. D. Fage, *A Short History of Africa.* Baltimore: Penguin Books, 1964. Paper. $1.95.

A scholarly survey of the various peoples of Africa followed by an interpretive chronological survey of their history to 1961; suggestions for further reading. Index. 280 pp.

*Singleton, F. Seth and John Shingler, *Africa in Perspective.* New York: Hayden Book Company, Inc., 1967. Paper. $3.96.

A readable, scholarly survey of the peoples, geography, history, and contemporary life of Africa south of the Sahara with special sections on the Congo and Nigeria, Ethiopia and Liberia, and South Africa. Excellent maps, charts, photos. Index. 310 pp.

Wilson, Margaret Welch, *Our African Neighbors.* Gastonia, North Carolina: Brumley Printing Company, n.d. Paper. $1.00.

A collection of brief descriptions of races, foods, traditional cultures, regional customs, proverbs, folktales, poetry, music, arts and crafts, with bibliographies and suggested projects. Index. 83 pp.

## GUIDES TO METHODS

"Africa" in *Grade Teacher,* October 1968, pp. 48-93. Reprint #91081. 40¢.

A classroom teaching program for elementary grades with a possible rationale for including it in a curriculum; has ideas and materials on folklore, songs, a game, a country (Ghana), several people; has a map on ancient civilizations, an excellent essay on using maps to teach African geography, and a limited bibliography of printed materials only; teaching ideas generally of a "show and tell" nature.

Beattie, John, *Understanding an African Kingdom: Bunyoro.* New York: Holt, Rinehart and Winston, 1965. Paper. $1.50.

A description of the methods used by the author in his study of the Nyoro focusing on his theoretical preparation, field work methods (including use of informants, quantification, observation, records), and writing procedures. No index. 61 pp.

Crookall, R. E., *Handbook for History Teachers in West Africa.* London: Evans Brothers Ltd., 1968. Paper. $4.50.

An in-depth description of a rationale and techniques for teaching history intended for teachers in West African schools. Includes chapters on "Why Teach History," basic principles and techniques, the use of written, audio, visual teaching aids, pupil activities (model-making, speaking, maps, etc.), relations with other subjects, a case study of the use of local history, and an appendix listing what the author feels are the best books, atlases, periodicals and other sources produced in Great Britain or Africa. Sample lesson plans and teaching suggestions included. Index. 270 pp.

Fenton, Edwin, *Race Relations in the Republic of South Africa,* a unit in *Studies in the Non-Western World, An Inquiry Approach.* New York: Holt, Rinehart & Winston, 1964. Paper. Free.

Student readings, transparency masters and teaching guides for a unit on apartheid; two booklets, each 29 pp.

*Hoon, Nancy M., *Introducing West Africal Literature Into Our Social Studies Classes.* Athens, Ohio: Cooperative Center for Social Science Education, Ohio University, 1967. Paper. $1.00.

Concise rationale for using West African literature in the social studies followed by detailed suggestions for the use of *Things Fall Apart, No Longer At Ease, Man of the People,* in studying about culture, culture change, and the clash of cultures. Annotated bibliography of selected West African literature. 31 pp.

Laughton, W. H., *Teaching About Our People.* London: Cambridge University Press, 1965. Hardcover.

A guide for teachers in Kenya schools that describes methods, sources of content, and types of presentation that can be used to teach about various aspects of local life; sections on teaching about the family, buying and selling, government, tribal wars, marriages, buildings, and communications. Index. 126 pp.

*Mamunes, George, *The New York Times Student Weekly in African and Asian Studies.* New York: New York Times Book and Educational Division, 1967. Paper.

A guide for teachers wishing to use current news sources in the classroom; includes suggested activities for teaching such topics as political instability, new nations, Nigeria, race and politics, and apartheid. 32 pp.

Milliken, Edith and R. E. Crookall, *Historical Model Making for African Schools.* London: University of London Press, Ltd., 1962. Hardcover. 15s.

Suggestions for using and directions for making models of historical sites (e.g., Zimbabwe, Elmina Castle, Kariba dam), buildings, ships, kraals, and homes of Africa south of the Sahara. Originally prepared for teachers in African schools. No index. 107 pp.

Odell, Clarence B., "Physical Framework of Africa," in *Cartograph Teaching Aids.* Chicago: Denoyer-Geppert Company, 1962. Vol. II, No. 3. Paper. 10¢.

A four-page, notebook-size description of the size, landforms, climate pattern and vegetation pattern of Africa; with full page color map of Africa and nine different exercises requiring use of maps.

*Teaching About World Regions.* Albany: The University of the State of New York, The State Education Department, Bureau of Secondary Curriculum Development, 1963. Paper. $1.50.

Descriptive list of teaching techniques and approaches for use in teaching about different regions of the world in the context of a traditional junior high school world geography course; includes 35 pp. of suggested techniques for use in teaching about Africa south of the Sahara. No index. 360 pp.

## GUIDES TO TEACHING AIDS

"Africa" in *Grade Teacher,* October, 1968, pp. 48-93. Reprint #91081. 40¢.

A classroom teaching program for elementary grades with a possible rationale for including it in a curriculum; has ideas and materials on folklore, songs, a game, a country (Ghana), several people; has a map on ancient civilizations, an excellent essay on using maps to teach African geography and a limited bibliography of printed materials only; teaching ideas generally of a "show and tell" nature.

Carter, Gwendolen M., *Changing Africa—A Study Guide to Africa South of the Sahara.* Washington: American Association of University Women, 1963. Paper. 35¢.

Bibliography of outstanding books on selected topics about Africa south of the Sahara, each topic introduced with a series of questions designed to direct the study of the topics; among the topics are geography, history, economic development, nationalism, and sections on selected nations in each region. 26 pp.

*Foreign Policy Association, *Handbook on Africa.* (Intercom— Vol. 8, No. 3). New York: Foreign Policy Association, May-June 1966. Paper. $1.00.

A guide for teachers, including background information on U.S. relations with Africa, African international organizations, a gazetteer, a list of recent publications and periodicals, a review of selected textbooks and teaching films, and a bibliography of selected books arranged by topics and regions. No index. 56 pp.

Kenworthy, Leonard S., *Free and Inexpensive Materials on World Affairs.* New York: Teachers College, Columbia University, 1965. Second Edition. Paper. $1.50.

Bibliography of free and inexpensive materials for use in teaching about a variety of topics in

world affairs such as education, health, music, race and culture, religions, etc., U.S. foreign policy, regions of the world, and the U.N. Six pp. devoted specifically to Africa. No index.

*Kenworthy, Leonard S., *Studying Africa in Elementary and Secondary Schools.* New York: Teachers College, Columbia University, 1965. Second Edition. Paper. $1.50.

A survey of things to teach about Africa and lists of stereotypes to dispel; suggested teaching techniques and important understandings to teach; includes an extensive bibliography of instructional materials as well as addresses of publishers and African information services and embassies in the United States. No index. 60 pp.

Schultz, Charles B., *Ten Questions and Answers that Focus on World Cultures.* Harrisburg: Pennsylvania Department of Public Instruction, 1966. Paper.

A brief rationale for the study of world cultures and 28 pp. of annotated references to written, audio and visual instructional materials. Cross references to all materials. 45 pp.

*Tolman, Lorraine E., *Journal of Education.* Boston: Boston University School of Education, October 1961, (Vol. 144, No. 1). Paper. $1.00.

Extensive annotated bibliography of written materials (fiction, biography, non-fiction, short stories, anthologies, folk tales) keyed by reading level; magazines and periodicals, teacher materials, pamphlets and audio-visual materials (especially films); bibliographical essays and teaching suggestions on South Africa and on changing Africa (using a variety of materials). Title and author index. 96 pp.

## PERIODICALS AND JOURNALS

*African Arts/Arts D'Afrique.* African Studies Center, University of California, Los Angeles, California, 90024. Published quarterly. $10/year.

A quarterly devoted to the graphic, plastic, performing, and literary arts of Africa. Includes many color prints, photographs, and other reproductions.

*African Bibliographic Center, *A Current Bibliography on African Affairs*. New York: Greenwood Periodicals, Inc. Paper. $20 per year/ $2.25 single issue.

A monthly bibliography of the latest publications in all fields of African studies and related topics; each entry annotated and arranged by subject; prices given; author index.

*African Forum*. American Society of African Culture, 401 Broadway, New York, New York, 10013. Published quarterly. $4.00/year.

A journal covering all aspects of Negro life in Africa, the Americas, and the rest of the world; focuses on political, economic, social, and literary fields.

*Africa Report*. African-American Institute, 505 Dupont Circle Building, Washington, D.C. 20036. Monthly, 9 issues yearly. $6.00/year.

Noted for its accuracy; an up-to-date factual report of Africa today in the context of its history; with monthly chronology of events; many illustrations.

*African Studies Bulletin*. African Studies Association, 622 West 113th Street, New York, New York, 10025. Three issues yearly. $20.00/year.

Scholarly articles dealing with research on African politics, history, anthropology, sociology, and economics; occasional reports on African studies in the U.S.

*Africa Today*. Africa Today Associates, Graduate School of International Studies, University of Denver, Denver, Colorado, 80210. Published bi-monthly. $5.00/year.

Presents opinions on current African economic, political, social, and literary developments.

*The Journal of African History*. Cambridge University Press, 32 East 57th Street, New York, New York 10022. Published quarterly. $14.50/ year.

*The Journal of Modern African Studies*. Cambridge University Press, 32 East 57th Street, New York, New York, 10022. Published quarterly. $9.50/ year.

Articles on all aspects of modern Africa, including politics, economics, society, and related subjects.

*African Affairs for the General Reader: A Selected and Introductory Bibliographical Guide—1960-1967*. New York: Council of the African-American Institute, 1967. 210 pp. Paper. $5.00.

A detailed annotated listing of the more than 80 English-language periodicals dealing with Africa south of the Sahara.

## BIBLIOGRAPHIES

*Africa*. New York: American Society of African Culture, n.d. Paper.

A 54-page mimeographed list of books on Africa available for study in the AMSAC library; unannotated; no prices; divided into sections on Africa in general, government, each region, and topics such as economics, education, religion and literature.

*Africa* (Addendum). New York: American Society of African Culture, June, 1965. Paper.

An unannotated mimeographed list of books available in the AMSAC library; no prices given; 18 pp.

*Africa: A List of Printed Materials*. New York: U.S. Committee for UNICEF, 1968. Paper. $1.00.

An annotated list of over 300 English-language materials published in nine countries; arranged by regions and graded for reading level. Some evaluative comments on each item. Includes publishers' addresses, prices, and author-title-subject index. 67 pp.

*Africa: A List of Printed Materials for Children*. New York: Information Center on Children's Cultures, 1968. Paper. $1.00.

A 76-page bibliography of materials on Africa suitable for children, each entry annotated, with grade levels suggested; prices included.

*African Bibliographic Center, *African Affairs for the General Reader: A Selected and Introductory Bibliographical Guide, 1960-1967*. New

York: Council of the African-American Institute, 1967. 210 pp. Paper. $5.00.

A selected bibliography of periodicals, articles, pamphlets, books and booklets on Africa; organized by topics and regions; annotated, with prices when known; with subject, title and author index. The most comprehensive, up-to-date bibliography available. 209 pp.

*Africa South of the Sahara—An Introductory List of Bibliographies.* Washington, D.C.: General Reference and Bibliography Division, Library of Congress, 1961. Paper.

A mimeographed, annotated list of bibliographies in print as of 1961. 7 pp.

*Book List on Africa for Canadians.* Ottawa: The Canadian National Commission for UNESCO, 1965. Paper.

A list of books, periodicals and other written materials on various topics related to Africa, each topic introduced by a brief description of the topic and its implication; in English and French; no prices provided; unannotated. 28 pp.

Castagno, A. A., *Reference Works and Surveys Dealing with Africa.* New York: Queens, College, 1963. Paper.

A mimeographed, annotated list of bibliographies, maps, travelogues, annuals, guides and surveys; prices not included. 6 pp.

Logasa, Hannah, *World Culture* (McKinley Bibliographies Volume III). Philadelphia: McKinley Publishing Company, 1963. Hardcover. $7.00.

Bibliography of scholarly, popular and student books arranged by topics such as geography, communication, ideas and isms, nations, religion, science; each topic is further sub-divided into a multitude of sub-topics. Index. 384 pp.

*Publications of the International African Institute.* London: International African Institute, 1965. Paper.

A list of the institute's publications on ethnography, languages, linguistics, history, and sociology with prices but no descriptions. 13 pp.

*Recommended List of Readings.* New York: National Council of the Churches of Christ in the U.S.A. October, 1967. Paper.

A mimeographed list of books on Africa south of the Sahara for the general reader; unannotated. 1 page.

*Rosenblum, Paul, *Checklist of Paperbound Books on Africa.* New York: Foreign Area Materials Center, 1967. Paper.

An unannotated bibliography of all paperbacks on Africa in print as of 1967; prices included; arranged by topics; includes index of publishers' addresses. 59 pp.

The World History Bibliography Committee of the NCSS, *World History Book List for High Schools,* (Bulletin #31). Washington: National Council for the Social Studies, 1962. Revised Edition. Paper. $1.50.

Annotated bibliography of books on all regions of the world, indexed by time period, topic and geographical areas (includes 30 on Africa). 145 pp.

# AN ANNOTATED BIBLIOGRAPHY OF INSTRUCTIONAL MATERIALS

The list of materials that follows is not complete. In spite of, and indeed because of, the tremendous advances in recent years in the technology of information dissemination and retrieval, and in the fields of educational materials and media, it has not been possible to identify, locate, and secure for examination or study every single material pertinent to teaching about Africa south of the Sahara.

Furthermore, no effort has been made to duplicate specialized bibliographies that already exist. Such is the case for 16mm films, paperbacks and library books. Since there already exist three excellent bibliographies of films on Africa, only a limited number of 16mm films are described here. Primarily, these are films that have become available in the past year or two. Because a number of complete bibliographies of paperbacks and other books on Africa south of the Sahara have been and continue to be published, this guide includes only English-language materials designed or advertised for instructional purposes.

Therefore, in searching for useful instructional materials, the following should also be consulted:

### FILMS

Committee of Fine Arts and the Humanities of the African Studies Association, *African Film Bibliography*. New York: African Studies Association (622 West 113th Street, New York 10025), 1966. 31 pp. Paper. $1.00.

Moyre, Claudia, *A List of Films on Africa*. Boston: Boston University African Studies Center, 1966. 41 pp. Paper.

*Film Catalogue*. New York: Council of the African-American Institute, n.d. 34 pp. Paper.

### BOOKS

*African Affairs for the General Reader: A Selected and Introductory Bibliographical Guide*. New York: Council of the African-American Institute (866 United Nations Plaza, New York 10017), 1968. 210 pp. Paper. $5.00.

Clark, Geraldine et al., *African Encounter*. Chicago: American Library Association, 1963. 69 pp. Paper. $1.50.

Rosenblum, Paul, *Checklist of Paperbound Books on Africa in Print November 1967*. Albany, New York: Foreign Areas Materials Center of the New York State Education Department, 1964. 59 pp. Paper.

United States Committee for UNICEF, *Africa: An Annotated List of Printed Materials Suitable for Children*. New York: Information Center on Children's Cultures, 1968. 76 pp. Paper. $1.00.

### INSTRUCTIONAL MATERIALS

"Handbook on Africa," *Intercom*, New York: Foreign Policy Association, 1966. (Vol. 8, No. 3) 80 pp. Paper. $1.00.

Kenworthy, Leonard, *Studying Africa in Elementary and Secondary Schools*, New York: Teachers College Press, Columbia University, 1965, Second edition. 60 pp. Paper. $1.50.

Tolman, Lorraine, "Africa: A Selected Bibliography with Related Instructional Aids for the Elementary and Secondary School," *Journal of Education*. Boston University School of Education, October 1961. 96 pp. Paper. $1.00.

Several precautions could be kept in mind when selecting instructional materials. First, the selection of these materials should follow, not precede, the development of the program of study in which they are to be used. No need exists today for a program or unit of study on Africa to be built around any specific commercial materials. Such a wide variety of materials is now available that this is completely unnecessary as well as unwise. Instead, a program should be designed, the learning objectives clearly delimited, and the individual lessons outlined in detail before instructional materials are selected. Only then will these materials be appropriate to the program objectives and fulfill their proper function in the learning process—as vehicles for learning than as ends in themselves.

Secondly, instructional materials should never be purchased or used sight unseen. They should be carefully examined and analyzed before any decisions are made regarding their use. A variety of different materials should be previewed before the purchase or rental of specific items is arranged.

Thirdly, the quality of available materials varies greatly. A few are excellent, but a great many are of borderline value. Thus, extreme care must be taken in selection. Probably no single material is perfect in all aspects—flawlessly accurate, well-balanced in approach, up-to-date in information, and of superior quality. However, careful preview and evaluation will help teachers detect major weaknesses as well as strengths; wise selection and use will then make it possible to employ a number of materials in combination that will enable the strength of one to fill the voids or correct the inaccuracies of another.

These materials are prone to several weaknesses. Many of them tend to give inaccurate impressions. This is sometimes a result of the intent of the materials being different from the user's frame of reference or intent. Generally, however, it merely reflects the ethnocentric biases of the producers themselves. One filmstrip on the Bantu of South Africa, for example, states in the very first frame that South Africa is a nation "...where racial conflict has resulted from the efforts of the Bantu and other dark-skinned peoples to improve their status." The impression given here is that the problem is the fault of the exploited for refusing to lie down and permit the exploitation to continue! Statements that leave impressions like this are common, especially in captioned filmstrips, narrated materials, and written texts or supplements, especially those produced before 1966.

Inaccurate impressions can also result from inferior research, poor editing or the sacrifice of content to the desire to make the material attractive or salable. An overemphasis on the exotic and unusual can create erroneous impressions, too. A film distributed by one East African nation shows little more than wild animals and African dancers; one could hardly blame anyone who views it for concluding that this particular country fits the Tarzan stereotype.

Many more inaccuracies are merely the result of the passing of time. What may have been true of Africa five years ago is not as likely to be true today. Since it may take that long to produce certain types of material, some are outdated before they become available. Therefore, it is most important to check the publication date of any material; in most instances anything produced or published before 1967 will be subject to some degree of inaccuracy.

Imbalance is a further problem. Visual materials are especially prone to this weakness, which at times this appears to be the result of poor preparation, but generally results from an overemphasis on one topic to the exclusion of others. At times, too, it is a result of deliberate efforts to create a specific impression that may be untrue in view of all the facts. African nations themselves have produced materials flawed by the wish to stress a "new image" while playing down existing impressions.

Thus, one filmstrip on economic activity includes only pictures of new factories, mills and transportation facilities which in reality are but a minor part of the economic scene of the region under study. Pictures of less complimentary but more typical aspects of its economy are omitted. Use of this filmstrip alone in the study of this region would lead surely to an erroneous impression about its economy. A number of misleading materials headline the fact that "Europeans ended the slave trade in Africa" while ignoring the fact that they also were largely responsible for stimulating it in the first place. An even more flagrantly unbalanced approach is found in those texts which treat African history only in relation to that of Western Europe or only after 1450.

A great many of these materials are heavily loaded with stereotyped words, phrases, ideas, or generalizations, especially those published before 1966. Words such as "native," "primitive," "backward," "heathen," and "uncivilized" abound in spite of their inaccurate connotations. Beliefs commonly but erroneously associated with Africa are also perpetuated. An elaborate filmstrip-record set talks about tigers in the jungles of this land. (There are none.) One otherwise useful set of transparencies carries decorative sketches that perpetuate outmoded stereotypes. And so on. In previewing materials, especially written ones, one should be particularly alert to the repeated use of words that connote erroneous stereotypes or generalizations that are in error.

No materials are completely free from these weaknesses, nor can their flaws be eliminated. They can, however, be minimized and even turned to effective classroom learning by wise selection and balanced use. This is essentially the responsibility of the classroom teacher. In the final analysis it is up to him and to the curriculum builder to select those materials that best fit their needs. To facilitate this, every effort has been made to list here all commercial materials known to be currently available. The basic content, structure, and emphasis is outlined for each. Judgments about their quality, however, are left to the individual educator, for these will largely depend on how he proposes to use them in his classroom.

The materials are arranged by regions of Africa south of the Sahara, and within each region, according to nations and/or subjects. Materials are labeled by type.

# AFRICA SOUTH OF THE SAHARA–GENERAL OVERVIEW

**WRITTEN MATERIALS**

### Student Texts

*Africa, Emerging Nations Below the Sahara.* Columbus: American Education Publications, Inc., 1966. Paper. 25¢.

Brief description of the land, peoples and current problems of Africa followed by brief case studies designed to stimulate thought and discussions. Topics include the tse tse fly, the effect of land redistribution on a Kikuyu farmer, the Masai, education of a young boy in Gabon; photos; chapter-end thought questions; statistical data on each nation; no index. 47 pp. (Reading level: 7-10)

Allen, William D., *Africa.* Grand Rapids: The Fideler Company, 1966. Hardcover. $3.95.

A brief description of the land, animals, history, peoples, economic activities, cities and social problems of Africa interspersed with many large, exceptionally clear, black and white photos and questions designed to guide reading; appendix includes information on map skills and problem-solving; glossary, index. 176 pp. (Reading level: 5-8).

Belasco, Milton Jay and Edward Graff, *The New Africa–History, Culture, People.* Bronxville: Cambridge Book Company, Inc., 1966. Paper. $1.45.

Review book-type survey of the land, peoples, and history of Africa south of the Sahara with special sections on current problems in Ghana, Nigeria, the Congo (K), Rhodesia and South Africa; section on international affairs; charts and maps; multiple choice questions, terms, map exercise and factual questions at end of each chapter; index. 154 pp. (Reading level: 9-12).

ben-Jochannan, Yosef et al., *Africa: The Land, the People, the Culture.* New York: William H. Sadlier, Inc., 1969. Paper. $1.95.

A regional survey of Africa treating the geography, history, economy of each major nation briefly; scores of color photos, excellent maps and some drawings; student activities and exercises included at the end of each unit; commences with detailed overview of Africa's geography and history and the peoples of central Africa. Regional studies emphasize urbanized, westernized Africa; words deemed offensive to Africans (such as "primitive") not used in text. Appendix has population data; glossary of terms. Index. 183 pp. (Reading level: 6-9).

Bohannan, Paul, *Africa and Africans,* Garden City: The Natural History Press, 1964. Paper. $1.25.

A popular survey of Africa, with half the book emphasizing the early history to 1900 and the period since 1960; and the other half describing African regions, arts, family organization, land and labor systems, politics, markets and religion; bibliography, index. 260 pp. (Reading level: 10-12).

Burke, Fred, *Sub-Saharan Africa.* New York: Harcourt, Brace and World, 1968. Paper. $1.35.

A history of Africa south of the Sahara emphasizing the period since 1500; chapters on the land and people, pre-European history, exploration, colonialism, the economics and politics of nation-building, and Africa's relations with the world. 17 maps, graphs, and charts, some photos (b/w); no index. 90 pp. (Reading level: 9-12).

Davidson, Basil, *A Guide to African History.* Garden City: Doubleday & Company, Inc., 1965. Paper. $1.45.

A brief, clearly written survey of the history of Africa south of the Sahara from pre-history, through the cities, kingdoms, states and empires of the pre-European period, the European penetration, slave trade, and imperialism to the independence movement in the 1960's; with several maps and sketches and a guide to pronunciation; index. 118 pp. (Reading level: 6-9).

Desai, Ram, *African Society and Culture.* New York: M. W. Lads Publishing Company, 1968. Paper. $2.95.

A brief summary of the land, various elements of culture (kinship, love, death, courtship), education, health, the status of women, and selected economic aspects of Africa south of the Sahara; photos, some maps and source materials; appendix has a glossary, list of selected proverbs, a gazetteer and extensive bibliography for teachers; no index. 130 pp. (Reading level: 7-10).

Eiselen, Elizabeth and Marguerite Uttley, *Africa.* Boston: Ginn & Company, 1966. Paper. $2.32.

Reprinted section in paperback form from the textbook *Lands and Peoples of the World*; chapters on the geography of the continent, North Africa, equatorial Africa, highland Africa, Southern Africa; over one-hundred colored maps, photos, charts; reference section including atlas maps and statistical tables; excellent questions inserted in text; index. 174 pp. (Reading level: 6-9).

Ewing, Ethel E., *The Cultures of Africa South of the Sahara.* Chicago: Rand McNally, 1967. Paper. $1.28.

A reprint in booklet form of the concluding unit of Ewing's *Our Widening World*; a section on the geography, history, and traditional culture (focusing on the Nupe) of Negro Africa; a section on its history from 1885 through independence followed by a section (15 pp.) on efforts at international cooperation in the world; many photos (b/w); pronouncing index. 79 pp. (Reading level: 10-12).

Foster, Philip J., *Africa South of the Sahara.* New York: The Macmillan Company, 1968. Paper.

A survey of Africa south of the Sahara with emphasis on contemporary Africa and its historic and geographic background; includes excellent but brief descriptions of the land and climate, people, history, and traditional life (pp. 1-84); emphasizes changing urban Africa, its religions, developments in education, the economic sphere, and the political realm. Suggestions for additional reading. Numerous maps, charts, photos (b/w). Index. 152 pp. (Reading level: 9-12).

Greig, Mary E., *How People Live In Africa.* Chicago: Benefic Press, 1963. Hardcover. $1.95.

Chapters on the land of Africa south of the Sahara, its peoples, and their history, with a special chapter on Nigeria, its history and life today; concludes with a section on Africa's future; includes summary of basic concepts and pronunciation index; sketches, photos, charts, and maps in color and black and white. 96 pp. (Reading level: 4-7).

Hapgood, David and Lindley J. Stiles, *Today's World in Focus: Africa.* Boston: Ginn & Company, 1965. Paper. $1.44.

Chapters on the land and history of central Africa, southern Africa, African village life, changing society, governments, African unity, economic development, socialism and foreign relations; emphasis throughout is on contemporary Africa; includes brief biographical sketches of leaders; photos, sketches, maps; short bibliography; no index. 122 pp. (Reading level: 9-12).

Jack, Elspeth, *Africa: An Early History.* London: George G. Harrap and Company, Ltd., (Distributed in the U.S. by International University Booksellers, Inc., 1968.) Paper. $1.50.

A brief survey of pre-European African history with short chapters on prehistoric Africa, Egypt, Axum, east coast kingdoms, Sudanic kingdoms, forest empires, the Bushmen, Zimbabwe, the Kongo, and the Bantu migrations. Clear maps, drawings and sketches. Concludes with notes to the teacher. Prepared for use in African schools. 86 pp. (Reading level: 6-9).

Joy, Charles R., *Emerging Africa.* (A Scholastic World Affairs Multi-Text). New York: Scholastic Book Services, 1967. Paper. 75¢.

A brief survey with small photos and maps of the land, peoples, and history of Africa followed by short country-by-country surveys of all nations on the continent and a description of selected problems of the future; includes chapter-end questions, terms to know, and suggestions for further reading, a gazetteer and index; with teachers' guide that suggests various approaches and audio-visual materials. 160 pp. (Reading level: 7-10).

Kimble, George H. and Ronald Steel, *Tropical Africa Today.* St. Louis: Webster Division, McGraw-Hill Book Company, 1966. Paper. $1.98.

Kimble's standard work edited and rewritten for secondary school students; includes chapters on the land, peoples, tradition and change, economic progress, political and social change, and the future; excellent maps, charts, photos, gazetteer, annotated list of recommended readings; index. 138 pp. (Reading level: 9-12).

Lengyel, Emil, *Africa in Ferment.* New York: Oxford Book Company, 1963. Paper. 50¢.

A brief survey of the land, resources, peoples, and religion of Africa followed by a short historical summary; sections on European colonies in Africa as of 1962 followed by country-by-country descriptions of the independent nations; chapter-end aids; few maps; no index. 92 pp. (Reading level: 9-12).

Mensoian, Michael and Hugh Brooks, *The Arab World/New Africa.* New York: William H. Sadlier, Inc., 1968. Paper. $1.95.

A survey of the Arab world followed by a survey of Africa south of the Sahara emphasizing especially its geography, peoples and history; has descriptions of major nations and/or regions followed by a survey of contemporary trends, problems and changes. Includes extensive chapter reviews, many photos (b/w), and several maps. Index. 194 pp. (Reading level: 6-9).

Murphy, E. Jefferson, *Understanding Africa.* New York: Thomas Y. Crowell Company, 1969. Hardcover. $4.95.

An up-to-date examination of Africa by the executive vice-president of the African-American Institute. Includes chapters on geography, ancient Africa, colonial conquest, people and nations, independence, Africa's role in world Affairs, Africa's future. Maps; illustrations; selected reading list; index. 209 pp. (Reading level: 6-9).

Nielsen, Waldemar, *Africa.* New York: Atheneum, 1966. Paper. $1.65.

An edited and somewhat revised version of Nielsen's *New York Times World Affairs Workshop* booklet on Africa; no illustrations; index. 169 pp. (Reading level: 10-12).

Nielsen, Waldemar, *Africa—World Affairs Workshop.* New York: *The New York Times*—Encyclopaedia Britannica Press, 1965. Paper. $1.00.

Summaries of interviews and personal descriptions of selected problems facing Africa south of the Sahara including those of colonialism, tribal loyalties, poverty, democracy, racial unrest, and the Cold War; some photos, index. 92 pp. (Reading level: 10-12).

Oliver, Roland and J. D. Fage, *A Short History of Africa.* Baltimore: Penguin Books, 1964. Paper. $1.95.

A scholarly survey of the various peoples of Africa followed by a chronological survey of their history to about 1961; suggestions for further reading; index. 280 pp. (Reading level: 12).

Rosberg, Carl G., *Africa and the World Today.* River Forest (Illinois): Laidlaw Brothers, Publishers, 1966. Paper. 75¢.

A very brief survey of the history of Africa south of the Sahara, its geography, selected aspects of traditional society, and the nature of the colonial impact; chapters on problems of nationalism, economic development, race problems in Southern Africa, and the implications of these for American foreign policy; chapter-end questions; some maps, cartoons, sketches. Teachers' guide lists additional materials and suggested activities, sources of data and test. 60 pp. (Reading level: 9-12).

Salkever, Louis R. and Helen M. Flynn, *Sub-Saharan Africa: Struggle Against the Past.* Chicago: Scott, Foresman and Company, 1964. Paper. $1.28.

A brief historical background followed by chapters on problems of economic development, pathways to growth, and Africa's relations with the rest of the world; some photos, maps and charts; chapter-end questions; no index. 72 pp. (Reading level: 10-12).

Savage, Katherine, *The Story of Africa South of the Sahara.* New York: Henry Z. Walck, Inc., 1961. Hardcover. $5.00.

A brief traditional survey of the history of Africa south of the Sahara commencing with the period of the slave trade to about 1900 followed by chapters on the history and development of South Africa, the creation of modern Ghana, the fight against federation in the Rhodesias, and on the Mau Mau in Kenya; several photos (b/w); index. 184 pp. (Reading level: 9-12).

Singleton, F. Seth and John Shingler, *Africa in Perspective.* New York: Hayden Book Company, Inc., 1967. Paper. $3.96.

A readable, scholarly description of Africa south of the Sahara that examines in depth the peoples, history, and search for unity in Africa, with special sections contrasting development in the Congo and Nigeria, in Ethiopia and Liberia, and within South Africa; also a special section on problems of political and economic development; superb maps, photos, charts, graphs, woodcuts, end-of-chapter questions and activities; good index. 310 pp. (Reading level: 10-12).

Stavrianos, Leften S. and Loretta Kreider Andrews, *Sub-Saharan Africa.* Boston: Allyn & Bacon, Inc., 1965. Paper. 99¢.

A reprint of the unit on Africa in Stavrianos' *Global History of Man* that treats the habitat, people, economic activities, culture, and government in terms of present conditions, historical origins, and prospects for the future; maps, charts, photos; end-of-chapter questions, terms, activities; brief bibliography; index. 80 pp. (Reading level: 9-12).

Williams, John A., *Africa–Her History, Lands and People.* New York: Cooper Square Publishers, Inc., 1962. Paper. $1.95.

A survey of the history of Africa emphasizing the period 1500 to 1950; special sections on peoples and creative arts; section including data and pictures on each nation; chronology; over 200 maps, photos, drawings, lithographs, and woodcuts from original sources (all b/w); no index. 128 pp. (Reading level: 9-12).

## Student Readings

Hoff, Rhoda, *Africa–Adventures in Eyewitness History.* New York: Henry Z. Walck, Inc., 1963. Hardcover. $3.75.

Excerpts from documents, diaries, letters, travel accounts, speeches, autobiographies, historical works, and other sources on early European contacts with Africa south of the Sahara, the colonial period, and independent Africa; no index. 174 pp. (Reading level: 9-12).

Moore, Clark D. and Ann Dunbar, *Africa Yesterday and Today.* New York: Bantam Books, Inc., 1968. Paper. 95¢.

A collection of edited excerpts from the writings of scholars (Kimble, Hance, Ottenberg, Fage, etc.) and others focusing on the structure of traditional African society, early African history, colonial systems, Africa since World War II, and the future of Africa; index. 394 pp. (Reading level: 10-12).

Nolen, Barbara, *Africa is People.* New York: E. P. Dutton & Company, Inc., 1967. Hardcover. $6.95.

Selections from African authors, political speeches, writings of anthropologists, explorers, and other observers of and participants in African life on traditional life, changes, and the impact of change in contemporary Africa south of the Sahara; index. 270 pp. (Reading level: 9-12).

Stavrianos, Leften S. et al., *Readings in World History.* Boston: Allyn and Bacon, Inc., 1962. Paper. $4.50.

Contains 88 pp. of excerpts from diaries, journals, biographies, speeches, and other sources describing African culture, economic development, recent poliitcal history, and early history (emphasizing especially the period of European exploration and the slave trade); no index. 910 pp. (Reading level: 9-12).

### Collections of Primary Sources

Betts, Raymond F., *The Scramble for Africa* (*Problems of European Civilization* series). Boston: D. C. Heath and Company, 1966. Paper. $1.95.

Historical interpretations focusing on the European perspective and the African perspective. 88 pp.

Curtin, Philip D., *Africa Remembered.* Madison: University of Wisconsin Press, 1968. Paper. $2.95.

A collection of selections from works by West Africans in the 18th and 19th century; includes introductions to each selection that explain the author's background and contributions; selections from former slaves writing about their travels and homelands in West Africa; some maps, woodcuts, and other illustrations. Extensive index. 363 pp.

Davidson, Basil, *The African Past.* New York: Grosset & Dunlap, 1964. Paper. $2.95.

Selections from ancient historians and contemporary observers and scholars, from Arab travelers, old chronicles, European diaries, letters, essays, and reports; focuses on ancient Africa south of the Sahara, early West and East Africa, the first European contacts, and the period since 1700; index. 392 pp.

Emerson, Rupert and Martin Kilson, *The Political Awakening of Africa.* Englewood Cliffs: Prentice-Hall, Inc., 1965. Paper. $1.95.

Excerpts from speeches and writings of African leaders and intellectuals on the topics of African self-identity, nationalism, political parties in Africa, and inter-African problems and policies; biographical sketches of authors included; no index. 174 pp.

Hodgkin, Thomas, *Nigerian Perspectives, An Historical Anthology.* London: Oxford University Press, 1960. Hardcover. $5.60.

Excerpts from documents, diaries, ancient, histories, chronicles, travelers' accounts, explorers' records, European government officials' writings on Nigeria from the origins of its peoples to the present; index. 340 pp.

Kohn, Hans and Wallace Sokolsky, *African Nationalism in the Twentieth Century.* Princeton: D. Van Nostrand Company, Inc., 1965. Paper. $1.45.

A narrative of the highlights of the nationalist movement, followed by excerpts from speeches, articles, and scholarly works illustrative of selected aspects of this movement; brief bibliography and chronology; index. 190 pp.

Marsh, Zoe, *East Africa Through Contemporary Records.* Cambridge University Press, 1961. Hardcover. $4.75.

Selections from explorers' accounts and other sources focusing on early Portuguese activities, exploration of the interior, missionary activities, various peoples and nations; several maps, drawings and plates; extensive bibliography; no index. 209 pp.

Oliver, Roland and Caroline Oliver, *Africa in the Days of Exploration.* Englewood Cliffs: Prentice-Hall, Inc., 1965. Paper. $1.95.

Excerpts from travelers' and explorers' accounts focusing on customs and traditional practices of the Africans prior to extensive European penetration; no index. 151 pp.

Perham, Margery and J. Simmons, *African Discovery: An Anthology of Exploration.* Evanston: Northwestern University Press, 1963. Hardcover. $3.95.

A collection of excerpts from the journals of James Bruce, Mungo Park, Hugh Clapperton, the Landers, David Livingston and others, with an introduction by the editors; index. 280 pp.

Richards, Charles, ed., *Some Historic Journies in East Africa.* Nairobi: Oxford University Press, 1961/1968. Paper.

A collection of edited excerpts from the journals of various explorers of East Africa such as Krapf and Rebmann, New, Burton, Speke and Grant, Baker, Livingston, Stanley, Thomson, and others. They describe such historic events as the discovery of Lake Victoria, Victoria Falls, the source of the Nile, the ascent of Kilimanjaro, the crossing of Masailand; includes some pictures, brief biography of each explorer. No index. 142 pp.

Richards, Charles and James Place, eds., *East African Explorers.* Nairobi: Oxford University Press, 1967. Paper.

Excerpts from the journals of twelve exploring parties and/or explorers with introductions; includes explorations of Krapf and Rebman, New, Austin, Lugard, McDonald, Casati, Burton, Grant, Teleki, von Hohnel and Gregory; selections on slavery at Malindi in 1863, escaping from the Masai, ascent of Mt. Kenya, etc. No index. 366 pp.

Wallbank, T. Walter, *Contemporary Africa: Continent in Transition.* Princeton: D. Van Nostrand Company, Inc., 1964. Revised edition. Paper. $1.45.

Following introductory description of contemporary Africa south of the Sahara (129 pp.) are excerpts from government documents, political speeches, and commission reports about colonial administration, unification of African territories, various racial policies; index. 191 pp.

Wallbank, T. Walter, *Documents on Modern Africa.* Princeton: D. Van Nostrand Company, Inc., 1964. Paper. $1.45.

Excerpts from 48 governmental documents, reports, and statements as well as from other sources relative to the history and government of Africa south of the Sahara, 1872-1964; emphasizes especially treaties, colonial policies, nationalism and independence, Europeans in Africa, and race relations; index. 189 pp.

## Fact Sheets

*African Fact Sheet.* New York: Division of Overseas Ministries, National Council of the Churches of Christ. Paper. Single copies free.

A series of 6-10 page mimeographed fact sheets, each on a specific African nation; each describes briefly geographic, historical, social, religious, and political conditions in that country; Congo (L), Nigeria, Tanganyika, Rhodesia, Malawi, Burundi, Zambia, South Africa, Ghana, Mozambique, Kenya, Botswana available. Published periodically.

*The African Mosaic: Black and White and Lots of Military Tan,* in *News Pointer* (April 1966). New York: Newsweek Educational Division, 1966. Paper.

A brief survey of current developments in Africa's economic growth, military takeovers, and the racial policies of Rhodesia and South Africa. 8 pp.

*Africa North and East,* Volume 2 of *The World and Its Peoples.* Chicago: New Horizons Publishers, Inc., 1967. Hardcover.

Surveys of the land, peoples, history, literature, and music of Spanish West Africa, Ethiopia, Somalia, Kenya, Uganda, Tanzania, Rwanda, Burundi, French Somaliland. 160 pp.

*Africa: Pattern of Sovereignty* (*Cartocraft Research Studies*). Chicago: Denoyer Geppert Company, 1968. Paper.

A survey of the evolution of national boundaries in Africa, of physical regions, and the new states of the continent; includes tables, maps. 16 pp.

*Background Notes.* Washington: Department of State, 1965 to date. Paper. 5¢ each.

Four- to 8-page, note-book size fact sheets (each including one full-page map) on the geography, people, history, government, political situation, economy, trade, U.S. aid received, and principal government officials for each African nation and dependency; bibliography of additional materials included for each. Published periodically.

Dostert, Pierre Etienne, *Africa, 1969.* Washington: Stryker-Post Publications, 1969. Paper. $1.75.

A concise historical background of the entire continent, followed by a country-by-country description of the terrain, contemporary history, government and politics, cultural heritage, and economy of Africa's 42 independent nations; brief notes on the dependent territories and a quick analysis of the present situation in Rhodesia; simplified maps of each country correlated with the text; full-page maps show vegetation belts and political divisions of the continent in 1905 and today; revised annually. No index. 89 pp.

*Focus.* New York: American Geographical Society. Paper. 26¢ each title.

Notebook size, six-page descriptions of individual African nations describing the geography, society, and economy of each nation; includes full-page of two-color maps on geographic features; issues on Niger, Nigeria, Gabon, Ivory Coast and most other nations now available. Published monthly.

Kimble, George H. T., *Africa* (reprinted from *The World Book Encyclopedia*). Chicago: Field Enterprises Educational Corporation, 1965. Paper. 25¢.

A brief survey of the land, life, peoples, languages, religion, education, arts, economic activities, and history of Africa; text with a multitude of maps, photos and charts, many in color; study aids. 39 pp.

*The New Africa,* CES (1967). Paper. $.50.

A 24" x 22" chart (punched and folded to fit a looseleaf notebook) that contains in chart form vital political, demographic, economic, and historical data for every African nation; also contains on reverse side a political map, photos, brief history of the continent and selected facts.

*Profiles of Newly Independent States, Geographic Bulletin No. 1.* Washington: U.S. Department of State, July 1964. Revised. Paper. 25¢.

A paragraph with independence date on each of 51 nations in the world (including 30 African nations) that have become independent since 1943; includes reference tables on area, population, and nationality forms; no index. 26 pp.

Rycroft, W. Stanley and Myrtle M. Clemmer, *A Factual Study of Sub-Saharan Africa.* New York: United Presbyterian Church, Commission on Ecumenical Mission and Relations, 1962. Paper. $1.00.

Descriptions of and statistics on geography, demography, culture, economy, society, and religion of Africa; includes maps, statistics on education, urban and rural population, per capita income, trade, population etc.; with bibliography; no index. 116 pp.

Thompson, Elizabeth M., *Other Lands, Other Peoples—A Country-by-Country Fact Book.* Washington: National Education Association of the United States, 1967. Paper. $2.00.

Seventy pages of descriptions of the location, size, geographical features, peoples, religion, cities, government, economy, education, and political history for each African nation; special notes on religions and national holidays; no index. 255 pp.

### Atlases

Ady, P. H. and A. Z. Hazlewood, *Africa, Oxford Regional Economic Atlas.* London: Oxford University Press, 1965. Paper. $7.00.

Sixty pages of text and statistics on population, agriculture, minerals, manufacturing, power, transport and foreign trade followed by 53 pages of full color maps on specific economic, social, and geographic topics on both regions and the continent as a whole; gazetteer; detailed index. 164 pp. Size: 7½" x 10".

*Africa,* (Atlas Plate 54) September 1960. Washington: The National Geographic Society, 1966. $1.00.

Full color 32" x 42" paper map of the entire African continent.

"Africa South of the Sahara," Section 6 of *Rand McNally's Illustrated Atlas of Today's World.* Sperling and Schwartz, Inc. Paper. $1.00.

A brief introduction to Africa south of the Sahara followed by a country-by-country survey with text, excellent maps, and charts of all the political units lying in Southern, Central, Equatorial, West and East Africa; no index. 95 pp.

Boyd, Andrew and Patrick van Rensburg, *An Atlas of African Affairs.* New York: Frederick A. Praeger, Publisher, 1963. Paper. $1.75.

Seventeen maps of the continent depicting geography, political history, and current conditions; 38 maps of various nations and regions; explanatory text on each facing page with some cross references to other relevant maps. 132 pp. Size: 5" x 8".

Cowan, L. Gray, *The Dilemmas of African Independence.* New York: Walker & Company, 1964. Paper. $2.25.

Eighty pages of introductory text on democracy, economic development and supra-nationalism in Africa; 75 pages of clearly-drawn color maps, charts and graphs on African society, cultures, geography, resources, commerce, aid, international relations; index. 162 pp. Size: 5½" x 8½".

Fage, J. D., *An Atlas of African History.* London: Edward Arnold Publishers, Ltd., 1963. Hardcover. $6.00.

Sixty-two black and white, detailed maps emphasizing the Sudanic states in different periods, the west coast, European exploration and imperialism, and modern economic development. Detailed index. Size: 8½" x 11".

Fordham, Paul, *The Geography of African Affairs.* Baltimore: Penguin Books, 1965. Paper. $1.45.

Text with 36 tables and 28 small maps interspersed; focuses on a general survey of the history and economic development of the continent (85 pp.) and then on regional studies on a country-by-country basis; index. 244 pp. Size: 4" x 7".

Fullard, Harold, *Philips' Modern College Atlas for Africa.* London: George Philip and Son, 1965. (Distributed by Denoyer-Geppert Company, Chicago.) Sixth edition. Hardcover. $4.50.

Thirty-one pages of climographs and full color maps on rainfall, climate, selected resources of the world; 42 pages of full-color maps of Africa and individual African nations; 64 pages of maps on other continents and nations; indexed. Originally intended for use in African schools. Size: 9" x 11½".

Gailey, Harry A., Jr., *The History of Africa in Maps.* Chicago: Denoyer-Geppert Company, 1967. Paper. $2.50.

Forty-six black and white maps of Africa and various regions of Africa; sections on geography and major historical events; each map accompanied by explanatory text on facing page. Size: 8½" x 11".

Healy, A. M. and E. R. Vere-Hodge, *The Map Approach to African History.* London: University Tutorial Press, Ltd. (Clifton House, Euston Rd., London N.W. 1), 1965. Third edition. Paper. 65¢.

Sixty-five black and white, clearly-drawn maps with detailed explanatory text on the highlights of African history and current problems; includes timeline of African history since 1800; index. Size: 6½" x 8".

Kitchen, Helen, *A Handbook of African Affairs.* New York: Frederick A. Praeger, Publisher, 1964. Paper. $2.25.

A country-by-country political guide of all independent and dependent territories in Africa, with vital statistics about the political system of each, followed by a description of the armies of African nations giving size, budget, sources of assistance, and defense agreements; includes charter of Organization of African Unity; several maps; no index. 322 pp.

Martin, Geoffrey J., *Africa in Maps.* Dubuque: Wm. C. Brown Company, Publishers, 1962. Paper. $2.50.

Fifty-eight black and white, easy-to-read maps of the geographic, historical, demographic, economic, and social features of the African continent; facing pages blank for student notes. Spiral bound. Size: 8½" x 11".

Peterson, Edwin L., *Cultural Geography Workbook–Afro-Asia.* Minneapolis: Burgess Publishing Company, 1962/1965. Paper. $4.00.

A series of student activities with 90 pages devoted to Africa; sections on Africa as a whole and on each major region; each section has 5-8 pages of information on the countries in it followed by a list of selected data on each country and 1-2 map locational assignments with directions and maps. 196 pp. (Reading level: 12).

## Periodicals for Students

*Tarikh.* New York: Humanities Press. $2.00/year.

A journal of African history published by the Historical Society of Nigeria for use by secondary school and first year college students. Articles accompanied by photos, charts, maps, and suggestions for further reading. Questions for discussion and advertisements of the latest British publications on Africa also included. Each issue averages 92 pp. Published May and November.

## Periodicals for Student References

*African Arts/Arts D'Afrique.* African Studies Center, University of California, Los Angeles, California, 90024. $10.00/year.

A quarterly devoted to the graphic, plastic, performing and literary arts of Africa. Each issue includes many color prints, photographs and other reproductions. Special student edition available. Published quarterly.

*Africa Report.* African-American Institute, 505 Dupont Circle Building, Washington, D.C., 20036. $6.00/year.

Noted for its accuracy; up-to-date, factual reports on Africa today in the context of its history; with monthly chronology of events; many illustrations. (Reading level: 10-12). Published 9 months a year.

## Related Periodicals

*Christian Science Monitor,* Christian Science Publishing Society, 1 Norway Street, Boston, Massachusetts, 02115.

Occasionally produces a special page or supplement on Africa or various regions of Africa.

*Current History.* Current History, Inc., 1822 Ludlow Street, Philadelphia, Pennsylvania, 19103. Monthly. $8.50.

Periodical review of current problems or trends in Africa; each year devotes a special issue to Africa such as: February 1968 *Africa*; March 1967 *West Africa.* (Reading level: 11-12).

*Headline Series.* Foreign Policy Association, 345 East 46th Street, New York, New York, 10017. Published 6 times a year. $4.00/year; 75¢/single copy.

Analysis of major foreign policy problems with maps, charts, discussion guides, and bibliographies. Among those now available are:

Kimble, George H. T., *Tropical Africa: Problems and Promises.* #147 (May-June 1961). Paper.

A survey of the sources of problems such as the land, resources and so on; and of industrialization, social change, education, and political revolution. 62 pp.

Montgomery, John D., *Aid to Africa: New Test for U.S. Policy.* #149 (Sept.-Oct. 1961). Paper.

A survey of U.S. policy and of African problems affecting the planning and use of U.S. aid; includes a survey of U.S. aid programs in Africa. 62 pp.

Rivkin, Arnold, *The New States of Africa.* #183 (June 1967). Paper.

A survey of African independence, the problems faced by these new countries, the role played by the military, and African-world, African-U.S. relations. 63 pp.

*Intercom.* Center for War/Peace Studies, 218 E. 18th St., New York, New York, 10003. Published six times yearly. $1.00 each.

Reference guide to world affairs field, latest ideas, programs, services, books, and pamphlets on Africa and other world areas; usually produces an annual issue devoted to Africa. *(Intercom* was formerly produced by the Foreign Policy Association.)

*National Geographic Magazine.* National Geographic Society, Washington, D.C., 20036.

A rich source of pictures and information about Africa south of the Sahara; since 1931 over 50 issues have been devoted in whole or in part to the peoples of this region; a bibliography and price list of those on Africa may be obtained directly from the Society.

*National Geographic School Bulletin.* National Geographic Society. 30 issues per year. $2.00/year

Each issue on a variety of topics especially interesting to students; frequently one or two articles with color pictures on various aspects of Africa south of the Sahara in each issue; each issue approximately 14 pages. (The February 5, 1968 issue, for example, featured a 5-page picture-essay on the Bushman.)

*New York Times Student Weekly.* New York Times Book and Educational Division, 229 West 43rd Street, New York, New York, 10036. This program is available for all secondary school students; supplemental guides and materials published periodically. A special 23-page supplement on Ghana and Nigeria (March 1967) focused on the problems of despotism and tribalism in these nations. A bibliography and suggested activities included.

## United States Government Sources

Many agencies of the federal government publish materials related to Africa south of the Sahara. The major sources are:

Superintendent of Documents
U.S. Government Printing Office
Washington, D.C.

Office of Media Services
U.S. Department of State
Washington, D.C.

Price lists and catalogs can be obtained from these sources on written request.

### Weekly News Magazines

Periodicals such as *Newsweek* and *Time* provide some coverage of events in Africa south of the Sahara and periodically publish supplemental materials exclusively on this region for use in secondary grades with their special student programs. In January 1968, for example, *Newsweek* published a special wall map on the East African Common Market; in March it distributed a dittoed map work sheet and a student supplement on current African problems. *Time* magazine periodically distributes similar materials. For further information write:

*Newsweek* Educational Division
444 Madison Avenue
New York, New York, 10022

*Time* Magazine Educational Division
Time and Life Building
Rockefeller Center
New York, New York, 10022

## AUDIO-VISUAL MATERIALS

### Maps

*Aero Raised Relief Map of Africa,* NYSTROM. $49.00.

45" x 49" plastic covered raised-relief map of Africa using traditional colors to indicate elevation; political boundaries and cities shown; highlands raised as high as ½ inch above surface of map.

*Africa,* Randmark V, RAND McNALLY. $25.00.

Wall map 60" x 66", color, showing relief and physical features as well as political boundaries, cities, transportation networks.

*Africa Study Series,* DENOYER. $102.75.

16 wall maps ranging in size from 25" x 36" to 44" x 37" on Ghana, Nigeria, Uganda, South Africa, East Africa, West Africa, Kenya, Tan-ganyika, Central Africa; population, winter climate, temperature-rainfall, vegetation, commerce, physical, political.

*Headline-Focus Wall Map,* CES. $9.00 per year.

28" x 38" color, twice monthly (15 copies per year); several each year on African subjects.

*Wenschow Relief-Like Map of Africa,* DENOYER. $27.25.

Wall map, 64" x 75" having three dimensional effect; shows relief and political features in color.

### Films

*African Continent: Tropical Region,* CORONET (1962). color, narration, 13 min. $162.50.

A filmed overview of the tropical region of Africa showing the principal geographic regions, peoples, history, cultures, agriculture, and natural resources. Concludes with themes of emergence of new nations and social change. Teacher's guide. (Collaborator: Professor Hibberd V. B. Kline, Jr.)

*Continent of Africa (Lands Below the Sahara),* EBF (1962). color, narration, 22 min.

A survey of the geography, peoples, economy, and colonial history of sub-Saharan Africa. Current themes of social change, economic development, and independence are stressed. (Collaborator: Professor Paul Bohannan.)

*Tropical Africa,* IFF (1961). color, narration, 29 min. $275.00.

A filmed introduction to Africa south of the Sahara emphasizing current trends and features—e.g., economic development, social change and political change. A graphic portrayal of the "becoming Africa."

### Film-loop/Sound

*Tropical Africa,* EALING (1967). 8mm, cartridged loop in color with narration and sound, 23 min. $175.00.

An introduction to Africa south of the Sahara filmed in 1965, emphasizing the contemporary life with its problems and prospects. A Julien Bryan International Film Foundation production.

## Filmstrips

*Africa: The Developing Continent,* BAILEY (1967). 5 fs., color, captioned, script. $42.00.

A series of five filmstrips on Africa dealing with the following topics: Geography of Africa, How African People Live, Transportation in Africa, Cultural Life in Africa, Earning a Living in Africa. Teachers' manual for the entire series with a paragraph for each frame.

*Africa, The Land of Developing Countries,* SVE (1965). 6 fs., 3 LP records, color, captioned, script. $39.75.

A series of six sound filmstrips dealing with the following regions: The Nile Valley, The Eastern Highlands, Southern Africa, The Congo Basin, The West Central Lowlands, Northwest Africa, and the Sahara. Each focuses on the land, peoples and economy. Script: seven individual manuals, one dealing with the entire series. Manuals consist of objectives, special features, utilization, and short paragraph for individual frames.

*Africa Today—Part One & Part Two,* AF (1968). color, non-captioned, script. $7.00 each.

Part I: General overview of the continent of Africa. Emphasis given to historical sites, street scenes, and buildings; some of the major cities of Africa, transportation, and political activities. Part II: General overview of the continent of Africa. Emphasis given to economic activities, products, and cultural life (education, religion, sports, art). Script: Introduction presenting the highlights of African history and geography. Short paragraph on individual frames of filmstrip. Suggested questions, activities, and references.

*The Continent of Africa,* McGH (1967). color, captioned, script. $8.50.

32 photos, 6 maps and one full caption. General overview of the continent of Africa. Introduc-

tion with emphasis on vegetation (5), life in northern Africa (9), West Africa (8), East Africa (7), southern Africa (7), conclusion (variations and progress in regions of Africa, 3). Map introduces each section of Africa. Captions: statements and questions.

*Profile of Africa—Part I and Part II,* SFS (1962). color, non-captioned, script. $6.00 each.

Part I: 49 photos and one overview map of the continent. Africa's past (9), the land (7), the people (8), housing (12), transportation and communication (13). Part II: 50 photos. General overview of the activities of the people of Africa. Ways of earning a living (10), markets (3), industries (4), health services (4), schools (4), religion (5), government—traditional modern (8), art and recreation (11). Scripts provide frame-by-frame description.

## Overhead Transparencies

*Africa,* EBF (1964). color. $32.00.

Three sets of small multi-color transparencies on Africa. Unit I: The Land (8), Unit II: The People (3), Unit III: History (5). With guide.

*Africa,* HAMMOND. color, script. $5.75.

Four transparencies: base map with rivers and political boundaries, physical features, place names; clear plastic for writing. Used in combination. Plastic frames provided with registration marks for alignment. Maps of entire continent. Notes to teacher deal with mechanics of using transparencies.

*Africa,* NYSTROM. color. $6.60.

Sculpture Relief Series (in color): two transparencies: physical map, overlay of political boundaries. Used in combination; a second set has (A) Base map with rivers and political boundaries and (B) physical features overlay in color.

*Africa,* RAND McNALLY. $5.00.

Ranvue Relief Outline Map Series. Three transparencies in paper frame. Base map with rivers and political boundaries, physical features map with rivers and political boundaries, place names map. Used in combination. Maps of entire continent.

*Africa and Australia* (Set IV), GINN. color, script. $9.50.

Five transparencies: Base map with rivers and physical features, annual rainfall, January/July temperature, population dot map, place names. Used in combination. Maps of entire continent.

*Africa and the Near East,* HAYES. $5.50.

A booklet of 14 transparencies and outline maps of Africa and various regions of Africa (e.g., West Africa, East Africa, South Africa); with teaching suggestions and geographical and population data for each nation (9 pp.).

*Africa in Perspective,* HAYDEN BOOK COMPANY, (1968). $35.00.

A set of 18 individual transparencies reproducing the maps in *Africa in Perspective.* Charts included when comparing Africa with selected countries of the world. Physical features (2), tribes (2), history (4), agriculture and mineral products (1), population density (1), African diseases (1), independence (3), income and literacy (2), urbanization (1), African religions (1).

*Alpha Map Transparencies: Africa,* ALLYN & BACON (1966). color, script. $60.00.

Thirty-three multi-color single transparencies: three base maps, and 30 maps pertaining to the physical (11), economic (11), and cultural (8) characteristics of Africa. Printed map with each transparency with reverse side containing description of data, suggested combinations of ' overlays, and suggested readings. Plastic registration guide provided. Used in combination. All maps are of entire continent.

*Africa: Political Geography and Nationalism* (Series AF-43), AEVAC (1968). $99.00.

A set of 13 multi-color transparencies having a total of 44 overlays; on political divisions (1968), regional associations, role of the U.N. and the League, independence sequence, colonial heritage, sketches of 4 nationalist leaders, Congress of Berlin, Nigeria, Republic of South Africa, O.A.U., structure of O.A.U., European possessions 1914. Extensive teaching guide of 64 pp.

*Northern Africa,* RAND McNALLY. $5.00.

Ranvue Relief Outline Map Series. Three transparencies in paper frame: base map with rivers and political boundaries, relief map with rivers and political boundaries, place names. Used in combination. Maps of Africa north of the equator.

*The New Africa,* CAMBRIDGE (1968). b/w. $1.50.

Set of 10 prepared masters for reproduction as class handouts or on acetate for use with overhead projector; includes charts, illustrations, maps; keyed to student text, *The New Africa.*

*World History: Unit I: Sub-Saharan Africa,* KEUFFEL & ESSER CO. (1966). $39.95.

A set of masters for 30 diazo charts and maps on Africa south of the Sahara, each with several overlays. Includes 3 base maps (outline, political, population-dot maps), 3 sets on Africa in the world, 10 on geography, 6 on the peoples, 11 on history. Large lettering, many colors. Each with teaching guide. May also be obtained already prepared at prices ranging from $1.75 to $10.25 per transparency depending on number of overlays, or $180.00 for entire set. Totals 200 sheets.

*World in Scope–Africa,* HAYDEN BOOK COMPANY (1968). two-color. $133.40.

Set consisting of two transparencies for each African nation. Physical maps provide data on climate and elevation. No key for elevation provided. Climograph. Political maps include an outline of country showing products and major cities, and data on religion, language, government, international alignment, and per capita output. Charts comparing United States with individual country in reference to demographic, social, and economic variables.

**Picture-cards**

*Africa,* FIDELER VISUAL TEACHING, INC. (1966). b/w. 48 plates, captions. 9¼" x 12¼". $3.95.

40 photos, 8 maps. Plates divided as follows: land, climate, animals, history, changing Africa, people, farming and grazing, natural resources, industry, transportation, cities of Africa, education and health.

*Children of Africa,* SVE (n.d.). color, heavy board. $8.00.

Set of 8 color photos 13" x 18" depicting scenes of children from various parts of Africa; background information and teaching suggestions printed on reverse side of each photo.

*New Nation English Wall Pictures,* NELSON (1962/1966). color, $5.00.

26½" x 38" multi-color sketches of life in Africa; 12 individual prints on heavy poster paper showing village market, family at home, economic activities, scenes outside houses, fishing, city street scenes, sports events, animal markets, life along a river, herding, inside a modern home, a coastal village. Pictures are stylized, emphasizing western influence. No identifying descriptions or narrative.

*West African Wall Pictures,* OXFORD (1958). color. $7.00.

Set of 8 paintings in color illustrating life in West African villages and cities; bound to flip over. Size 3' x 2'.

## Outline Maps

*Map Reading Africa,* MILLIKEN PUBLISHING CO. (12 transparencies and 28 master duplicating dittoes). $5.95.

Transparencies on Africa, each with identical spirit masters for duplication. The remaining 16 spirit masters are exercises and text to be used with maps. Includes both North Africa and Africa south of the Sahara.

*Outline Maps of Africa,* TEACHERS PUBLISH-ING CORPORATION. (63 spirit masters outline maps). $8.20.

Master maps on Africa: 59 maps of individual countries of Africa with 4 maps of the world, Eastern Hemisphere, Africa and North Africa; 34-page teachers' guide; 2 pages on how to use

outline maps, 32 pages on suggested activities and topics.

## Games

*Adi (Count and Capture),* WORLD WIDE (n.d.) $10.95.

A two-man game played in Ghana and other African nations for hundreds of years; indoors a "muffin-pan" type game board is used—outdoors small holes are scooped in the dirt to serve as a gameboard; includes wooden game board, marbles, directions.

## AFRICA SOUTH OF THE SAHARA–GENERAL TOPICS

### Land

*(Written materials)*

Money, D. C., *Africa: Human Geography.* London: University Tutorial Press, Fourth edition: 1967. (distributed in U.S. by International University Booksellers, Inc.). Paper. $1.20.

A booklet of student exercises and descriptions of Africa's people and geography; extensive use of maps, photos, drawings, charts, graphs; chapters on northwest Africa, Nigeria, the Congo (K), East Africa, southern Africa, and South Africa. Many different types of student activities designed to help students develop geographic concepts relative to Africa. No index. 48 pp. (Reading level: 10-12).

Pritchard, John M., *Studying Africa–Book One: Its Physical Features.* London: Longman's, Green & Company, Ltd., 1966. Paper. 8s 6d.

Designed for use in the middle grades of African secondary schools, this colorful survey focuses on the relief, geologic formations, and other physical features of the continent; includes a multitude of geographic maps and diagrams, questions, glossary; teachers' guide contains data for teacher and suggested activities. 48 pp.

Pritchard, John M., *Studying Africa–Book Two: Its Weather and Climate.* London: Longman's, Green & Company, Ltd., 1967. Paper. 5s 9d.

Also designed for use in the middle grades of African secondary schools, this focuses on earth-sun relations, wind, rain, weather, climate types, and vegetation in Africa; many colorful diagrams and drawings (including climographs); with questions; teachers' guide has data for the teacher and suggested activities. 32 pp.

*Africa, the Awakening Giant: The Impact of Its Geography,* (Honor Roll #701), HONOR PRODUCTS CO., (1967). teachers' guide. $20.00.

A programmed exercise in small plastic machine, manually operated. Overview of the topography, climate, vegetation, products, and people of the entire continent of Africa. 200 frames. Teachers' guide: introduction, how to use programmed materials, and test.

*(Filmstrips)*

*Africa: Climate and Vegetation,* MES, (n.d.). 42 frames, color, captioned, script. $10.00.

30 photos, 9 maps, and 3 drawings. General overview of the climatic zones and vegetation of the entire continent: location of climatic zones (5), tropical rainforest (9), tropical grasslands (12), deserts (11), subtropical and Mediterranean (5). Sections deal with location, major characteristics, vegetation, and products. Captions: statements explaining frames.

*Africa: Physical Features,* MES, (n.d.). 35 frames, color, captioned, script. $10.00.

15 photos, 14 maps and 4 drawings. Combination of maps and photos depicting the major physical features of Africa. An emphasis on geological history and mineral deposits. Captions: statements explaining frames.

*African Jungle,* VEC, 36 frames, b/w, captioned. $4.00.

Thirty-four photos and 2 full captions. Terrain and vegetation, animals and insects (9), natural resources (2), people (dress, housing, daily activities, transportation, and recreation, 17). Captions: statements explaining frames. Several questions included. Full captions: vocabulary and summary.

*What is the Jungle,* VEC, 44 frames, b/w, captioned. $4.00.

41 photos, 2 maps, and one full caption. No specific region treated. Divided in three sections: evergreen forest (15), savanna (13), and monsoon regions (13). Topics: vegetation, products, and animals. Captions: statements explaining frames. Full caption: vocabulary.

*A Look at the Geography of Africa,* BF, (1966). 51 frames, color, captioned, script. (*Africa: Developing Continent* Series—No. 1.) $6.00.

39 photos, 11 maps, and one full caption frame. Maps include Africa and various regions in Africa. Major emphasis on physical features: rivers (Nile and Zambezi), mountain and lakes region, jungle, plains, and Kalahari Desert (30); on vegetation and animals (8), ancient Egyptian ruins (5), and types of people (4); summary (3). Captions explain frames. Script supplements captions.

*(Transparencies)*

*Africa (The Land—Unit 1),* EBF, (1963). color, script.

8 transparencies: comparative map of U.S. and Africa, outline map with rivers, lowlands, highlands, precipitation, vegetation, principal products, production chart ("Africa and Rest of the World"). All maps of entire continent. Can be used individually or as overlays. Registration marks for alignment provided. Notes to teacher. Part of larger set priced at $32.

*Alpha Map Transparencies: Africa,* ALLYN & BACON, (1967). color, guide.

20 multi-colored, single sheet transparencies on all aspects of African geography including climate, mineral resources, manufacturing, relief, vegetation, land forms, and so on. Part of larger set. Each has descriptive guide. Total set $60.

*World Geography: Africa* (258-658), GAF, (1964). $4.25.

Outline base map with overlays showing yearly rainfall, climate, vegetation. Three colors. No guide.

*World Geography* (#258-657), GAF, (1964). $4.25.

Outline transparency with overlays of landforms, boundaries, people per square mile. Three colors. No guide.

*World History: Unit 1–Sub-Saharan Africa.* KEUF-FEL & ESSER CO., (1966).

13 sets of transparencies on various features of Africa south of the Sahara. Includes sets on Africa's position in the world, Africa and the U.S. compared, regions, elevation, climate types, vegetation zones, agriculture, agricultural products, mineral resources, development, per capita income, and transportation. May be obtained for prices ranging from $2.65 to $9.25 depending on number of overlays, or as total package for $39.95.

## People

### *(Written material)*

Feldman, Susan, *African Myths and Tales.* New York: Dell Publishing Company, Inc., 1963. Paper. 50¢.

A brief introductory analysis of African myths and tales followed by collections on such themes as the creation, origin of death, tricksters, dilemmas and morals, and human adventure; also a section of tales that explain how different things or customs came to be; tribal origins identified—heavy emphasis on West and central Africa. Bibliography of sources. No index. 318 pp. (Reading level: 9-12).

Kaula, Edna Mason, *The Bantu Africans.* New York: Franklin Watts, Inc., 1968. Hardcover.

A description of the Bantu peoples who inhabit central and South Africa with many photos (b/w); chapters on early African history, on rituals, growing up, customs, religion and changes coming about today; brief one-page essays on nations there today. Pronunciation guide. Index. 90 pp. (Reading level: 6-9).

Turnbull, Colin M., *Tradition and Change in African Tribal Life.* Cleveland: The World Publishing Company, 1966. Hardcover. $5.95.

An analysis and description of life in Africa south of the Sahara describing the organization and activities of the family, clan and tribe among a variety of peoples (Pygmies, Bushmen, Ik, BaNdaka) at various stages of life: childhood, growing up, adulthood, old age; numerous photos (b/w), bibliography, index. 271 pp. (Reading level: 9-12).

### *(16 mm film)*

*Africans All,* IFF (1965). color, narration, 23 min.

A portrayal of the peoples of Africa. Commences with an animated description of popular misconceptions about this area and its peoples and then surveys them in all their diversity and color.

*Leaders and People of Africa,* McGH (1967). color, narration, 15 min.

An excellent introduction to contemporary Africa; begins with series of shots of various peoples, cities, leaders; focuses on selected leaders of conservative and radical leanings; notes major problems.

### *(8 mm loop/sound)*

*Africans All,* EALING (1967). 8 mm, cartridged loop in color with narration and sound; 23 min. $150.00.

Diversity and color of Africa shown via animation and photos. A Julien Bryan International Film Foundation film.

### *(8 mm loop)*

*Africa–Culture Groups,* GATEWAY. color, script, 4 min. $12.00.

Provides a comparison of four different culture groups in Africa showing different physical types, economic activities, and dress. Major emphasis on type of agriculture practiced by each group.

*People of Africa,* ICF (n.d.). color, super 8, script to be issued, 4 min. $16.00.

Provides examples of the variety of peoples of Africa, concerning physical characteristics and dress. Also shows the variety between the modern and traditional groups.

*(Filmstrips)*

*Africa: Human Resources,* MES (n.d.). 35 frames, color, captioned, script. $10.00.

23 photos, 4 maps, 6 drawings, and 2 full captions. North African and Arab contacts (9), European contact, colonization and impact (12), Negro Africa (7), modern contrasts (4). Captions: statements explaining frames. Full caption summary.

*An African Home Near the Equator,* CF (1957). 22 frames, color, captioned. $6.00.

19 photos, one map and 2 full captions. Follows a day in the life of an African boy on his return from school. School (2), village (2), weapons (3), preparing meals (5), family life (7). Captions: statements explaining frames. Full captions: notes to teacher and vocabulary.

*African Children at School,* EG (1962). 40 frames, color, captioned, script. (*The Continent of Africa: Children of Africa Series*–No. 160I). $6.00.

All frames show students at school. Depicts various types, levels and languages used in mission, public, and Moslem schools. 21 frames show classroom situation. Captions: statements and questions which explain frames.

*African Farm Children,* EG (1962). 35 frames, color, captioned, script. (*The Continent of Africa: Children of Africa Series*–No. 160A). $6.00.

Deals with farming, daily activities, villages and markets of rural Africa. Includes products and landscape of rural Africa. Major regions: East Africa (13), South Africa (6), Angola (6), Niger (4), Uganda (3). Also included are Chad, Congo. Captions: statements and questions which explain frames.

*The Babies of Africa,* EG, (1962). 41 frames, color, captioned, script. (*The Continent of Africa: The Children of Africa Series*–No. 160A). $6.00.

40 photos and one map. People of various regions of Africa depicting housing, markets, and daily home activities. Southern Africa (18), Central Africa (8), Western Africa (7), Eastern Africa (4), Northern Africa (3). Captions: statements and questions which explain frames.

*Children of the African Deserts,* EG (1962). 42 frames, color, captioned, script. (*The Continent of Africa: Children of Africa Series*–No. 160H). $6.00.

Characteristics of the southern fringe of the Sahara region. Topics: daily and economic activities (14), people (4), terrain (4), desert animals (4), transportation (4), housing (4), recreation (2). Kano and Timbuctu included (3). Captions: statements and questions which explain frames.

*Children of Equatorial Africa,* CF (1957). 23 frames, color, captioned. $6.00.

20 photos, one map and 2 full captions. Depicts the daily family life and activities of young children in an African village. Captions: statements explaining frames. Full captions: notes to teacher and vocabulary.

*Children of Non-African Origin,* EG (1962). 40 frames, color, captioned, script. (*The Continent of Africa: Children of Africa Series*–No. 160D). $6.00.

Daily activities of non-African people from various regions of Africa. Major groups: Portuguese (10), English (10), Indian (8), Afrikaners (4). People from Asia, Europe and Middle East also included. Captions: statements and questions which explain frames.

*Children of Rural Africa,* EG (1962). 39 frames, color, captioned, script. (*The Continent of Africa: Children of Africa Series*–No. 160F). $6.00.

Emphasis on people, villages and markets of rural Africa. Major emphasis on West Africa (21), Angola (5), Uganda, and South Africa (5), Congo, Upper Volta, Zanzibar and East Africa (8). Captions: statements and questions which explain frames.

*Children of Urban Africa,* EG (1962). 41 frames, color, captioned, script. (*The Continent of Africa: Children of Africa Series*–No. 160E). $6.00.

Description of daily activities (markets, cooking, housing) of children in urban areas of Africa. Regions depicted: West Africa (15), Central Africa (10), South Africa (8), Angola (5), East Africa (3). Captions: statements and questions which explain frames.

*Faces of African Children,* EG (1962). 40 frames, color, captioned, script. (*The Continent of Africa: Children of Africa Series*–No. 160B). $6.00.

Emphasis on the faces of African children and their dress. Depicts children from various tribes and regions of Africa. Contrast of people and dress in Africa. Captions: explanatory statements and questions.

*How People Live in Africa,* BP (1966). 36 frames, color, captioned, script. $6.62.

32 photos and 4 maps. Overview of the entire continent. People of Northern Africa (4), people of Sub-Sahara Africa (3), animals of Northern Africa (5), animals of Sub-Saharan Africa (2), economic activities (8), Lake Victoria and Mt. Kenya (3), cities and villages of Northern Africa (3), urban centers of Sub-Saharan Africa (4). Captions: statements explaining frames. Script explains and supplements captions. Frames numbered.

*How the African People Live,* BF (1966). 32 frames, color, captioned, script. (*Africa: Developing Continent* Series–No. 3). $6.00.

31 photos and one full caption frame. Major emphasis on the buildings of Africa: housing (village and urban) (11), government (6), churches (4), modern urban centers (7), summary frames (3). Captions explain frames. Script supplements captions.

*Modern Children in Africa,* EG (1962). 42 frames, color, captioned, script. (*The Continent of Africa: Children of Africa Series*–No. 160C). $6.00.

Emphasis on tribal groups and Moslem religion. Market and economic activity (16), indentification and dress (15), religion, housing and villages of Moslem groups (11). Kano and Timbuctu included. Captions: statements and questions which explain frames.

*Natives of Africa,* CG (1951). 40 frames, b/w, non-captioned, script. $4.50.

12 frames showing various aspects of the life of the Bedouim, 13 on the first pygmies of the Congo, 15 frames on the Basuto of Lesotho. Script has detailed comments on subject of each frame.

*(Transparencies)*

*Alpha Map Transparencies: Africa,* ALLYN & BACON (1967).

5 multi-color, single sheet transparencies depicting population, tribes, diets, health and literacy. Part of larger set. Each transparency has descriptive guide. Set price $60.00.

*Africa* (*The People–Unit II*), EBF (1963). color, script. $32.00 for series.

3 transparencies: population map, major language map, chart of the major religions of Africa and percentage of population. All maps of entire continent. Can be used individually or as overlay. Registration marks provided for alignment. Notes to teacher.

*World History: Unit 1–Sub-Saharan Africa,* KUEFFEL & ESSER CO. (1966).

6 sets of transparencies on African society including indigenous races, language groups, major religions, literacy rates, family structure, and area and population. Charts and maps with multiple overlays. May be obtained as part of masterbook for $39.95 or as prepared spectra transparencies individually priced depending on number of overlays.

### Economy

*(16 mm film)*

*The Economy of Africa,* McG-H (1966). color, narration, 15 min.

Depicts selected aspects of African economic growth and problems facing future development. Shows agricultural and industrial development. Teachers' guide.

*Economic Development in Africa,* SB (1964). 29 frames, color, captioned. $3.00.

27 photos and 2 full captions. Emphasis on impact of modernity on the traditional societies of Africa and of contrast between the traditional and modern. Transportation (6), farming (4), housing (9), dress (3). Modern influences and their outward manifestations (4), traditional wood carving (1). Captions: statements explaining frames. Full captions: definitions and statements concerning economic development and modern changes.

*Economic Development in Africa,* BUDEK (1964). 40 frames, color, non-captioned. script. $6.00.

Transporting goods to market (6), plowing the land (4), houses (10), storage of crops (3), the proper clothing (7), toys and games (5), other indications of economic change (5). Script: introduction, descriptive paragraph for each frame. Each category is introduced by a short paragraph.

*The Economy of Africa,* McGH (1967). 38 frames, color, captioned, script. $8.50.

33 photos, 2 maps and 3 full captions. General economic situation of Africa: basic economic activities (5), agricultural development (13), development of urban life (8), industrial development (9), conclusion, factors for progress (3). Captions: statements and questions.

*Farmers of Africa,* CG (1951). 42 frames, b/w, non-captioned, script. $4.50.

Depicts the steps in the production of cotton in the Sudan (14), of palm oil in Nigeria (14), and of fruit in South Africa (14); script has detailed explanation of each frame.

*Farming in Equatorial Africa,* CF (1957). 29 frames, color, captioned. $4.95.

20 photos, one map, and 2 full captions. Topography and climate (1), past economic activities (3), traditional farming (5), modern farming and education (9), products (6), markets (3). Captions: statements explaining frames. Full captions: notes to teacher and vocabulary.

*Occupations in Equatorial Africa,* CF (1957). 26 frames, color, captioned. $4.95.

23 photos, one map, and 2 full captions. Contrasts the old and new occupations and changes occuring in Africa within a short period of time. Traditional occupations (10), modern occupations (13), concluding frame (bygone days and the new dawn). Captions: statements explaining frames. Full captions: notes to teacher and vocabulary.

*Transportation in Africa,* BF (1966). 34 frames, color, captioned, script. (*Africa: Developing Continent Series*–No. 4). $6.00.

32 photos, one map, and one full-caption frame. Modern and traditional water transportation (canoe and ship) (9), use of animals (6), air transportation (6), auto-trucks (6), Suez Canal (3), summary (3). Captions explain frames. Script supplements captions.

*Transportation in Equatorial Africa,* CF (1957). 28 frames, color, captioned. $6.00.

25 photos, one map, and 2 full captions. Traditional modes (human carriers, trails and trackless fields) (6), animal- and man-powered vehicles (2), modern transportation (10), role of the Congo River and water transportation (7). Captions: statements explaining frames. Full captions: notes to teacher and vocabulary.

*What the Africans Do to Earn a Living,* BF (1966). 39 frames, color, captioned, script. (*Africa: Developing Continent Series*–No. 2). $6.00.

36 photos and 3 full caption frames. Major emphasis on agriculture and agricultural products (10), handicrafts (8), tourism (6), markets (3), mining (2), general occupations (5), summary (4). Captions explain frames. Script supplements captions.

*(Transparencies)*

*Alpha-Map Transparencies: Africa,* ALLYN & BACON (1967).

12 multi-color, single sheet transparencies on various aspects of Africa's economic life including agriculture, manufacturing, mineral resources, etc. Part of larger set. Each accompanied by guide. Total set costs $60.00.

*World History: Unit I—Sub-Saharan Africa,* KEUF-FEL & ESSER (1966).

7 sets of multi-overlay transparencies on various aspects of African economic development including resources, agriculture, agricultural products, transportation networks, economic development, and per capita income. Part of masterbook priced at $39.95 or available separately as spectra transparencies.

*(Charts)*
*Africa* (#218), PICTORIAL CHARTS. single sheet, color, 36" x 45". $2.00.

Consists of 11 maps: large map of the economic and mineral products of Africa and 10 small insert maps dealing with political, economic, social, and physical aspects of Africa.

*African Lands,* PICTORIAL CHARTS. single sheet, color, 36" x 45". $2.00.

2 maps: large map of the major economic activities found in Africa. Small maps of racial distribution for individual countries of Africa.

**Art**

*(Written material)*
Glubok, Shirley, *The Art of Africa.* New York: Harper & Row, Publishers, 1965. Hardcover. $4.50.

Text with b/w full-page photos of samples of African art. 48 pp.

*(Kit)*
*African Arts Study Kit: Series 1,* UCLA (1969). $85 per subscription.

Each subscription includes 30 copies of each of 3 printed 16-page 8½" x 11" booklets with photos (color and b/w) and text on a selected aspect of music, art, poetry, sculpture of a particular people of Africa; two film strips on masks, Nigerian ritual dance; a 12" LP record of Ghanaian master drum; a folio of Congolese art; 30 copies of a desk map of Africa; teaching guides.

*(Reproductions)*
*Africa (Unit 2-1),* ALVA (1969). sculptures. $30.00.

Reproductions in ceramic of a dance mask, ceremonial cup, and dance headgear from West Africa; includes 30 student activity folders with exercises requiring coloring of drawings; emphasis is on design. Teaching manual included.

*Africa (Unit 2-2),* ALVA (1969). Sculpture. $37.00.

Reproductions in ceramic of a crocodile, ceremonial cup, and Bateke figure; includes 30 student activity folders requiring student completion of maps, questions, and diagrams. Extensive student reading also included; focus is on geography, tradition and culture. Teaching manual.

*African Sculpture,* ALVA (1968). Sculpture. $50.00.

9 reproductions of outstanding examples of African sculpture cast in ceramic; includes laughing mask, two antelope headgear (Mali), carving of a man dressing his beard (Ivory Coast), ibis (Nigeria), a cup and a number of gold weights (Ashanti).

*African Reproductions,* UM (n.d.)

A large catalog of African masks, figures, carvings, and ornaments from which reproductions may be made. Prices per item range from $5.00 to $50.00; catalog on request.

*African Art Objects,* MPM (n.d.)

A large collection of African masks, sculptures, castings, and carvings from which reproductions can be made on order; reasonable prices; catalogs on request.

*(Filmstrips/records)*
*African Art and Culture,* WSP (1968). 3 color filmstrips and records. $45.60.

Each of the 3 filmstrips is in color and without captions; each has a 12" LP record which describes the frames and is keyed to the filmstrip. (One side of each record is for 33⅓ player and has audible sound; other side has same text but inaudible sound for use in automatic synchronized projector-players.)

*African Art: Set I,* MLEAT (1968). 20 slides, color, non-captioned, script. $15.00.

Twenty color slides of masks and figures made by selected peoples of West Africa only; 14 slides show masks, 6 show figures or figurines; 5 slides from Nigeria, 8 from Congo (K), and the rest from other West African nations; each slide numbered and labeled with place of origin; short, descriptive script accompanies set.

*African Art,* MPA (1969). 26 slides, colors, captions. $15.00.

One map of Africa and 25 slides of different objects in the museum's collection, including masks, figures, castings, bronze work, and carvings of wood, stone, gold, ivory; objects from Mali, Guinea, Liberia, Ghana, Nigeria, both Congos, Ivory Coast; printed descriptions and bibliography.

*African Masks and Art,* AMNH (n.d.). color, 2" x 2" slides.

A large color slide collection of a wide variety of African carvings, sculptures, masks, pottery, and musical instruments; 70¢ per duplicate (60¢ if 10 or more are ordered); price lists available on request.

*African Arts: Set I,* LOWIE (1968). 25 slides, color, non-captioned, script. $15.00.

Color slides of excellent quality showing close-ups of different types of art of West Africa only; most of the slides show either masks or figures (figurines), although there are also photos of headpieces, dolls, and a plaque; about 1/3 of the photos are of art done by various peoples in the Congo (K), another 1/3 are from the Ivory Coast; 5 are from Nigeria and the rest scattered among other West African nations; printed on each slide is a brief description of the object shown, including its size, purpose and makers. Detailed script gives tribe, location, use of objects.

*African Arts: Set II,* LOWIE (1968). 25 slides, color, non-captioned, script. $15.00.

Each slide is a close-up view of an African sculpture, carvings, headdress mask, or other work of art including a brass procession, pulley frame, pestle; primarily from the Ivory Coast, Upper Volta, Congo Brazzaville and Congo Kinshasa. Detailed script on each slide; each slide labeled with maker and purpose of object.

*African Arts: Set III,* LOWIE (1969). 25 slides, color, non-captioned, script. $15.00.

Slides of figures, masks, headdresses, animals, carved hooks, cups, lock, etc. from peoples of the Congo (K), Liberia, and other West African nations; each slide labeled with brief description; detailed printed descriptions of each slide also included.

*African Arts: Set IV,* LOWIE (1969). 25 slides, color, non-captioned, script. $15.00.

Slides depicting carved serpents, masks, figures and objects (animal heads, cups, spoons, doors, processions, gold weights); from the Congos, Nigeria, Ghana, and other West African nations; each slide labeled; detailed printed description of each slide.

## Literature

*(Written material)*

Hughes, Langston, ed., *Poems from Black Africa.* Bloomington, Ind.: Indiana University Press, 1963. (Fifth Edition 1968). Paper. $1.75.

A collection of over 80 poems from black Africa representing most African nations; brief biographical sketch of each author. No index. 160 pp. (Reading level 9-12).

Litto, Fredric M., ed., *Plays from Black Africa.* New York: Hill and Wang, 1968. (A Mermaid Dramabook). Paper. $1.95.

Six plays, in English, by black Africans; from full length to one act, serious and comic plays on such themes as the conflict between traditional society and change, the presence of the white man, and the struggle of man for survival, livelihood, and psychological security and expression. Brief description of each playright included. No index. 317 pp. (Reading level: 9-12).

Moore, Gerald and Ulli Beier, *Modern Poetry From Africa*. Baltimore: Penguin Books, 1966. Paper. 95¢.

A collection of 104 poems accompanied by brief notes on each author; a detailed introduction that treats Negritude in its historical context and its expression in the poems included in this collection. Index of first lines. 192 pp. (Reading level: 9-12).

Rive, Richard, ed., *Modern African Prose*. New York: Humanities Press, Inc., 1967. Paper. $1.25.

A collection of short excerpts from longer novels and stories by Africans intended for use in African classrooms. This includes authors from all parts of Africa south of the Sahara, including the Republic of South Africa. Selections on such themes as beauty in nature, social and racial discrimination, local customs, education, and daily life. 214 pp.


## Music

### *(Written material)*

Dietz, Betty Warner and Michael Olantunji, *Musical Instruments of Africa*. New York: The John Day Company, 1965. Hardcover. $5.95.

A description with b/w pictures of different types of musical instruments; accompanying record demonstrates sounds of these instruments. 116 pp.

### *(Filmstrips/record)*

*Folk Songs of Africa*, SB (1964). Filmstrip #1 (40 frames) Filmstrip #2 (31 frames). color, non-captioned, script, Record: (part I- 15 min. Part II- 20 min.). $19.75.

Side I: 29 photos, one map and 10 music sheets. Divided into people of Africa (traditional and modern) (5), characteristics of land (3), musical instruments (13), types of African music (19).

Side II: 12 African songs (31). Script provides directions, general characteristics of African music, information concerning each song.

### *(Records)*

*African Drums* (FE4502 AB), FOLKWAYS, 11 bands, script. $6.79.

Side 1: 5 bands. Side 2: 6 bands. An anthology of drum music from the continent of Africa. Only drums featured with selections from Nigeria, Congo, Ruanda, French Equatorial Africa, and South Africa. Script provides introduction and background material on drum music. Notes on individual bands.

*African Music* (FW8852), FOLKWAYS. 12 bands, script. (1939). $5.79.

Side 1: 6 bands. Side 2: 6 bands. Vocal and instrumental music from various sections and tribes in Africa. Sudan, Mali, the Cameroons, and Nigeria are represented. Script: background material and extensive notes on individual bands.

*African Music from the French Colonies* (KL205), COLUMBIA. 8 bands, script. $5.98.

Vocal and instrumental music sampled from a wide area of Africa. Side 1: samples taken from the Sudan to the Atlantic Coast paralleling the influence of Moslem religion. Side 2: samples from Madagascar to Central Africa. Script: introduction and notes on individual bands.

*Africa South of the Sahara* (FE 4503), 2 vols. FOLKWAYS. 38 bands, script. $13.90.

Vol. 1, Side A: 21 bands. Side B: 9 bands. Vol. 2, Side C: 9 bands. Side D: 8 bands. A wide sampling of the vocal and instrumental music from various peoples and countries of Africa. Script: introduction with notes on individual bands.

*Folk Music of Africa*, AFRICAN-AMERICAN INSTITUTE. 23 bands. script.

Side 1: 11 bands. Side 2: 12 bands. Provides a sample of various types of folk music. Selected African songs sung by Pete Seeger, Addiss and Crofut, and Ibn El Badya, with narrations. Script: notes on African folk music and songs.

*Miriam Makeba* (LPM 22679), RCA, 14 bands. $3.98.

Side 1: 7 bands. Side 2: 7 bands. Popular treatment of predominantly African folk songs.

*Negro Folk Music of Africa and America* (FE4500), 2 vols., FOLKWAYS. 24 bands. script. $13.58.

Vol. 1, Side A: 5 bands. Side B: 5 bands. Vocal and instrumental music from the various countries of Africa. Vol. 2, Side C: 7 bands. Side D: 7 bands. Music from Latin America and the United States with emphasis on Haiti and the United States. Provides a wide sampling of Negro music from three continents. Process of selection places emphasis on similarites of music. Script: introduction with notes on each band.

*The World of Miriam Makeba* (LPM 2750), RCA. 12 bands. $3.98.

Side 1: 6 bands. Side 2: 6 bands. Collection of popular American and African folk songs.

*(Tapes)*
*African Concert* (No. 209), WTE. 11 min. $2.75.

Selections depicting the variety of music found in Africa and the varied musical types. Narration: introduction only; remainder of tape is music.

*The Guitars of Africa* (No. 131), WTE. 22 min. $2.75.

Discussion of the introduction and spread of the guitar in Africa and the variations caused by local influences. Examples of African calypso and varied styles which have developed. Selections from Uganda, Kenya, and South Africa.

*Talking Drums,* (No. 47), WTE. approx. 15 min. $2.75.

Discussion of the use and construction of drums, characteristics of "drum language." Drum music used to illustrate narrator's comments.

## Education

*(Filmstrips)*
*Cultural Life in Africa,* BF (1966). 33 frames, color, captioned, script. (Africa: Developing Continent Series—No. 5) $6.00.

31 photos and 2 full caption frames. Modern aspects of life in Africa. Schools (11), library and museums (7), religion (5), recreation (4). Summary frames (4). Captions explain frames. Script supplements captions.

*Learning for Modern Living in Equatorial Africa,* CF (1957). 27 frames, color, captioned. $6.00.

25 photos and 2 full captions. The role of education in Africa; types of schools and conditions under which teachers must work. Shows desire of all to read and write. Captions: statements explaining frames. Full captions: notes to teacher and vocabulary.

*(Pictures)*
*Africa: Challenge for the Future,* UNESCO, b/w, non-captioned, script. 11½" x 11½". $1.00.

12 photos on education in Africa dealing with its problems, progress, and future developments.

## History

*(Written materials)*
Chijioke, F. A., *Ancient Africa.* Ikeja: Longman's of Nigeria, Ltd., 1966. Paper. 4s 6d.

A descriptive survey of the history of Africa emphasizing the empires of the West African savanna with some attention to ancient Egypt, Carthage, the Moslem invasions, and East Africa; drawings, photos, maps and study questions; originally prepared for upper elementary students *in* Africa; no index. 48 pp.

Chu, Daniel and Elliott Skinner, *A Glorious Age in Africa.* Garden City: Doubleday & Company, Inc., 1965. Paper. $1.45.

A brief story with maps and sketches of the empires of Ghana, Mali, and Songhay; personalized approach emphasizing the exploits of great leaders such as Sundiata, Mansa Musa, and Sunni Ali; index. 120 pp. (Reading level: 6-9).

Davidson, Basil, *African Kingdoms.* New York: Time Incorporated, 1966. Hardcover. $3.95.

A description of ancient African kingdoms in the Nile Valley, the West African Sudan, the forest states, and of the arts of ancient Africa;

many color photos; a time-line of ancient empires; maps; index. 191 pp. (Reading level: 9-12).

Davidson, Basil, *The Lost Cities of Africa*. Boston: Little, Brown and Company, 1959. Paper. $2.25.

A survey of kingdoms and cities of ancient Africa which poses questions about a variety of aspects of their past and describes historical and archeological evidence bearing on these questions; extensive bibliography; index. 366 pp. (Reading level: 10-12).

Dobler, Lavinia and William A. Brown, *Great Rulers of the African Past*. Garden City: Doubleday & Company, Inc., 1965. Paper. $1.45.

A description in story form of the exploits of Mansa Musa (Mali); Sunni Ali Ber (Songhay); Askia Muhammed (Songhay); Affonso I (Kongo); and Idris Alaoma (Bornu); occasional sketches; pronunciation guide; index. 120 pp. (Reading level: 6-9).

Hatch, John, *Africa—The Rebirth of Self-Rule*. London: Oxford University Press (distributed in U.S. by the Humanities Press), 1967. Hardcover. $1.95.

A short summary of ancient Africa followed by chapters on European seizure and on each region; regional chapters stress influence of colonial governments on the people and their culture and the movement for independence; many clear maps, photos (b/w) and drawings. Index. 135 pp. (Reading level: 9-10).

Hughes, Langston, *The First Book of Africa*. New York: Franklin Watts, Inc., 1964. (revised). Hardcover. $4.80.

A brief survey of Africa focusing on ancient history, white explorers and missionaries, "primitive peoples," and art and homelife in "primitive Africa"; half of book devoted to changes underway in Africa, touching on problems in Kenya, South Africa, the Congo, Guinea, Liberia, and Ghana. Many photos (b/w). Appendix has data on nations. Index. 82 pp. (Reading level: 6-9).

Jack, Elspeth, *Africa: An Early History*. London: George G. Harrap and Company, Ltd. (distributed in U.S. by International University Booksellers) 1968. Paper. $150.

A brief survey of African history prior to the coming of Europeans; chapters (4-8 pp. each) on pre-history and early man, Egypt, Axum, trade across the Sahara and along the East coast, kingdoms of West Africa, Zimbabwe and the Bantu migrations; a final chapter on the coming of Europeans; several sketches; large, clear maps. Suggested student questions. No index. 86 pp. (Reading level: 6-9).

Kaula, Edna Mason, *Leaders of the New Africa*. Cleveland: The World Publishing Company, 1966. Hardcover. $3.95.

Brief biographical narratives of leaders (including Senghor, Nkrumah, Ahmadu Bello, Seretse Khama, Luthuli) of new African nations, with descriptions of their countries and peoples and the story of how each became independent. Pencil drawings of many leaders included. Appendix containing data on independence for each nation. Index. 192 pp. (Reading level: 7-10).

Labouret, Henri, *Africa Before the White Man*. New York: Walker & Company, 1962. Hardcover. $3.95.

A survey of the societies, trade, and kingdoms of the Sudan and the West African coast with some brief attention to Ethiopia, central Africa, Monomotapa and the Zulu; several maps included; no index. 138 pp. (Reading level: 6-9).

Rosenthal, Ricky, *The Splendor That Was Africa*. Dobbs Ferry: Oceana Publications, Inc., 1967. Hardcover. $1.25.

A rather detailed, scholarly account of the ancient West African empires of Mali, Ghana, and Songhai designed to eliminate erroneous impressions about Africa; several maps; bibliography; glossary; index. 86 pp. (Reading level: 10-12).

Shinnie, Margaret, *Ancient African Kingdoms*. New York: St. Martins' Press, 1965. Hardcover. $4.95.

A description of selected kingdoms in Egypt, Kush, the West African Sudan, the forest regions and in east-central Africa; many photos; sketches of archeological finds; maps; index. 126 pp. (Reading level: 10-12).

Vlahos, Olivia, *African Beginnings.* New York: Viking Press, 1968. Paper. $4.95.

A detailed ancient history of Africa south of the Sahara, based on archeological and other evidence and of the kingdoms and empires of pre-European Africa south of the Sahara; special sections on contemporary life among selected African peoples (Bushmen, Pygmy, Lovedu, Tonga, Nilote, Herero, Kikuyu, Nyakyusa, etc.). Index. 286 pp. (Reading level: 7-12).

*(16 mm films)*

*Dr. Leaky and the Dawn of Man,* EBF (1967). color, narration. (2 versions: 26 min. @ $327.50; 50 min. @ $500).

A National Geographic Society production detailing Leaky's search for the origins of man in Africa; depicts evidence unearthed by Leaky and dramatic reconstruction of skull remains.

*Negro Kingdoms of Africa's Golden Age,* ATLANTIS (1968). color, narration. (17 min.) $150.00.

Use of scenes of West African geography and of carvings, bronzes, iron work, and old woodcuts and drawings to tell the story of West Africa's ancient past; focuses on the climate, geography, history, technology, political structure, and religion of the empires of old Ghana, Mali, and Songhai; recounts the destructive effect of the slave trade.

*The Old Africa and the New: Ethiopia and Botswana,* McG-H, (1967). color, narration. (15 min.)

Brief survey of selected physical features; study of Ethiopia, its terrain, Coptic church, government, poverty, and pageantry; study of Botswana's independence celebration.

*(8 mm film loops)*

*The Boer War,* THORNE FILMS. b/w, script, 4 min. $12.50.

Depicts several fighting scenes from the Boer War, contemporary recreations.

*Italian Conquest of Ethiopia,* THORNE FILMS. b/w, script, 4 min. $12.50.

Footage of original motion picture showing the departure of Italian troops, the preparation of Ethiopian troops, the modern weapons of the Italian army, the defeat and takeover of Ethiopia.

*(Filmstrips)*

*Africa: The French Community,* CAF (n.d.). 41 frames, b/w, captioned. $6.00.

28 photos, 6 maps, 2 drawings and 5 full captions. Deals with French colonialism and the evolution of the French Community. Depicts French relationships with African states in French Community in areas of trade, aid, and organization. Captions: statements explaining and supplementing frames.

*Focus on Africa,* NYT (April 1966). 52 frames, b/w, captioned, script. $7.95.

46 photos, 4 maps and 2 full captions. Separated into sections dealing with contemporary Africa: independence and problems (10), struggle and transition (11), Africa of the Equator (10), Africa of the South (7), troubled outlook (10), summary (1). Script shows each frame and provides paragraph which describes and supplements frame. Captions: statements explaining frames.

*The New Africa,* VEC (n.d.). 29 frames, b/w, captioned. $6.00.

26 photos, 2 maps and one full caption. Population and language (3), independence (1), problems and needs of "new Africa": education (4), government (5), economics (8), summary (5). Captions: statements explain and supplement frames.

*(Filmstrip/record)*

#1 *Early Art,* WSP (1968). 65 frames, color, non-captioned, recorded (non-banded) narrative, 19 min.

Sixty-one photos, 4 maps; divided into peoples of east and central Africa (8), Victoria Falls (1), ancient rock art (7), ruins in Nile Valley and East Africa (8), drawings of historical interest (11), West African sculpture—figures and bronzes (26); recorded narrative briefly describes peoples of east-central Africa; origins and migration of early man; the ancient kingdoms of Kush, Ethiopia, coastal parts, Zimbabwe, Timbuktu; early art objects and African culture and the influence of art styles on noted Western artists. Some musical background.

#2 *African Art & Culture,* WSP (1968). 63 frames, color, non-captioned, recorded narrative. 19 min.

Starts with several objects of art (3), market and museum scenes (2), sunset (1), tree (1), and a sequence on carving (5), followed by 51 photos of individual carvings or sculpture in wood, gold, bronze; includes figures, stools, ornaments, etc.; recorded narrative explains carving techniques, role of sculpture in culture, different objects—their functions, composition and origin.

#3 *African Art & Culture,* WSP (1968). 62 frames, color, non-captioned, recorded narrative. 19 min.

Mask (1), drawing (1), African wearing a mask (1), masks (54), drawings (3), scenery (2). Recorded narrative explains function of masks in African cultures, how they were worn, and the different varieties of masks. Occasional musical background.

*(Slides/records)*
*Emerging Africa in the Light of its Past: Land, People, and History* (Unit 1), CHR (1965). 40 slides, color, script, record. $29.95.

34 photos, 6 maps and photos. The interrelation between the natural environment and the history of sub-Saharan Africa in the formation of the various cultures. Topics include physical environment, pre-history, racial composition and diversity, origin of culture groups, and cultural history. Script: text of record, notes and bibliography keyed to topics covered. Record: 30 minutes keyed to slides.

*Emerging Africa in the Light of its Past: From Exploration to Independence* (Unit 2), CHR (1965). 40 slides, color, script, record. $29.95.

37 photos and 3 maps. Impact of Europe on Sub-Saharan Africa. Divided into four periods: changes in Africa during the Age of Exploration, effects of slave trade with Americas, European colonization, and independence movement after World War II. Script: text of record, notes and annotated bibliography keyed to topics covered. Record: 30 minutes keyed to slides. Explains and supplements slides.

*(Records)*
*Africa and the Origin of Man,* AMIE (1967). 12" LP. $4.95.

Introduction via lecture and occasional question and answer to a series of records on African history; lectures explain archeological evidence relative to early African history, focusing on writings of ancient scholars, investigations of Leaky, archeology as a science, activities and accomplishments of "near man" and Stone Age man in East Africa. Brief teaching ideas listed on enclosure.

*Africa Lost and Found,* AMIE (1968). $2.95.

A presentation by three Afro-Americans of a nationalistic interpretation of African history which attempts to "set the record straight"; focuses on an asserted effort by Europeans to dehumanize Africa and cover up its past, and on a survey of significant features of African history including hypothesized black African origins of Egyptian civilization, black African penetration and racial intermixture in Asia, southern Europe, Greece; African (Arabian) origins of the European Renaissance, cultures of the Western Sudan, impact of the slave trade.

*African Origins 500-1492.* SILHOUETTES. nonbanded, no script (19 min.) $12.50.

One side of a 12" LP (Vol. 1 of "Silhouettes in Courage") that deals exclusively with the African origins of black American culture; mixes narration with "interviews" of known participants on the period 500 to 1492; excellent use of music; focuses on trade, learning, and empires in pre-European Africa; original account of culture and value systems of Africans; excellent description of indigenous and traditional slavery before the slave trade.

*(Transparencies)*

*Alpha Map Transparencies: Africa,* ALLYN & BACON (1967).

2 multi-colored, single-sheet transparencies on colonialism and decolonialism. Part of larger set. Each has descriptive guide. Cost of entire set is $60.00.

*Africa (Past and Present—Unit III),* EBF, (1963). color, script. $10.00.

5 transparencies: Kingdoms and Empires of Africa, Colonial Africa (1939), Independent Countries (1945), Independent Countries (1959), Independent Countries (1962). All maps of entire continent. Can be used individually or in combination as overlays. Registration marks provided for alignment. Notes to teacher. Part of larger set priced at $32.00.

*World History: Unit I—Sub-Saharan Africa,* KEUFFEL & ESSER CO. (1966).

Set of 11 maps depicting various aspects of African history: major kingdoms, coastal exploration, exploring the interior, the quest for the Niger, search for sources of the Nile, exploration of Central and Southern Africa, the African slave trade, areas controlled by Europe, settlement 1875, European dependents 1914, independence. Available as master for $39.95 or as pre-made spectra transparencies for prices ranging between $3.25 and $9.25, depending on number of overlays.

*Africa Before European Impact: 1000 A.D., Africa: 1885, Africa: 1924, Africa: 1966.* NYSTROM. color. $13.00.

Knowlton-Wallbank World History Maps. KW31 consists of one transparency with two maps: (a) races 1000 A.D. and trade routes; (b) extent of European colonization and exploration routes. KW32 is also one transparency with two maps: (a) colonial division of Africa in 1924; (b) Independent countries in 1966.

*Africa Before European Supremacy (About 1815)/ The Partition of Africa,* RAND MCNALLY. Color. $5.00.

Ranvue World History Map Series. Single transparency with paper frame and clear plastic overlay. Maps: (a) Africa before European supremacy about 1815, showing the extent of European control and the kingdoms of Africa; (b) the partition of Africa (1885 and 1889), showing the colonies under European control.

*World History: Africa* (#258-628), GAF (1964). $4.50.

Base outline with overlays showing African political boundaries 1850, 1914, 1963. Three colors. No guide.

*(Pictures)*

*The Changing Map of Africa,* BRITISH INFORMATION SERVICES (Jan. 1967). single sheet.

Front: map of Africa with tables providing name, area, population, and political status of all the countries of the continent of Africa. Back: political and economic relationships. Synopsis of various economic unions and organization between countries of Africa.

*The Slave Trade and Its Abolition, (Jackdaw #12),* JACKDAW Paper. $2.95.

Reproduction of 15 pictures, posters, and primary sources dealing with the slave trade and its abolition.

*(Tapes)*

*Africa: Continent of Change* (P-125), WASHINGTON TAPES (1966). 15 min. $10.00.

Discussion by Fred Hadsel of the U.S. State Department of the changes taking place in Africa. Topics include political changes, economic and social progress, political union among African nations, foreign influences in Africa, the importance of Africa.

*David Livingston,* (#48), WTE. 28 min. $2.75.

Story of the life of David Livingston from his childhood in England to his death in Africa.

# WEST AFRICA

## GENERAL

### Overview

*(Written materials)*

Davidson, Basil, *A History of West Africa 1000-1800.* London: Longman's Green & Company, Ltd., 1965. Paper. 11s 6d.

An introduction to West African history with equal space devoted to each of three periods—1000-1500, 1500-1600, 1600-1800; chapters on regions and empires; many illustrations, photos, and maps; questions, timeline; prepared for African secondary students; index. 312 pp.

Higson, F. G., *A Certificate Geography of West Africa,* London: Longman's Green & Company, Ltd., 1967. Hardcover. 14s.

An introduction to the geography of West Africa that focuses on the physical features such as climate, weather and vegetation; peoples, economic development, and selected countries (Liberia, Guinea, Ghana, Nigeria, and several others); includes several photos, many maps and charts, questions; prepared for African secondary schools and teacher training institutions; index. 223 pp.

Webster, J. B., A. A. Boahen, and H. O. Idowa, *The Revolution Years: West Africa Since 1800.* London: Longman's Green & Company, Ltd., 1967. Paper. 12s 6d.

The concluding volume of a history designed for West African secondary students; includes chapters on the 19th century Sudanic and coastal kingdoms, relations with Europe, resistance to colonial rule, and the return to independence; many illustrations, photos, and maps, with bibliographies and activities at the end of each chapter; prepared for African secondary school students; index. 342 pp.

*(16 mm film)*

*West Africa: Tropical Lowlands,* McG-H (1966). color, narration, 14 min.

Describes the peoples of various West African nations and surveys different ways they make a living. Also shows recent economic developments. With maps. Teachers' guide.

*(Filmstrips)*

*West Africa,* EAV (n.d.). 42 frames, b/w, non-captioned, script. $3.75.

38 photos and 4 maps. Divided by climatic regions: *Savanna:* topography (1), cities and villages (3), transportation (2), agricultural products (10), mining (2). *Tropical Rain Forest:* topography (2), agriculture (11), fishing (2), urban areas (2), economic activities (3). Script provides paragraph for each frame. Produced in England.

*West Africa,* McG-H (1967). 38 frames, color, captioned, script. $8.50.

34 photos and 4 maps. Introduction, new nation problems (2), arid and semi-arid Northern Region (10), humid tropical regions (dealing with farming, lumbering and transportation) (15), urbanization (8), allocation of resources and economic growth (3). Captions: statements and questions.

*(Filmstrip/record)*

*The West Central Lowlands,* SVE (1965). 61 frames, color, non-captioned, script, record. *(Africa, The Land of Developing Countries Series A—239-5R).*

51 photos, 6 maps and 4 full captions. Location, size, and physical features (7), agriculture and industry (22), people and how they live (10), transportation (7), important cities (9). Script follows record (18 min.). Full captions: review question and map study exercise. Part of a set of 6 costing $39.95.

*(Slides/records)*

*Emerging Africa in the Light of Its Past: West Africa—Patterns of Traditional Culture (Unit 3),* CHR (1967). 40 slides, color, script, record. $29.95.

35 photos and 5 maps. Description of West Africa's culture that was established before contact with the European and the traditional

culture patterns still in existence. Topics: natural environment, history, economic activities, religion, family, and political organization. Script: text of record, notes, and annotated bibliography keyed to topics. Record: 30 minutes, keyed to slides. Explains and supplements slides.

*Emerging Africa in the Light of Its Past: West Africa Today–Patterns of Change.* (Unit 4), CHR (1967). 40 slides, color, script, record. $29.95.

38 photos and 2 maps. Deals with the impact of European contact after the period of the slave trade on the traditional culture of West Africa and the interrelationship between the European forces and traditional forces to the post-independence period. Topics: government, religion, economic activities, family organization, and African literature. Script: text of record: notes, annotated bibliography keyed to topics. Record: 30 minutes. Explains and supplements slides.

*(Transparencies)*
*Western Africa,* HAMMOND. color, script. $6.50.

Maps of Western Africa. Four transparencies: base map with rivers and political boundaries, physical features, place names, clear plastic for writing. Used in combination. Plastic frames provided with registration marks for alignment. Notes deal with mechanics of using transparencies.

*(Tapes)*
*Africa Soviet Style,* THE CENTER FOR THE STUDY OF DEMOCRATIC INSTITUTIONS. (n.d.) 30 min. $5.00.

Yaw Turkson, First Counsellor of the Embassy of Ghana in Washington, explains to the Center staff that the Soviet model is better adapted to African nations for bridging the gap between their political ideals and social and economic realities.

*Introduction to West Africa,* U.S. DEPARTMENT OF STATE, (n.d.) 28 min.

Hendrick van Oss, Deputy Director, Office of West African Affairs of the U.S. State Department, describes the geography, politics and economics of West African nations and U.S. relations with them.

*(Records)*
*Folk Tales From West Africa* (FC7103), FOLKWAYS. 5 bands. $4.15.

Side 1: "The Cow-Tail Switch" and "Youhde Goes to Town." Side 2: "Talk," "Throw Mountains," and "Don't Shake Hands with Everybody."

*African Folk Tales: Vol. 1,* CMS (1968). $4.98.

Bertha Parker tells three traditional folktales: "Umusha Mwaice" (The Little Slave Girl—a variation of Cinderella) (19 min.); "The Hunter and the Elephant" (8 min.); and "How Beans Come to Have a Black Spot on Them" (11 min.).

*African Folk Tales: Vol. 2,* CMS (1968). $4.98.

Three more African folktales narrated by Bertha Parker: "The Pigheaded Ruler" (19 min.); the "Legend of the Wandering Tribe" (10 min.); "A Giant on His Back" (9 min.); these give insights into traditional African society and culture.

## Economics

*(8 mm loop)*
*Agriculture in West Africa,* ICF (1967). color, super 8, script to be issued, 4 min. $16.00.

Depicts the land, methods of farming, and products raised in the wet and dry parts of Africa. Emphasis on the use of hand labor in farming.

*Labor in West Africa,* ICF (1967). color, super 8, script to be issued, 4 min. $16.00.

Varied economic activities of the people of West Africa. Examples provided from farms, villages, and cities of West Africa. Emphasis on hand labor.

*Markets in West Africa,* ICF (1967). color, super 8, script to be issued. 4 min. $16.00.

Provides a cross-sectional view of the various types of markets present in West Africa. Contrasts modern and urban markets with traditional and rural markets. Products also included.

*Peanuts–Important Product of West Africa,* ICF (1967). color, super 8, script to be issued, 4 min. $16.00.

Traces the route of the peanut from hand harvesting and processing to export. Shows the combination of human and machine labor used in Africa.

*Progress in West Africa,* ICF (1967). color, super 8, script to be issued, 4 min. $16.00.

Depicts the physical changes occuring in West Africa. Major emphasis on examples of new developments in urban housing, transportation, and industry.

*Rubber Plantation in West Africa,* ICF (1967). color, super 8, script to be issued, 4 min. $16.00.

Layout of a plantation and tapping of rubber trees introduces the major portion of the film, which deals with the processing of raw rubber in a modern plant. No treatment of people, housing, or organization of plantation.

*Transportation in West Africa,* ICF (1967). color, super 8, script to be issued. 4 min. $16.00.

Shows the various types of roads and means of transportation utilized in West Africa. Depicts animal, human, and mechanical means of transportation.

### Life

*(Written material)*

Beti, Mongo, *Mission to Kala,* New York: Humanities Press, Inc., 1966. Paper. $1.00.

Written in 1957, this novel is set in the southern Cameroons. It relates the adventures of a youth sent to a nearby village and who, while there, becomes idolized by the local populace because of his education. It presents a detailed picture of village life, pastimes, and ceremonies. 183 pp.

Conton, William, *The African.* New York: Humanities Press, Inc., 1966. Paper. $1.00.

This is a fictitious autobiography of Kisimi Kamara of Songhai, an equally fictitious British colony in West Africa. It traces his studies in England and his rise to political power later

in his homeland, providing excellent insights into African views of whites, to family organization and kinship and to West African politics. Originally published in 1960. 213 pp.

Ekwensi, Cyprian, *Lokotown and other Stories.* New York: Humanities Press, Inc., 1967. Paper. $1.00.

An anthology of short stories about various aspects of life in village and urban Africa.

Ekwensi, Cyprian, *People of the City.* New York: Humanities Press, Inc., 1965. Paper. $1.00.

This novel, written in 1954, is set in a West African city. It describes the problems and temptations of urban life and reflects an African concern for freedom and independence. It also reflects inadequate housing conditions, some local customs, and changing life of the people. 156 pp.

Guillot, René, *René Guillot's African Folk Tales.* New York: Franklin Watts, 1964. Hardcover. $3.95.

Collected folk tales from West Africa, including tales about creation, individual initiative, lore about people and animals. Translations from Guillot's previous works. No commentary or introduction. No index. 160 pp. (Reading level: 6-12).

Oyono, Ferdinand, *Houseboy.* New York: Humanities Press, Inc., 1967. Paper. $1.00.

Translated from the French in 1966. Presented as a diary of an African servant, it suggests the ways in which white colonials mistreated the Africans and discriminated against them. Much of the story is built around a love affair which results in the tragic death of the principal character. 140 pp.

*(8 mm loop)*

*City Life in West Africa,* ICF (1967). color, super 8, script to be issued. 4 min. $16.00.

Overview of an African city, showing its various functions and types of structures. Contrasts old and new parts of city, depicts street scenes, markets and new construction. Examines impact of Europeans.

*Dinner in West Africa,* ICF (1967). color, super 8, script to be issued, 4 min. $16.00.

Traces the preparation of a meal for a West African family in an urban setting—buying the food (markets and products), preparing a meal (kitchen and family dining room), eating.

*Homes in Africa,* ICF (1967). color, super 8, script to be issued, 4 min. $16.00.

Depicts the various types of housing in wet and dry Africa. Examples of various styles both modern and traditional; type of construction materials used. Influence of Arab and European styles also noted.

*Rural Life in Arid West Africa,* ICF (1967). color, super 8, script to be issued, 4 min. $16.00.

Shows the meager means of transportation, the emphasis on human power; depicts housing and activities of the people and influence of the Arabs on language and religion.

*Semi-Nomadic Life in Dry West Africa,* ICF (1967). color, super 8, script to be issued, 4 min. $16.00.

Overview of semi-nomadic settlement. Emphasis on housing and raising of cattle. Shows housing conditions and the herding of cattle by men and boys.

*Town Life in West Africa,* ICF (1967). color, super 8, script to be issued, 4 min. $16.00.

Shows a river town—the housing, streets, transportation activities, and living conditions. Comparison with *City Life in West Africa.*

### Music

*(Records)*

*Folk Tales From West Africa,* FOLKWAYS, 5 bands, script. $4.15.

Side 1: Reading of the "Cow-Tail Switch" and "Younde Goes to Market" folk tales. Side 2: Reading of "Throw Mountain" and "Don't Shake Hands with Everyone." Script: notes on each folk tale on jacket of the record.

*Olantunji—Flaming Drums,* COLUMBIA. 6 bands, script. $3.98.

Side 1: 3 bands, side 2: 3 bands. Popular treatment of vocal and instrumental music from Africa. Primary emphasis on West Africa. Script: notes on each band.

*Olantunji Zungo,* COLUMBIA. 7 bands, script. $3.98.

Side 1: 3 bands; side 2: 4 bands. Music illustrates examples of the merging of Latin, jazz and West African music. Script: general introduction. No notes on individual bands.

*The Voices and Drums of Africa,* MONITOR, 18 bands, script. $3.79.

Side 1: 9 bands; side 2: 9 bands. Music divided into three groups: Monaque and his African Ensemble playing music from the Cameroons; Kante Facelle and his African Ensemble playing music from Dahomey, Niger and Guinea; Keita Fodeba and his African Ensemble playing music from Guinea and Casamance. Script: general notes on each of the ensembles featured in the album. No notes on individual bands.

## COUNTRIES OF WEST AFRICA

### Cameroons

*(Filmstrips)*

*The Republic of Cameroon,* EG (1962). 45 frames, color, captioned, script, (*Continent of Africa: Countries of the Congo Basin Series*—155C). $6.00.

Forty-one photos, one map and 3 full captions. General overview of the country. Topics included: terrain and vegetation (10), tribes and economic activities (10), urban centers (13), agriculture and agricultural products (6), resources (2). Captions: statements explaining frames. Full captions: review (2) and summary questions (1).

*A Teacher Visits Africa: Cameroon Urban Life,* VEC (n.d.). 39 frames, color, captioned. $6.00.

Thirty-five photos, 2 maps and 2 full captions. Arrival in country (4), vegetation (4), housing (2), markets (6), city of Yaounde (6), mission schools (5), a parade in the city (6). Captions: statements explaining frames.

*(Records)*

*Psalms of the Cameroons* (FR8910), FOLKWAYS. 13 bands, script. $5.79.

Side 1: 8 bands; side 2: 5 bands. Collection of psalms sung by the people of the Cameroons. Script: provides English translation of the psalms.

*Music of the Cameroons* (FE4372), FOLKWAYS. 23 bands, script. $6.79.

Side 1: 9 bands; Side 2: 14 bands. Vocal and instrumental music of the Bafut tribe of the highlands of the Cameroons. Script: background material and notes on individual bands.

*Bulu Songs from the Cameroons* (FE4451), FOLK-WAYS. 17 bands, script. $6.79.

Side 1: 9 bands; side 2: 8 bands. Vocal and instrumental music of the Bulus of the Cameroons. Script: background material with notes on individual bands.

## Dahomey

*(Filmstrip)*

*The Republic of Dahomey,* EG (1964). 46 frames, color, captioned, script, (*Continent of Africa: Countries of the Guinea Coast Series*—156A). $6.00.

Forty-two photos, one map and 3 full captions. General overview of the country with an emphasis on agriculture: terrain and vegetation (6), transportation (6), people (religion, education, economic activity) (8), urban centers (products and people) (6), and agriculture and agricultural products (16). Captions: statements explaining frames. Full captions: review (2) and summary questions (1).

*(Record)*

*Dahomey Suite for Oboe and Piano* (FS3855), FOLKWAYS. script. $5.79.

Side 1: The Dahomey Suite. Blending of the non-harmonic structures of West African songs with the harmonic-polyphonic language of contemporary music.

Side 2: Samples of African music to provide a comparison with the "Afro-European" idiom of

the Suite. Both vocal and instrumental music. (Samples not confined to West Africa.) Script: introduction with notes on each band.

## Gambia

*(Filmstrip)*

*Gambia & Portuguese Guinea,* EG (1962). 47 frames, color, captioned, script, (*Continent of Africa: Countries of West Africa Series*—157A). $6.00.

43 photos, 2 maps and 2 full captions. Separate general overviews of each country. Gambia (21) and Portuguese Guinea (22). Topics include terrain and vegetation, people and religions, agriculture and agricultural products, capitals, transportation. Captions: statements explaining frames. Full captions: summary questions (2).

## Ghana

*(Written material)*

Achebe, Chinua, *Man of the People.* New York: John Day, 1966.

A novel about the rise and fall of a demagogue in a West African state. It offers excellent insights into the nature of the political process in newly developing states and describes the political education of the electorate.

Bleeker, Sonia, *The Ashanti of Ghana.* New York: William Morrow & Company, Inc., 1966. Hardcover. $3.25.

A description of the culture, history, family life, arts and crafts, and government of the Ashanti; illustrated by drawings; index. 160 pp. (Reading level: 6-9).

Boateng, E. A., *Ghana: Junior Atlas.* London: Thomas Nelson and Sons, Ltd. (distributed in U.S. by Humanities Press), 1965. Hardcover. $1.25.

First 16 pp. of this 8½" x 11" atlas include full-color maps of Ghana's physical features, regions, rainfall, vegetation, agriculture and forestry, resources, and population; also 2-page relief map of West Africa as well as maps of West Africa's wind systems, vegetation, population, and transportation and economy; remaining pages include maps of other regions of the world. Index. 33 pp.

Brown, Godfrey N., *An Active History of Ghana, Book Two: Since 1844.* London: George Allen & Unwin, Ltd., 1964. Paper.

A description of the history of Ghana from 1844 to independence, using documents, maps, charts, and photos as integral parts of the learning activities; study questions and exercises are built into the narrative; prepared for upper elementary level students in Ghana; no index. 143 pp.

Brown, Godfrey N. and Philip M. Amono, *An Active History of Ghana, Book One: From Earliest Times to 1844.* London: George Allen & Unwin, Ltd., 1965. Paper.

A study of the history of Ghana from the discovery of iron to 1844; includes many illustrations, maps and charts as well as exercises, study questions, and activities built into the text to involve the students actively in its study; section on biographies of early leaders; prepared for upper elementary level students in Ghana; no index. 143 pp.

Lobsenz, Norman, *The First Book of Ghana.* New York: Franklin Watts, Inc., 1964. Hardcover. $1.98.

An overview of Ghana stressing its geography, climate, people, and economy; numerous photos (b/w). Index. 88 pp. (Reading level 6-9).

Sale, J. Kirk, *The Land and People of Ghana.* Philadelphia: J. B. Lippincott Company, 1963. Hardcover. $2.93.

A description of the geography, people (especially the Ashanti and the Europeans), history, and culture of Ghana; with photos; index. 159 pp. (Reading level 9-12).

Selormey, Francis, *The Narrow Path: An African Childhood.* New York: Frederick A. Praeger, Publishers, 1966. Hardcover. $4.95.

An account of childhood in Ghana told in the first person; describes vividly the life and adventures of Kofi and his family and gives insights into many aspects of their lives, including education, religion, family organization. No index. 184 pp. (Reading level: 7-10).

Zemba, Lydia Verona, *Ghana in Pictures.* New York: Sterling Publishing Company, Inc., 1966. Hardcover. $1.00.

A brief survey of the history of Ghana followed by descriptions of its government, geography, people, economy, and society; many photos; no index. 64 pp. (Reading level: 6-12).

*(16 mm film)*
*Family of Ghana,* CF (n.d.) b/w., narration, 30 min.

Personalized description of life in a village on the coast of Ghana; focuses on conflicts between tradition and change as illustrated in the lives of a father and son.

*Ghana,* McG-H (1967). color, narration, 13 min.

Survey of Nkrumah's record; aspects of local government, including destoolment of old chief and enstoolment of new chief; ceremonies at military barracks; interview with U.S. Ambassador to Ghana; future problems.

*(Filmstrips)*
*Ghana: Land and People,* EG (1967). 47 frames, color, captioned, script. (*Continent of Africa: Countries of the Guinea Coast Series*—156B). $6.00.

43 photos, one map and 3 full captions. Major emphasis on people and modern influences. Terrain and vegetation (5), transportation and construction (9), history (4), modern influences (religion, education, dress) (20), markets (people and products) (5). Captions: statements explain frames. Full captions: review (2) and summary questions (1).

*Ghana,* CG (1962). 28 frames, color, non-captioned, script. $7.50.

27 photos and one map. Overview of the country. Accra and surrounding area (8), agriculture and agricultural products (6), northern Ghana—farming and houses (5), industrial development (7), and education (1). Script provides title and paragraph for each frame.

*Ghana–Part I*, BUDEK (1961). 31 frames, color, captioned, script. $6.00.

29 photos and 2 full captions. Divided into three distinct categories: terrain and vegetation (8), modern and traditional buildings (12), seaport and city of Accra (9). Captions: statements explaining frames. Full captions: history of modern Ghana. Script: descriptive paragraph supplementing each frame.

*Ghana–Part II*, BUDEK (1961). 38 frames, color, captioned, script. $6.00.

36 photos and 2 full captions. Emphasis on economic activities of the people of Ghana. Transportation (10), fishing (9), economic activities (7), handicrafts (6), celebrations in Ghana (4). Captions: statements explaining frames. Full captions: people and products of Ghana. Script: descriptive paragraph for each frame. Supplements captions.

*Ghana: Industries, Products, Cities,* EG (1964). 44 frames, color, captioned, script, (*Continent of Africa: Countries of Guinea Coast Series*–156C). $6.00.

42 photos and 2 full captions. Emphasis on city of Accra and agriculture. Agricultural products, (people and products, limited landscape) (12), ports and products (7), mineral resources (2), Accra (functions, buildings, education, people) (21). Captions: statements explain frames. Full captions: review (1) and summary questions (1).

*Accra-Ghana,* EG (1962). 45 frames, color, captioned, script. (*Continent of Africa: Historic Cities of Africa Series*–158A). $6.00.

43 photos and 2 full captions. General characteristics of the city. Modern structures and government buildings (13), markets and traditional sections (7), modern industrial influence (4), transportation (6), seaport and facilities (6), police force (4), and youth groups (3). Captions: statements explaining frames. Full captions: review and summary.

*How Kwaku Lives in Ghana.* WSP (n.d.). 58 frames, b/w, captioned. $4.00.

57 photos and one map. Follows the daily activities of a young boy in Ghana. Dress of people, including dress worn by village chief (11), family chores and food (20), fishing and daily activities of village (8), education and vocational training (18). Captions: statements explaining frames.

*(Chart)*

*Ghana,* PICTORIAL CHARTS. Single sheet, color, 30" x 40". $2.00.

Large map of Ghana showing the elevation and system of communication. Chart on the work cycle of the cocoa farmers and of chief exports. Information dated.

*(Tapes)*

*Ghana: A Case Study,* CENTER FOR THE STUDY OF DEMOCRATIC INSTITUTIONS (n.d.). 1 hour. $5.00.

Recording of a discussion held at the Center by Daniel Apter. Examination of questions associated with the shift from democratic institutions to military and dictatorial regimes. Focuses on the ethnic and social history and political development in Ghana.

*Ghana and Uganda,* WTE (n.d.). 25 min. $2.75.

An interview with nationalists from Ghana and Uganda discussing the social, economic, and political problems facing independent Ghana and "soon to be independent" Uganda.

*Ghana,* SOUNDS OF LEARNING, INC. (n.d.). (2 parts), 30 min. $5.00 each.

Discussion of the political, social, and economic aspects of Ghana and Ghana's point of view on these questions. Topics are history, economic development, and social progress. Selections of music from Ghana at end of tape.

*(Record)*

*Ashanti Folk Tales from Ghana* (FC7110), FOLK-WAYS. 6 bands. $4.15.

Side 1: "All Stories are Anansi's" "Anansi, the Oldest of Animals," and "Nyame's Well." Side 2: "Two Feasts for Anansi," "Anansi Plays Dead," and "The Porcupine's Hoe."

## Guinea

*(16 mm film)*
*African Village,* CF (n.d.). color, narration. 17 min.

Life in a tiny Kissi settlement in Guinea, emphasizing especially patterns of social change and continuity.

*(Filmstrips)*
*Guinea,* DON BOSCO (n.d.). 30 frames, color, non-captioned, script. $6.00.

Overview of Guinea: Terrain and vegetation (5), village life (9), Conakry (8), products and economic activities (7). Script: descriptive paragraph for each frame.

*Republic of Guinea* EG, (1962). 49 frames, color, captioned, script. (*Continent of Africa: Countries of West Africa Series*–157B). $6.00.

46 photos, one map and 2 full captions. General overview of the country. Terrain and vegetation (13), agriculture and agricultural products (15), tribal groups and major economic activities (8), minerals (2), and Conakry (markets, industries, and transportation) (8). Captions: statements explaining frames. Full captions: review (1) and summary questions (1).

## Ivory Coast

*(16 mm film)*
*Republic of the Ivory Coast,* (*The Peoples of Africa Series*), UNITED WORLD (1967). b/w, narration, 20 min.

Depicts export-oriented economy and products of the Ivory Coast. Emphasis on growth and potential, economic ties with France. Also included are scenes of an Independence Day celebration in a small town, illustrating a blending of modern and traditional life in the Ivory Coast.

*(Filmstrips)*
*The Ivory Coast,* DON BOSCO (n.d.). 30 frames, color, non-captioned, script. $6.00.

General overview of the country depicting climate (5), animals (2), products (7), villages and people (5), Moslem religion (4), city of Abidjan (5). Script provides descriptive paragraph for each frame.

*Republic of the Ivory Coast–Land and People,* EG (1962). 46 frames, color, script. (*Continent of Africa: Countries of West Africa Series*– 157C). $6.00.

Forty-three photos, one map and 2 full captions. Terrain and vegetation (10), population and ethnic groups (10), city of Abidjan (5), transportation and communication (7), education (7), traditional culture (4). Captions: statements explaining frames. Full captions: review (2).

*Republic of the Ivory Coast–Industries, Products and Cities,* EG (1962). 46 frames, color, captioned, script. (*Continent of Africa: Countries of West Africa Series*–157D). $6.00.

44 photos and 2 full captions. Divided between agriculture and urban centers. Agriculture and agricultural products (14), Abidjan (buildings, industries and products) (20), Buoake (surrounding regions, markets and products) (10). Captions: statements explaining frames. Full captions: review (1) and summary questions (1).

*(Record)*
*The Baoule of the Ivory Coast,* FOLKWAYS. 23 bands, script. $6.79.

Side 1: 9 bands; side 2: 14 bands. Vocal and instrumental music of the Baoule of the Ivory Coast. Religious and ceremonial music included. Script: background notes with notes on individual bands.

## Liberia

*(Written material)*
Rottsolk, James E., *The Story of Liberia,* Cincinnati: McCormick-Mathers Publishing Company, Inc., 1967. Paper. $1.32.

A narrative (written as the adventures of a boy) of life in Liberia, its villages, cities, schools, and rubber plantations; geography, history and economic and social conditions are infused in the narrative; maps and photos; glossary; pro-

nunciation guide in the text; index. 124 pp.
(Reading level: 6-9).

*(Filmstrips)*

*Liberia,* BUDEK (n.d.). 50 frames, color, captioned, script. $6.00.

36 photos, 13 captions, and one map. Provides a general overview of Liberia. Filmstrip divided by full title frames into the following categories: rubber (4), life on the plantation (12), urban life (12), getting about in Liberia (1), new developments—iron mining (4), shipping the iron ore —Freeport (2), areas untouched by Moslem influence (4). Captions: statements explaining frames. Full captions: introduction and supplement (6), title frames (7). Script: introduction plus descriptive paragraph for each frame.

*Liberia and Togo.* EG (1962). 52 frames, color, captioned, script. (*Continent of West Africa Series*—157E). $6.00.

48 photos, 2 maps and 2 full captions. General overview of each country. *Liberia* (26): people, tribes, and economic activities (11), agricultural products (5), capital of Monrovia (8), history (1), and vegetation (1). *Togo* (22): terrain and vegetation (4), agriculture and agricultural products (5), city of Lome (6), people (2), and mining (1). Captions: statements explaining frames. Full captions: summary questions (2).

*How Duce Lives in Liberia.* WSP (n.d.). 47 frames, b/w, captioned. $4.00.

45 photos and 2 maps. Follows the life and activity of a 12-year-old boy in a village in Liberia. Introduction (5), use of palm tree products (12), the village, including construction of houses and people of (15). Captions: statements explaining frames.

*(Record)*

*Folk Music of Liberia* (FE4465), FOLKWAYS. 11 bands, script. $6.95.

Samples of the vocal and instrumental music of Liberia. Instruments and music taken from the various tribal groups. Script: introduction and notes on individual bands.

## Mali

*(Written material)*

Niane, D. T., *Sundiata: An Epic of Old Mali.* New York: Humanities Press, 1967. Paper. $1.25.

An English translation of a narrative about the life and exploits of a great king of ancient Mali as told by an African minstrel or annalist; includes many asides that reflect the culture of the Mandingo; no index. 96 pp. (Reading level: 9-12).

*(16 mm film)*

*Daily Life of the Bozo People,* (#10 *African Village Life*), IFF (1967). color, background sound, no narration, 15 min.

Shows daily activities of the Bozo peoples who live along Niger River in Mali—house building, weaving at hand loom, preparing food, washing, fishing.

*Fishing on the Niger River,* (#1 *African Village Life*), IFF (1967). color, background sound, no narration. 17 min.

Shows Bozo people of Mali engaged in fishing activities on Niger River—preparing nets and boats, fishing with nets, cleaning and drying nets, cooking fish; market place. Brief shots of community building.

*Building A Home,* (#2 *African Village Life*), IFF (1967). color, background sound, no narration. 7 min.

Shows the Bozo peoples of Mali engaged in constructing a home from wood and straw.

*Building a Boat,* (#3 *African Village Life*), IFF (1967). color, background sound, no narration, 7 min.

Shows Bozo peoples of Mali assembling a boat— shaping the wood, setting and pinning the sides to the hull; details of final steps.

*Onion Farming,* (#4 *African Village Life*), IFF (1967). color, background sound, no narration, 7 min.

Shows Dogon people of Mali engaged in various aspects of onion farming, including irrigation of terraced fields and preparing harvested onions.

*Herding Cattle,* (#5 *African Village Life*), IFF (1967). color, background sound, no narration, 7 min.

Description of Peul peoples of Mali herding cattle across Niger river.

*Hunting Wild Doves,* (#6 *African Village Life*), IFF (1967). color, background sound, no narration, 7 min.

Shows Dogon peoples of Mali preparing rope, climbing cliffs, capturing doves, and descending. Also brief shots of cliff dwellings and houses.

*Cotton Growing and Spinning,* (#9 *African Village Life*), IFF (1967). color, background sound, no narration, 7 min.

Shows Dogon peoples of Mali engaged in picking cotton, carding and spinning it into thread. Also brief shots of housing.

*(Filmstrips)*

*Republic of Mali,* EG (1965). 46 frames, color, captioned, script. (*Continent of Africa: Countries of Moslem Africa Series*–159E). $6.00.

43 photos, one map, and 2 full captions. Urban centers (people, buildings and markets) (18), agriculture (people and products) (9), handicraft (5), topography (4) and population composition (4), and transportation. Captions: statements explaining frames. Full captions: summary and review questions.

*Timbuktu: Republic of Mali,* EG (1962). 48 frames, color, captioned, script, (*Continent of Africa: Historic Cities of Africa Series*–158H). $6.00.

45 photos, one map, and 2 full captions: history (5), Tuaregs (5), Songhai (2), Moslem religion (4), buildings (8), central market (people and products) (8), foods (9), camel caravans and salt trade (4). Captions: statements explaining frames. Full captions: review and summary.

*(Record)*

*Music of Mali,* (FE4338), FOLKWAYS. 5 bands, script. $6.79.

Side 1: 1 band; side 2: 4 bands. First side deals with the music played at a funeral at Dini. Side two records wedding songs and Tuareg minstrels at Timbuktu. Script: introduction with notes

from a diary describing the scenes where the music was recorded.

*(8 mm film loops)*

*Africans of the River Niger,* EALING (1968). six 8 mm cartridged loops in color, no sound, super 8. $21.50 each; regular $18.50 each.

Adapted from films produced by Julien Bryan and the International Film Foundation. Titles are:

*River Bank Village.* (4 min.)
Life of the Bozo of Mali showing men weaving, women doing household chores.

*Building a House.* (4 min.)
Bozo men build house of branches and reed thatching on stilts.

*Building a Boat.* (3½ min.)
Bozo men assemble large canoe and waterproof it.

*Fishing.* (4 min.)
Bozo community fishes the river Niger using a variety of techniques, including a huge net.

*Trading Smoked Fish.* (4 min.)
Bozo sell surplus of smoked fish at local markets, where they get money for basic necessities.

*Preparing a Meal.* (4 min.)
Bozo housewife prepares a meal of rice and fish which is then served to the men and boys.

*(8 mm loops/sound)*

*African Village Life,* EALING (1968). 8 cartridged 8 mm loops in color with sound, super 8.

Adapted from films produced by Julien Bryan and the International Film foundation. Titles are:

*Building a House.* (7 min.) $59.00.
Bozo tribesmen of Mali construct home on stilts from reeds and branches.

*Building a Boat.* (7 min.) $59.00.
Bozo assemble a large canoe.

*Onion Farming.* (7 min.) $59.00.
The Dogon of Mali harvest onions and prepare them for trading with their neighbors.

*Cotton Growing and Spinning.* (7 min.) $59.00. Dogon techniques of cotton growing and spinning.

*Hunting the Wild Doves.* (7 min.) $59.00. With rope made from bark of Baobab tree, Dogon men scale cliffs to capture wild doves.

*Herding Cattle.* (7 min.) $59.00. The Peul of the Fulani move cattle across the Niger.

*Daily Life of the Bozo.* (15 min.) $98.00. Shows various occupations of these people.

*Fishing on the Niger.* (17 min.) $110.00. Depicts Bozo engaged in fishing, using a variety of techniques.

## Mauritania

*(16 mm film)*

*The Islamic Republic of Mauritania,* (*The People of Africa Series*), UNITED WORLD (1967). b/w, narration, 20 min.

General overview of the country. Emphasis placed on development of natural resources, the impact of lack of water and of nomadic life, and modernization projects.

*(Filmstrip)*

*The Islamic Republic of Mauritania,* EG (1965). 47 frames, color, captioned, script, (*Continent of Africa: Countries of Moslem Africa Series—* 159E). $6.00.

43 photos, one map and 3 full captions. General overview of the country, farms, and farm products (10), urban centers (5); and topography, transportation, nomads, animals, imports-exports, education and fishing (28). Captions: statements explaining frames. Full captions: review (2) and summary (1).

## Niger

*(16 mm film)*

*Republic of Niger,* (*The Peoples of Africa Series*), UNITED WORLD (1967). b/w, narration, 20 min.

Depicts the lack of water in Niger. Examples of search for water, economic activity, and daily

life of the nomads of southern and northern Nigeria and the desert towns and cities. Also examines impact of modernization.

*(Filmstrip)*

*The Republic of Niger,* EG (1962). 47 frames, color, captioned, script, (*Continent of Africa: Countries of Moslem Africa Series—* 159H). $6.00.

43 photos, one map and 3 full captions. Broad coverage of varied activities and characteristics of Niger. Agriculture and products (12), population (10), urban centers (5), education (6), markets, housing and transportation (10). Captions: statements explaining frames. Full captions: review (2) and summary (1).

## Nigeria

*(Written material)*

Achebe, Chinua, *No Longer At Ease.* New York: Humanities Press, Inc., 1966. Paper. $1.00.

A 1961 novel about a Christian Ibo, the grandson of the fictitious Okonkwo of Achebe's earlier novel, caught up in a changing world. Educated in England and a member of the Nigerian civil service during colonial rule, Obi finds life in a bribery-ridden urban society beset with all the problems of clash between the new and old. Excellent portrayal of Ibo life, of the paternalistic attitude of the English and of life in the city. 170 pp.

Achebe, Chinua, *Things Fall Apart.* New York: Humanities Press, Inc., 1966. Paper. $1.00.

A novel (first published 1958) about a Nigerian Ibo, Okonkwo, who is exiled from his village. Upon his return he finds that missionaries have converted many villagers and great changes have taken place, changes he finds hard to accept and with which he comes into tragic conflict. An fine depiction of Ibo customs and life and the impact on individuals of the introduction of new religions and governments. 187 pp.

Aluko, T. M.,*One Man, One Matchet.* New York: Humanities Press, Inc.. 1966. Paper. $1.00.

A novel written in 1964 about relations between Africans and their white rulers and between various types of African leaders themselves. The story is set in western Nigeria shortly after World War II and involves the struggles of two Africans for local political support in a variety of issues. 197 pp.

Aluko, T. M., *One Man, One Wife*. New York: Humanities Press, Inc., 1967. Paper. $1.25.

This 1959 novel concerns the inhabitants of a small village in Western Nigeria and the problems evolving from the conflict between their customs and the teachings of the missionaries. 201 pp.

Ekwensi, Cyprian, *Burning Grass*. New York: Humanities Press, Inc., 1966. Paper. $1.00.

This novel describes the life of the Fulani and touches on some changes introduced by the white man. It describes many tribal customs and rites while detailing the wanderings of its hero, Sunsaye. 150 pp.

English, M. C., *An Outline of Nigerian History*. Ibadan: Longman's of Nigeria, Ltd., 1959. Paper. 7s 9d.

A detailed history of Nigeria for Nigerian upper secondary school students; approximately half of the book is devoted to pre-European history; questions follow each chapter; some maps and plates; index.

Forman, Brenda Lu and Harrison, *The Land and People of Nigeria*. Philadelphia: J. B. Lippincott Co., 1954. Hardcover. $3.25.

A survey, with black and white photos, of Nigeria, its geography, history, peoples, government, education, arts, and economy; concludes with description of each major region; index. 160 pp. (Reading level: 9-12).

Grant, James, *A Geography of Western Nigeria*. London: Cambridge University Press, 1960. Paper.

A description of the geography of the western region of Nigeria presented as an account of an imaginary journey starting at Ibadan; many maps, charts, photos (b/w), city diagrams, student exercises and activities; focuses on climate, population distribution, settlement patterns,

selected resources (cocoa, timber, rubber), farming, industry, and transportation. Designed for use in Nigerian schools. No index. 15 pp. (Reading level: 7-10).

Iloeje, N. P., *A New Geography of Nigeria*. Ikeja: Longman's of Nigeria, Ltd., 1956. Paper. 12s 6d.

Description and analysis of physical setting, economic development, regional geography of Nigeria with chapter summaries, exercises and questions; extensive use of maps, graphs, charts, photos, and diagrams; prepared for upper secondary students in Nigerian schools; index. 260 pp.

Kenworthy, Leonard S., *Profile of Nigeria*. Garden City: Doubleday & Company, Inc., 1960. Hardcover. $2.95.

A text on the peoples, customs, social conditions, government, geography, and economy of Nigeria; numerous clear black and white photos; index. 96 pp. (Reading level: 6-9).

Munonye, John, *The Only Son*. New York: Humanities Press, Inc., 1966. Paper. $1.00.

This novel is set in eastern Nigeria. It is the story of a woman's devotion to her youngest son and his growing up and leaving her for the religion and education of the white man. Family organization customs, rites, and the impact of Christianity are vividly described. An extensive view of traditional life in eastern Nigeria. 202 pp.

Mwapa, Flora, *Efuru*. New York: Humanities Press, Inc., 1967. Paper. $1.50.

This is a novel depicting the role of women in Nigeria. Emphasis is placed on trading, marriage customs, raising children and village life. 281 pp.

Oboli, H. O. N., *Beginning Geography in Eastern Nigeria*. Ikeja: Longman's of Nigeria, Ltd., 1965. Paper. 4s 6d.

A combination workbook, study guide, and text on Nigeria's geography that emphasizes land use, population distribution, trade, and economy; includes considerable material on neighboring nations; numerous charts, graphs, maps, pictures and student activities; concludes with section on "The World in Space." For use in Nigerian elementary schools. 106 pp.

Soladoye, E. E., ed., *Nigeria: Junior Atlas.* London: Thomas Nelson and Sons, Ltd., (distributed in U.S. by Humanities Press), 1965. Paper. $1.00.

First 20 pp. of this 8¼" x 11" atlas include full color 2-page maps of Nigerian administrative divisions by region; special maps on rainfall, products, vegetation; street maps of major cities; photos; various maps on West Africa; remaining 10 pp. includes full color maps of other regions of the world. Index. 33 pp.

Spicer, E., *The Peoples of Nigeria.* Ikeja: Longman's of Nigeria, Ltd., 1962. Paper. $1.00.

Brief (7-10 pp. each) descriptions of eight different cultural groups which occupy Nigeria, including the Hausa, Fulani, Kanwi, Yoruba and Ibo; some photos and drawings included. Prepared for use in Nigerian upper elementary schools. 71 pp.

Walker, Barbara K. and Warren S., *Nigerian Folk Tales.* New Brunswick: Rutgers University Press, 1961. Hardcover. $4.00.

A collection of Nigerian Yoruba folktales centering on the themes of demon lovers, moral fables, trickster tales, fertility tales, and tales which explain the nature of things. Bibliography. No index. 113 pp. (Reading level: 7-12).

*(16 mm films)*

*Africa is My Home,* ATLANTIS (n.d.) color, narration, 23 min.

Portrayal of the conflict between the traditional and the modern as seen through the eyes of a young Ibo girl; reflects the impact of the colonial experience and the desire for national identity.

*African Girl...Malobi,* ATLANTIS (1967). color, narration, 11 min. $110.00.

The Ibo people of southern Nigeria are described through the eyes of a young girl. A recurrent theme is the drive for education at all ages. Food production, community enterprise, markets and trading, social change, and urbanization also are depicted. Teachers' summary.

*Hausa Village,* CF (n.d.) b/w, narration (22 min.).

Daily life in a village in northern Nigeria; depicts farming and fishing activities of inhabitants and shows preparation for a wedding ceremony; shows Muslim way of life.

*Nigeria: Problems of Nation Building.* ATLANTIS (1967). color, narration, 22 min. $200.00.

Geography, pre-colonial and colonial history, religion, language, and economic development are analyzed in this realistic appraisal of the problems of national unity. Emphasis is placed on tribal hostilities and conflict between traditional and innovative segments of society. Helps explain Biafran secession. Teachers' summary.

*Nigerian Unity,* McG-H (1967). color, narration, 20 min.

Description of Lagos, of the resources of Nigeria; problems of tribalism and 1967 civil war; focuses on Emir of Kano, his pageantry and government, and on problems of unity.

*West Africa (Nigeria),* EBF (1962). color, narration, 22 min.

The history, geography, societies, and economy of each of Nigeria's three main regions are shown and contrasted. Emphasis is placed on the problems of economic development and shaping national unity. Teachers' guide. (Collaborator: Professor Paul Bohannan.)

*(Filmstrips)*

*Nigeria,* BUDEK (1965). 40 frames, color, non-captioned, script. $6.00.

General overview of the various sections of Nigeria. Major emphasis on the following topics: major cities of Nigeria (7), villages (4), modern structures (2), markets (4), savanna landscape (3), transportation (5), people (6), agriculture (7), industry (2). Script: introduction and descriptive paragraph for each frame.

*Profile of Nigeria,* SFS (1961). 50 frames, color, non-captioned, script. $6.00.

Forty-nine photos and one map. General overview of the country. Introduction (1), land (4), people (5), housing and living (6), transportation and communication (8), markets and earning a living (12), health and education (5), religion (2), government (2), arts (2), recreation (4). Script provides a frame-by-frame description.

*Village Life in Northern Nigeria,* CG, (1953). 27 frames, color, non-captioned, script. $7.50. Shows village activities including cooking, weaving, farming (18), urban life (7), wet and dry seasons (2). Script has detailed description of each frame.

*Contrasts in Nigeria,* EBF (1961). 45 frames, color, captioned. $6.00.

37 photos, 4 maps, and 9 full captions. Comparison of northern and western Nigeria with major emphasis on urban centers of the regions and of the contrast between traditional and modern aspects of life. Kano (7), surrounding area of Kano (11), Western Region (5), Ibadan (old and new) (5), modern Lagos (4). Captions: statements explaining frames. Full captions: introduction (3) and summary.

*In the Tropics Part I: Savanah and Hot Grasslands (Nigeria).* UNITED WORLD (n.d.). 43 frames, color, non-captioned, script. $4.00.

43 photos. Scenes centered around the Kadunda/Kano areas. Topics include: climate (10), countryside (8), products (15), human activities (9). Script: introduction and descriptive paragraph for each frame. Quality of this and following film fair; colors slightly washed out.

*In the Tropics Part II: The Coast and Rain Forest (Nigeria).* UNITED WORLD (n.d.). 31 frames, color, non-captioned, script. $4.00.

The coastal region and rain forest of Nigeria, divided as follows: Coastal region—physical and cultural aspects (6), products (16), human activities (9). Script provides introduction and descriptive paragraph for each frame.

*Nigeria,* SB (1965). 31 frames, color, captioned. $3.00.

27 photos and 4 full captions. Cities and villages (7), housing (4), terrain and climate (3), tribes, religion, and education (5), agriculture

and agricultural products (6), transportation (2), coal (1). Full captions: information on size, location, vegetation. Captions: statements explaining frames.

*Nigeria: Industries and Products,* EG (1964). 47 frames, color, captioned, script. (*Continent of Africa: Countries of Guinea Coast Series–* 156F). $6.00.

44 photos and 3 full captions. Products and related industries. Agricultural products and food processing (17), animal husbandry and related industries (8), cash crops and processing (6), mineral resources (6), industries (7). Captions: statements explaining frames. Full captions: review (2) and summary questions (1).

*Nigeria: Land, Transportation, Communication,* EG (1964). 46 frames, color, captioned, script. (*Continent of Africa: Countries of the Guinea Coast Series–*156D). $6.00.

42 photos, one map, and 3 full captions. Major emphasis on physical geography: terrain, vegetation and climate (20), transportation (11), postal and radio communication (7), palm oil (4). Captions: statements explaining frames. Full captions: review (2) and summary questions (1).

*Lagos: Federation of Nigeria,* EG (1962). 46 frames, color, captioned, script. (*Continent of Africa: Historic Cities of Africa Series–*158D). $6.00.

43 photos, one map, and 2 full captions. Map shows location of city. Major emphasis on population, physical structure, and industries, tribes, language and religious groups (14), modern and traditional buildings (9), functions of city (2), industries (8), port (3), suburban areas (3) and education (4). Captions: statements explaining frames. Full captions: review and summary.

*Nigeria: Important Cities,* EG (1964). 48 frames, color, captioned, script, (*Continent of Africa: Countries of Guinea Coast Series–*156G). $6.00.

45 photos and 3 full captions. Comparison and contrast between Lagos and Kano. *Lagos:* mod-

ern buildings (9), transportation (4), education (4), industries (3), and people (2). *Kano:* traditional buildings (6), tribes and religious groups (5), industries and products (12). Captions: statements explaining frames. Full captions: review (2) and summary questions (1).

*Nigeria: Other Cities,* EG (1964). 46 frames, color, captioned, script, (*Continent of Africa: Countries of Guinea Coast Series*—156H). $6.00.

44 photos and 2 full captions. Comparison of cities and regions of Nigeria. *Ibadan:* modern structures (6), T.V. station (5), industries and products (6), local markets (4), and education (3). *Enugu:* products (5). *Port Harcourt:* (3). *Kaduna and Benin:* industries, products, education and markets (12). Captions: statements explaining frames. Full captions: review (1) and summary questions. (1).

*Nigeria: People,* EG (1964). 44 frames, color, captioned, script. (*Continent of Africa: Countries of the Guinea Coast Series*—156E). $6.00.

42 photos and 2 full captions. Major emphasis on religious groups and education. Population and language (4), people of urban areas (5), Yoruba (4), Fulani (3), recreation (5), religious groups (10), education and government services (11). Captions: statements explaining frames. Full captions: review (1) and summary questions (1).

*Village Life in Northern Nigeria,* CG (1951). 25 frames, color, non-captioned. $8.50.

Comparison of village and town in northern Nigeria. Village: house construction (3), daily activities (5), agriculture and agricultural products (9). Town: general view (including Kano) (2), transportation, street scenes, and markets (4), seasons (2). Script provides title and paragraph on each frame.

*Nigerian Arts and Crafts,* UNITED WORLD (n.d.). 38 frames, color, non-captioned, script. $6.00.

Examination of the various types of arts and crafts found in Nigeria. Working in wood (5), in metal (5), in leather (5), in cotton (10); miscellaneous crafts—mostly pottery and architecture

(13). Script: introduction and descriptive paragraph for each frame.

*(Filmstrip/record)*
*Nigeria: What You'd See There—Part I,* BF (n.d.). 41 frames, color, non-captioned, script, record. set $25.00.

39 photos and 2 maps. Record (10 min.). Introduction (3), dress (7), schools (3), housing (13), Lagos (11), economic development (3). Script follows record.

*Nigeria: What You'd See There—Part II,* BF (n.d.). 41 frames, color, non-captioned, script, record. set $25.00.

40 photos and one map. Record (9 min.). Cities of Nigeria (9), products and markets (11), fishing (5), transportation (6), government activities (3), sights in Nigeria (6). Script follows record.

*(Charts)*
*Nigeria,* PICTORIAL CHARTS. single sheet, color, 30" x 40" $2.00.

Large map of the country showing elevation, major economic activities, and communication. Notes on the techniques of oil palm production, and on the steps toward self government. Information dated.

*Nigeria—Headline-Focus Wall Map #11,* CES (1966).

Large (28" x 38") color wall chart of Nigeria with descriptive test inserted in one corner ("Democracy bows out"); map contains drawings and explanatory notes on economic, political, and social problems as of February 1966.

*(Records)*
*This is My Country: Nigeria,* WILSON (1968). 1 side of 12" LP (or tape). 19 min.

Introduced by narrative description of Nigeria's location, followed by interview with a Nigerian that briefly covers family life and structure, how people make a living, education, religion (stressing difference between city and village life), higher education, form of government, current political problems.

*Drums of the Yoruba of Nigeria* (FE4441), FOLK-WAYS. 13 bands, script. $6.79.

Side 1: 4 bands; side 2: 9 bands. Record of the various types of drums and music produced by the Yoruba people of West Africa. Script: introduction with notes on each band.

*Olantunji, Drums of Passion,* COLUMBIA. 8 bands, script. $3.98.

Side 1: 4 bands; side 2: 4 bands. Olantunji's impressions of the folk and dance music of Nigeria. Script: general introduction. No notes on individual bands.

*Olantunji High Life,* COLUMBIA. 10 bands, script. $3.98.

Side 1: 5 bands; side 2: 5 bands. The term "high life" refers to the popular music and dance which developed in Ghana and Nigeria seventy years ago. Album provides samples of "high life" music. Script: general discussion of music. No notes on individual bands.

*Hausa,* WORLD. script. $2.45.

Six 7" records, part of the World Foreign Language Series, giving English and Hausa pronunciation of general expressions and vocabulary. Script: 27-page English-Hausa dictionary.

### Senegal

*(16 mm film)*

*Senegal* (*The People of Africa Series*), UNITED WORLD (1967). b/w, narration, 20 min.

Emphasis on economic activities and natural resources. Stress is placed on the need for modern equipment for development of cash crop industries and for Senegal to achieve its potential; comparison of modern and industrial Dakar with traditional countryside.

*(Filmstrips)*

*The Republic of Senegal: Land and People,* EG (1962). 48 frames, color, captioned, script, (*Continent of Africa: Countries of West Africa Series*—157F). $6.00.

44 photos, one map, and 3 full captions. Ter-rain and vegetation (5), population and tribes (3), dress (4), religion (3), French and non-African influence (6), education and health services (9), occupations (7), daily activities and recreation (7). Captions: statements explaining frames. Full captions: review (2) and summary questions (1).

*Republic of Senegal: Industries and Products,* EG (1962), 45 frames, color, captioned, script, (*Continent of Africa: Countries of West Africa Series*—157G). $6.00.

43 photos and 2 full captions. Agriculture and agricultural products (9), fishing and fishing industries (14), animal husbandry (4), lumbering (4), mineral products (4), imports-exports (8). Captions: statement explaining frames. Full captions: review (1) and summary questions (1).

*Republic of Senegal: Transportation and Cities,* EG (1962). 46 frames, color, captioned, script. (*Continent of Africa: Countries of West Africa Series*—157H). $6.00.

43 photos and 3 full captions. Major emphasis on the city of Dakar: history (2), transportation and communication (14), modern buildings, markets, recreation, and historical buildings (27). Captions: statements explaining frames. Full captions: review (2) and summary questions (1).

*(Records)*

*Wolof Music of Senegal and Gambia,* (FE4462), FOLKWAYS. 10 bands, script. $6.79.

Side 1: 5 bands; side 2: 5 bands. Vocal and instrumental music of the Wolof people from both Senegal and Gambia: Script: background material with notes on individual bands.

*The Music of the Diola—Fogny of the Casamance, Senegal* (FE4323), FOLKWAYS. 10 bands, script. $6.79.

Side 1: 4 bands; side 2: 6 bands. Instrumental and vocal music of the Fogny which are part of the Diola bribe of the Southwestern section of the Republic of Senegal. Script: background notes and notes on individual bands.

## Sierra Leone

*(Written material)*

Cran, M. I. and Geoffrey Williams, *Sierra Leone Atlas.* London: Thomas Nelson and Sons, Ltd. (distributed in the U.S. by Humanities Press), 1966. Paper. $1.00.

First 12 pp. of this 8½" x 11" atlas include full color physical, vegetation, and rainfall maps of Sierra Leone and maps on its population, agriculture; also included are maps of West Africa's wind systems, vegetation, population density, and economy; maps of continent's rainfall, temperature, and mineral resources; remaining pages on other regions of the world. Index. 25 pp.

Dalton, K. G., *A Geography of Sierra Leone.* London: Cambridge University Press, 1965. Paper.

A description of Sierra Leone's people and countryside presented as an imaginary journey; focuses on Freetown and its suburbs, coastal and inland villages, transportation, climate, selected resources and products (iron, rice, cattle, diamonds, cocoa, timber) and selected features of the landscape; many photos (b/w), maps, charts, graphs, student exercises included. Prepared for students in Sierra Leone. No index. 63 pp. (Reading level: 7-10).

Peters, Lenrie, *The Second Round.* New York: Humanities Press, Inc., 1967. Paper. $1.25.

Set in Sierra Leone, this novel explores the difficulties that face an idealistic African doctor who returns to his country to contribute to its progress but finds the conditions there hardly what he had expected. 193 pp.

*(Filmstrips)*

*Sierra Leone,* EG (1962). 45 frames, color, captioned, script, *(Continent of Africa: Countries of West Africa Series*–157I). $6.00.

42 photos, one map and 2 full captions. General overview of the country: terrain, vegetation and animals (11), ethnic groups (7), farming and farm products (11), natural resources (9) and transportation (4). Captions: statements explaining frames. Full captions: review (2) and summary questions (1).

*Profile of Sierra Leone,* SFS (1961). 51 frames, color, non-captioned, script. $6.00.

48 photos and 3 maps. General overview of the country: transportation (14), economic activities (13), people (8), settlements (2), history (2), modern agricultural training (6). Script provides a frame-by-frame description.

*People of Sierra Leone,* SFS (1962). 34 frames, color, non-captioned, script. $6.00.

33 photos and one full caption. Shows the work of the West African Institute for Oil Palm Research. Photos show the various phases of research and the growing of palm oil. Full caption: title frame. Script: provides title and description of each frame.

*(Record)*

*Music of the Mende of Sierra Leone* (FE4322), FOLKWAYS. 10 bands, script. $6.79.

Side 1: 5 bands; side 2: 5 bands. Vocal and instrumental music of the Mende tribe. Work, religious, and celebration songs are included. Script: introduction and notes on individual bands.

## Spanish Territories

*(Filmstrip)*

*Spanish African Territories,* EG (1962). 43 frames, color, captioned, script, *(Continent of Africa: Countries of Moslem Africa Series*–159J). $6.00.

37 photos, 2 maps, and 4 full captions. Divided into Spanish West Africa (11), Spanish Sahara (11), and Spanish Guinea (15). Topics include: people, topography, economic activities, and products. Captions explain frames. Full captions: review (3) and summary (1).

## Upper Volta

*(Filmstrip)*

*The Republic of Upper Volta,* EG (1964). 49 frames, color, captioned, script, *(Continent of Africa: Countries of Guinea Coast Series*–156I). $6.00.

Forty-five photos, one map, and 3 full captions.

General overview of the country, with emphasis on Bobo-Dioulasso. Population and tribes (8), agriculture and agricultural products (6), transportation (6), public services (3), minerals (2). Bobo-Dioulasso: industries, imports-exports (10), buildings, markets, and people (10). Captions: statements explaining frames. Full captions: review (2) and summary questions (1).

*(Record)*
*Tuareg Music of the Southern Sahara* (FE4470), FOLKWAYS. 13 bands, script. $6.79.

Side 1: 7 bands; side 2: 6 bands. Instrumental and vocal music of the Tuaregs. Dominance of women in music reflects the matrilineal organization of the Tuaregs. Script: introduction with notes on individual bands.

## EAST AFRICA

### GENERAL

#### Overview

*(Written material)*
Carpenter, Frances, *The Story of East Africa*. Cincinnati: McCormick-Mathers Publishing Company, Inc., 1967. Paper. $1.32.

A survey of Uganda, Kenya, and Tanzania in story form that deals with the land, peoples, cities, animal life, religion, magic, arts, and independence; many photos; several maps and charts; a timeline, glossary, and index. 140 pp. (Reading level: 6-9).

Hickman, G. M. and W. H. G. Dickins, *The Lands and Peoples of East Africa, A School Certificate Geography*. London: Longman's, Green and Company, Ltd., 1965. Hardcover. 15s.

An introduction to the geography of East Africa that focuses on selected problems and then on various regions (the coast, plateaus, highlands) and various resources; includes a number of photos and over 70 maps, charts, drawings, and tables; end-of-chapter problems; glossary; prepared for African secondary schools and teacher training institutions; index. 232 pp.

Lobsenz, Norman, *The First Book of East Africa*. New York: Franklin Watts, Inc., 1964. Hardcover. $1.98.

An overview of East Africa followed by studies of Kenya, Tanganyika, and Uganda; brief chapters on tribes, wild life, the Rift valley, fossil beds, the tse-tse fly, Swahili, and East Africa's future; numerous photos (b/w), especially of people. Index. 88 pp. (Reading level: 6-9).

*( 16 mm films)*
*East Africa (Kenya, Tanganyika, Uganda)*, EBF (1962). color, narration, 21 min.

East Africa's varied geography, economy, and peoples are illustrated, with strong emphasis placed on the problems of social change in newly independent nations. Teachers' guide. (Collaborator: Professor Paul Bohannan.)

*East Africa: Tropical Highlands*, McG-H, (1966). color, narration, 15 min.

A survey of the physical features of the nations of East Africa pointing out the great variations in topography and how these result in economic differences. Social contrasts are featured in a short study of Nairobi and the Masai. Excellent maps. Teachers' guide.

*(Filmstrips)*
*East Africa*, EAV (n.d.). 43 frames, b/w, non-captioned, script. $3.75.

39 photos and 4 maps. Provides a general overview of three countries: Uganda (12), Kenya (13), Tanganyika and Zanzibar (14). Topics include: topography, products, resources, urban centers. Script provides a descriptive paragraph for each frame. Produced in England.

*East Africa*, McG-H (1967). 36 frames, color, captioned, script. $8.50.

31 photos, 2 maps, one drawing, and 2 full captions. Introduction—highlands and climate (6), coastal, inland, and southern East Africa (9), major activities of highlands (17). Conclusion: training and modern development (4). Captions: statements and questions.

*East Africa–Land of Contrast,* EG (1965). 46 frames, color, captioned, script, (*Continent of Africa: East Africa–Land of Safaris Series–* 146C). $6.00.

42 photos and 4 maps. Terrain (with emphasis on Mt. Kenya, Kilimanjaro, and Great Rift Valley) (10), modern structures (5), vegetation and animal life (11), people and farming (16). Captions explain frames.

*East Africa: A Regional Survey,* CG (1956). 26 frames, color, non-captioned, script. $7.50.

26 photos. Divided into three sections: coastal settlements, water transportation, and products (7); plateau–village markets, terrain, products (12); development: economic (3), political and educational (3), transportation (1). Script provides title and paragraph for each frame.

*The East African Coast,* BUDEK (1964). 34 frames, color, non-captioned, script. $6.00.

34 photos. General survey from north to south along the east coast of Africa. Arab Africa (10) showing the modern harbors, villages, ancient ruins, Suez Canal. Africa south of the Sahara (24) showing harbor and street scenes from Zanzibar, Dar-es Salaam and Tanganyika, former colonial structures, and coastal plain of Mozambique. Script: introduction and descriptive paragraph for each frame.

*The East African Coast,* SB (1964). 28 frames, color, captioned. $3.00.

25 photos and 3 full captions. Emphasis on man-made structures. Arab and European influences (10), villages (4), rivers and irrigation (6), ports and canal (5). Captions: statements explaining frames. Full captions: history and description.

*East and Southeast Africa,* BUDEK (1964). 43 frames, color, non-captioned script (also available in slides). $6.00.

Filmstrip and script divided as follows: The land (7), vegetation (7), soils and soil erosion (7), economic activities (9), religion and early settlements (4), architecture and settlements (5), roads and transportation (4). Countries and people not identified. General overview of the regions indicated. Script provides title and descriptive paragraph for each frame.

*East and Southeast Africa,* SB (1964). 29 frames, color, captioned. $3.00.

Topography and vegetation (11), farming (6), local markets (3), housing and villages (4), transportation (4), fishing (1). Captions: explain frames.

*Journey Down the Nile,* CG (1962). 30 frames, color, non-captioned, script. $7.50.

28 photos, one map, and one drawing. From Owens Dam to Alexandria Harbor, depicting characteristics of the river and the village people and economic activities along the river. Script provides title and paragraph for each frame.

*Life Along the Nile,* EBF (1961). 40 frames, color, captioned, $6.00.

29 photos, 2 maps, and 9 full captions. Traces the Nile River from its source near Lake Victoria to Cairo, depicting the countries, people, and major economic activities. Uganda (6), Ethiopia (3), Khartoum (2), and Egypt (18). Captions: statements explaining frames. Two full captions for summary.

*Living in Eastern and Southern Africa,* SVE (n.d.). 66 frames, color, captioned. $6.00.

50 photos, 7 maps, and 9 full captions. Natural environment (8), agriculture and agricultural products (16), mining (11), transportation (5), cities and villages (10). Captions explaining frames. Full captions: questions for discussion.

*The Region: Tanganyika, Kenya, Uganda.* EBF (1952). 51 frames, color, captioned. $6.00.

38 photos, 2 maps, and 11 full captions. Emphasis given to highland and coastal regions. Major emphasis on terrain. Physical terrain (21), urban centers and capitals (10), shipping (dhows) (7). Captions: statements explaining frames. Full captions: introduction and summary questions.

*(Filmstrip/record)*

*Eastern Highlands,* SVE (1965). 63 frames, color, non-captioned, script, record, (*Africa, The Land of Developing Countries* Series—A-289-2R).

52 photos, 6 maps, and 5 full captions. Record (20 min.). Location, size and physical features (9), agriculture and industry (9), people and how they live (17), transportation (5), animals of Eastern Highlands (5), important cities (11). Script follows record. Part of a six-filmstrip series costing $39.75.

*(Slides)*

*East Africa,* EAV. 30 slides, color.

27 photos and 3 maps. General overview of the region. Terrain and vegetation (5), people (2), government (3), farming (7), transportation (3), animals (3), markets and settlements (4). No script or captions to identify content of frame or region. Two maps not identified.

*East and Southeast Africa,* BUDEK. 43 slides, color. $20.00.

Overview of East and Southeast Africa. Terrain and vegetation (15), animals (2), farming (9), people (5), cultural history (3), housing (5), transportation (4). No script or captions to identify slides.

*(Chart)*

*The East Africa Common Market,* NEWSWEEK. Single sheet 30" x 45."

Consists of two maps: large map of the continent of Africa with all countries; nations comprising the East Africa Common Market identified. Smaller map showing just the countries in the Common Market and their major products. Notes on the development of economic cooperation and the formation of the Common Market. (Newsweek Map of the Month for January, 1968.) Accompanying spirit master with map of Africa and map research and discussion questions.

## People

*(Written material)*

Cook, David, ed., *Origin East Africa.* New York: Humanities Press, Inc., 1967. Paper. $1.00.

An anthology of stories, plays and poems by East Africans, a Nigerian, an American, and a Briton on a variety of themes of contemporary importance.

Fox, Lorene, *East African Childhood: Three Versions.* Nairobi: Oxford University Press, 1967. (distributed in U.S. by Humanities Press). Paper. $1.00.

Three narratives by Africans of their youth in East Africa stressing various aspects of their training and education, the customs and ways of living of their different peoples, and the impact of change; includes *The Valley Between— A Muluyia's Story; At Home in the Village: Growing Up in Acholi;* and *Thorns In the Grass: The Story of A Kamba Boy.* Glossary; no index; 139 pp.

*(16 mm film)*

*A Giant People: The Watussi,* EBF (1949). b/w, narration, 11 min.

A day in the life of a young prince is used to illustrate aspects of the social structure, culture, and economy of the Watussi. A leopard hunt and harvest dance are events in the day of this exotic tribe.

*(Filmstrips)*

*East Africa: People, Crops, Cattle.* CG (1956). 25 frames, color, non-captioned, script. $7.50.

Buganda, Masai, and Bahima tribes and their housing (9), agriculture and agricultural products (6), economic activities (5), people (5). Script provides title and paragraph for each frame.

*Native Tribes* (Tanganyika—Kenya—Uganda), EBF (1952). 52 frames, color, captioned. $6.00.

42 photos, 2 maps, and 8 full captions. Deals with the Masai and Sonyo tribes. Masai: economic life (9), rituals and traditions (10), geographic setting (8). Sonyo: customs, daily activities, rituals (12), and geographic setting including terrain and housing (3). Captions: statements explaining frames. Full captions: introduction, review, and summary questions.

*(Records)*

*Bantu Music of British East Africa* (KL 213), COLUMBIA. 8 bands, script. $5.98.

Side 1: 5 bands; side 2: 3 bands. Collection of the variety of music found in East Africa among the various Bantu groups and the types of instruments used. (Music is vocal and instrumental.) Script: introduction and notes on each band with reference to the individual instrument used.

*Songs of the Watutsi* (FE4428), FOLKWAYS. 12 bands, script. $6.79.

Side 1: 6 bands; side 2: 6 bands. Vocal and instrumental music of the Watutsi of Ruanda. Script: background material with notes on individual bands.

*Swahili,* WORLD. Script. $2.45.

Five 7" records, part of the World Foreign Language Series, giving English and Swahili pronunciation of general expressions and vocabulary. Script: 24 page English-Swahili dictionary.

*(Tapes)*

*Drums of East Africa* (M51), WTE. Approximately 21 min. $2.75.

Discussion of various types of drums, their construction and use by tribes from Tanganyika, Uganda, and Kenya. Good description of instrument with follow-up selection to illustrate the selections recorded.

*Tribal Music of East Africa* (No. 52), WTE. 25 min. $2.75.

Thirteen selections of music from the various tribal groups in Kenya. Narrator discusses the story of the music, the key instruments, the tribe, and the influence of European colonization on the music. Primarily vocal selections.

**Flora and Fauna**

*(Filmstrips)*

*All About Ostriches,* EG (1965). 41 frames, color, captioned, script. (*Continent of Africa: East Africa—Land of Safaris Series—*146F). $6.00.

35 frames on the ostrich with a sequence of 14 shots showing an ostrich egg hatching. Terrain (3), and use of ostrich feathers (3). Captions: statements explaining frames.

*Animals and Birds* (Tanganyika, Kenya, Uganda), EBF (1952). 54 frames, color, captioned. $6.00.

43 photos, 2 maps, and 9 full captions. 28 frames are close-ups of animals, 12 provide view of animals with landscape, and 2 are concerned with the physical terrain of the region. Captions: statements and questions explaining frames. Full captions: introduction, review and summary.

*Museum Collecting Safari—I (Birds),* EG (1965). 41 frames, color, captioned, script. (*Continent of Africa: East Africa—Land of Safaris Series—* 146D). $6.00.

Major emphasis on expedition and procedures used to gather birds. Terrain and vegetation (7), animals (19), expedition procedures (15). Captions: statements explaining frames.

*Museum Collecting Safari—II (Insects, Plants, Reptiles),* EG (1965). 47 frames, color, captioned, script. (*Continent of Africa: East Africa—Land of Safaris Series—*146E). $6.00.

Collection of specimens (22), insects of East Africa (13), plant life (11), terrain (1). Captions: statements explaining frames.

*Organizing a Museum Expedition,* EG (1965). 38 frames, color, captioned, script. (*Continent of Africa: East Africa—Land of Safaris Series—* 146A). $6.00.

All frames are concerned with the preparations required for a field trip to East Africa by an ornithologist. Emphasizes equipment, administrative procedures, and personnel needs required for trip. Pictures taken in U.S.A. and of personnel involved. Captions: statements explaining frames.

*Plants & Flowers* (Tanganyika, Kenya, Uganda), EBF (1952). 47 frames, color, captioned. $6.00.

39 photos, 2 maps, and 6 full captions. The individual plants and flowers found in the region (26), physical terrain and climate (4), flora of the region in the context of the landscape (9). Captions: statements explaining frames. Full captions: introduction, review and summary questions.

*Safari to East Africa,* EG (1965). 46 frames, color, captioned, script. (*Continent of Africa: East Africa–Land of Safaris Series* 146B). $6.00.

42 photos, 4 maps. Major emphasis on areas visited on way to East Africa. Trip to Africa (35) showing major American and European cities. Africa (7) showing arrival in Africa and city of Nairobi. Captions: statements explaining frames.

*Treetop Adventure,* EG (1965). 36 frames, color, captioned, script. (*Continent of Africa: East Africa–Land of Safaris Series–*146I). $6.00.

Photos of animal life in East Africa from "treetop" position. Treetop area and countryside (10), explanation of Treetop (4), animals as seen from Treetop (22). Captions: statements explaining frames.

## COUNTRIES OF EAST AFRICA

### Ethiopia

*(Filmstrips)*
*Ethiopia,* SB (n.d.). 26 frames, color, captioned. $3.00.

22 photos, one map, and 3 full captions. History (3), religion (2), topography (3), agriculture and agricultural products (6), city of Addis Ababa and villages (5), people (2), fishing (1). Full captions: information on topography, climate, and history. Other captions: statements explaining frames.

*Ethiopia and Eritrea,* EG (1962). 47 frames, color, captioned, script. (*Continent of Africa: Countries of Moslem Africa Series–*159C). $6.00.

43 photos, 2 maps, and 2 full captions. Major emphasis on Ethiopia (40), Addis Ababa (14), population and composition (8), education (7),

agriculture and agricultural products (5), topography (4), and transportation; Eritrea (3). Capital and products. Captions: statements explaining frames. Full captions: review and questions.

*(Recordings)*
*Amharic,* WORLD. Script. $2.45.

Five 7" records, part of the World Foreign Language Series giving English and Amharic pronunciation of general expressions and vocabulary. 23-page English-Amharic dictionary.

*Folk Music of Ethiopia* (FE4405), FOLKWAYS. 11 bands, script. $6.79.

Side 1: 6 bands; side 2: 5 bands. Vocal and instrumental music which samples the diverse music of the various ethnic groups of Ethiopia. Script: background materials and notes on each band.

*Religious Music of the Falashas* (FE4442), FOLKWAYS. 7 bands, script. $6.79.

Side 1: 4 bands; side 2: 3 bands. Jewish religious prayer songs of the Falashas of Ethiopia commemorating religious holidays. Primarily vocal. Script: background notes and explanation.

*This is My Country: Ethiopia,* WILSON (1968). 1 side of a 12" LP (or tape). 19 min.

Introduced by a narrative description of the location of Ethiopia; interview of Ethiopian concerning family life in his nation, how people make a living, schools and education, form of government, current problems; concludes with suggestions for further study of Ethiopia.

### Eritrea

*(Filmstrip)*
*Eritrea–The African Votes,* VEC (n.d.). 22 frames, b/w, captioned, script. $4.00.

17 photos, 2 maps, and 3 full captions. Preparation and election of a new representative assembly by the people. Maps and captions deal with history (4). Captions: statements explaining frames. Full captions on vocabulary.

## Kenya

*(Written material)*

Clarke, P. J. H., *Kenya: Junior Atlas.* London: Thomas Nelson and Sons, Ltd. (distributed in U.S. by Humanities Press), 1967. Paper. $1.00.

First 12 pp. of this 8½" x 11" atlas include full color 2-page maps of Kenya's administrative district; maps of population, agricultural patterns, economy, rainfall; physical and political maps of East Africa; maps of rainfall, temperature, vegetation for entire continent; remaining 10 pp. include maps of other regions of the world. Index. 25 pp.

*Colonial Kenya: Cultures In Conflict.* Middletown, Conn.: American Education Publications, 1968. Paper. 30¢.

A selection of excerpts from novels, travel literature, autobiographies, and other sources interwoven with specially written cases to explore the the clash of English and Kikuyu culture in Kenya between 1900 and 1955; emphasizes the defining of progress, the difference between science and superstition, land ownership, and internal revolt. Adapted from the Harvard Social Studies Curriculum Project materials. Questions and bibliography included. Teaching guide and test separate. 63 pp. (Reading level: 7-10).

Gatheru, R. Mugo, *Child of Two Worlds.* Garden City: Doubleday and Company, Inc., 1965. Paper. $1.25.

An autobiographical account by a Kikuyu who grew up in Kenya prior to World War II, secured an education against tremendous odds, went to Nairobi (where he was a victim of British racial discrimination), and from there went to India, Britain, and the United States to complete his education. Excellent insight into traditional Kikuyu life and the problems of living under colonial rule. 222 pp.

Kenworthy, Leonard S., *Profile of Kenya.* Garden City: Doubleday & Company, Inc., 1963. Hardcover. $3.25.

A description of Kenya, touching on all aspects of life in this country; large, clear photos (b/w); index. 128 pp. (Reading level: 6-9).

Kenyatta, Mzee Jomo, *My People of Kikuyu.* Nairobi: Oxford University Press, 1966. Paper. $1.00.

This brief description (first published in 1942 and reprinted here without substantial revision) touches on early Kikuyu history, government, chieftanship and other topics; it concludes with a brief biography of Chief Wangomibe, a leader of the Kikuyu prior to their subjection by the British. No index. 59 pp. (Reading level: 7-12).

Ngugi, James, *The River Between.* New York: Humanities Press, Inc., 1967. Paper. $1.00.

This is a novel about the conflicts between two groups of Kikuyu—the Christians and those struggling to adhere to traditional tribal religion and customs. Customs cherished by the tribe are condemned by the Christians. An excellent examination of Kikuyu life, customs, and legends. 160 pp.

Ngugi, James, *Weep Not, Child.* New York: Humanities Press, Inc., 1966. Paper. $1.00.

A tragic tale of an African family in modern Kenya which reflects the turmoil in the African community fed by the desire to re-take their land from the Whites. Depicts not only traditional life but also some of the factors that led to the Mau Mau uprisings. Written in 1964. 154 pp.

*(16 mm film)*

*Kenya—Multi-racial Experiment,* McG-H (1967). color, narration, 18 min.

A survey of the impact of the slave trade on West Africa, focusing on life in Dahomey today and current events in Kenya. Includes the background of the coming of whites and Asians to Kenya and current efforts of the government to redistribute property and land among its peoples. Suggests the conflict existing between Kenya's economic interests and its nationalistic desires. (ABC—*Africa*).

*Kenya: Industries and Products,* EG (1962). 41 frames, color, captioned, script. (*Continent of Africa: East Africa Series*–154B). $6.00.

38 photos and 3 full captions. Major emphasis on agriculture: farming (11), grazing (5), products (domestic consumption and export) (23). Captions: statements explaining frames. Full captions: review (2) and summary (1).

*Kenya: Land and People,* EG (1962). 48 frames, color, captioned, script. (*Continent of Africa: East Africa Series*–154A). $6.00.

44 photos, one map, and 3 full captions. Terrain and vegetation (12), modes of transportation and transportation links (9), people (13), wild animals (10). Captions: statements explaining frames. Full captions: review (2) and summary (1).

*Kenya: Principal Cities,* EG (1962). 43 frames, color, captioned, script. (*Continent of Africa: East Africa Series*–154C). $6.00.

40 photos and 3 full captions. Nairobi: functions and buildings (10), Mombasa: history, buildings and their functions (10), port facilities (8). Nakuru: buildings and surrounding countryside (9). Kisumu: housing (native and European) (3). Captions: statements explaining frames. Full captions: review (2) and summary (1).

*The Kenya Highlands,* SB (1962). 20 frames, color, captioned. $3.00.

18 photos, one map, and one full caption. Pre-independence. Nairobi (3), Mau-Mau country and internment camp (5), European settlements and farms (9), local settlements (3). Captions: statements explaining frames. Full captions: description of highlands.

*Highlands of Kenya,* EBF (1961). 43 frames, color, captioned. $6.00.

33 photos, 2 maps, and 8 full captions. Climate and vegetation (3), Kikuyu farmers (5), Masai (6), wild animals (3), impact of modernity or modernization (11), Nairobi (5). Captions:

statements explaining frames. Full captions: introduction and summary.

*Nairobi to Nakuru,* EG (1965). 48 frames, color, captioned, script. (*Continent of Africa: East Africa–Land of Safaris Series*–146G). $6.00.

Depicts a trip from Nairobi to Nakuru. Nairobi (2), Nakuru (2). Kikuyu–daily activities, dress, and economic activities as seen along the road to Nakuru (27); Lake Nakuru and flamingos (17). Captions: statements explaining frames.

*Profile of Kenya,* SFS (1962). 50 frames, color, non-captioned. Script. $6.00.

47 photos and 3 maps. General overview of the country. Divided into Kenya and its past (5), the land (7), the people (5), types of houses (3), cities (2), earning a living and products (5), markets and factories (5), transportation (7), schools (3), religion (3), government (3), recreation (5). Script provides frame-by-frame description and suggestions for the use of the filmstrip.

*(Filmstrip/record)*

*How People Live in Kano, Nigeria and Nairobi, Kenya,* SVE (1966). 53 frames, color, non-captioned, script, record (13 min.). $9.50.
45 photos, 3 maps, 2 drawings, and 3 full captions. Film and narration by students in Kano and Nairobi: Band I (2 min.) introduction (5), Band II (5 min.) Kano–general characteristics of the land and people (23). Band III (6 min.) Nairobi–emphasis on modern buildings, schools, churches (25). History of both cities included. Script: follows record. Also available without record.

*(Slides)*

*The Masai of Kenya and Tanzania,* AMNH (n.d.). color. $11.40.

A set of 19 color slides showing the topography, housing, kraals, people of the Masai; 8 of these feature Masai warriors; may be purchased separately or as a set; descriptive list available.

*(Records)*

*The Great Elephant Joke–Big Drum, Little Drum,* AMIE (1968). $4.95.

Two Kikuyu folktales with sound effects—
"Big Drum, Little Drum" is a story about a
drum family (19 min.); "The Great Elephant
Joke" is a story about an elephant who made
friends with a man (19 min.).

*Songs from Kenya* (FW8716), FOLKWAYS, 8
bands, script. $5.76.

Side 1: 4 bands; side 2: 4 bands. Contemporary
music from Kenya sung by the David Nzomo
Trio. Script: Facsimile of the sheet music used.

*(Tape)*
*Kenya, An Emerging Nation* (P127), WASHING-
TON, (1966). $10.00.

An interview with the Ambassador of Kenya.
Topics discussed: independence, political parties and leadership, tribal and national loyalty,
economic development, European settlers and
their role in Kenya, positive and negative aspects of colonialism, the Cold War.

*(Pictures)*
*Living in Kenya,* SILVER BURDETT, (1966).
color, script. $10.80.

12 photos and text. Pictures can be grouped
into the following general categories: animals
(3), social and economic activities (12), families
(4). Script: Teacher's manual providing introduction, lesson for each picture, and references.

## Malagasy

*(Filmstrips)*
*Madagascar,* DON BOSCO. 43 frames, color, non-
captioned, script. $6.00.

Provides "tour" of Madagascar showing the
major cities, people and their activities, markets, and products. Cities (8), markets and villages (8), people (9), products (7), transportation (2), terrain (2). Script: descriptive paragraph for each frame.

*Malagasy Republic,* EG (1962). 43 frames, color,
captioned, script. (*Continent of Africa: East
Africa Series*—154D). $6.00.

40 photos, one map, and 2 full captions. General overview of the country: terrain, vegetation

and climate (9), resources (7), transportation
(5), farming (8), people (8), city of Malagasy
(3). Captions: statements explaining frames.
Full captions: review (1) and summary (10).

## Malawi

*(Record)*
*Music Malawi—1962 (Nyasaland),* OPERATION
CROSSROADS AFRICA, 15 bands, script.
$3.00.

Side 1: 7 bands; side 2: 8 bands. Music recorded
at a secondary school in Nyasaland. Songs are
primarily nationalistic. Script: notes on individual bands.

## Somalia

*(Filmstrips)*
*Central African Republic, Republic of Chad and
Somali Republic,* EG (1962). 55 frames, color,
b/w, captioned, script. (*Continent of Africa:
Countries of Moslem Africa Series*—159B).
$6.00.

49 photos, 3 maps, and 3 full caption frames.
General overview of the three countries dealing
with topography, people, agricultural and industrial activities, transportation, and urban centers. Chad (19), Central African Republic (14),
Somali (16). Somali is in black and white. Captions: statements explains frames. Full captions:
questions.

*Somalia,* BUDEK (1962). 49 frames, color, captioned, script. $6.00.

45 photos, 3 full captions, and one map. General overview of the country of Somalia. Introduction (3), the capital (6), nomadism (3),
daily life (7), building and industry (6), veter-
inary services (3), provincial towns (15), old
and new problems (3). Captions: statements
explaining frames. Full captions: introduction
and supplement (3).

## Sudan

*(Filmstrips)*
*Nile Basin—Sudan,* EAV (n.d.). 36 frames, b/w,
non-captioned, script. $3.75.

32 photos and 4 maps. Agriculture and agricultural products (12), markets (2), animals (2), fishing (4), transportation (7), activities of the people (5). Script provides descriptive paragraph for each frame. Produced in England.

*The Republic of Sudan,* EG (1965). 47 frames, color, captioned, script. (*Continent of Africa: Countries of Moslem Africa Series*—159I). $6.00.

44 photos, one map, and 2 full captions. General overview of the country: people (12), terrain and vegetation (9), economic activities and products (10), urban centers (7), education and transportation. Captions: explain frames. Full captions: review (1) and summary (1).

*(Record)*

*This is My Country: Sudan,* WILSON (1968). 1 side of a 12" LP (or tape). 19 min.

Introduced by a narrative description of the location of Sudan; interview of a Sudanese national briefly covering such topics as family life, education, children's life, recreation, religion, economy, government; concludes with description of the major problems facing Sudan today—illiteracy and communication-transportation.

**Tanzania** (see also Zanzibar)

*(Written material)*

Kaula, Edna Mason, *The Land and People of Tanganyika.* Philadelphia: J. B. Lippincott Company, 1963. Hardcover. $2.93.

A description of the geography, peoples, customs, wildlife, history, and current conditions in Tanganyika and Zanzibar; photos; index. 160 pp. (Reading level: 9-12).

*(16 mm film)*

*Other Side Up,* ROBECK (n.d.) b/w, narration, 30 min.

Filmed in Tanzania. Shows changes in government and society since independence; reveals distrust, suspicion and prejudice of black Africans and Europeans toward each other; problems of both groups attempting to live together. Uses interviews, scenes at integrated schools,

college students, and social clubs. (Originally produced for BBC-TV.)

*(Filmstrips)*

*A Lion Hunt (Tanganyika),* EG (1965). 38 frames, color, captioned, script. (*Continent of Africa: East Africa—Land of Safaries Series*—146J). $6.00.

Depicts a hunting expedition by white hunters in Tanganyika: the hunt (30, seven of which show a taxidermist at work), other animals of the region (3), the Masai (5). Captions: statements explaining frames.

*Tanganyika,* CG (1964). 30 frames, color, non-captioned, script. $7.50.

28 photos and 2 maps. Divided into coastal and plateau regions and deals with settlements, topography, products and people: coastal region (7), plateau (21). (Plateau subdivided into East Mountain Belt, volcanic country, savanna grasslands, savanna woodlands and sukumaland.) Script provides titles and paragraphs for each frame.

*Tanganyika—Industries, Products, Cities,* EG (1962) (1962). 41 frames, color, captioned, script. (*Continent of Africa: East Africa Series*—154F). $6.00.

38 photos and 3 full captions. Agricultural products (13), mining (4), Dar-es-Salaam (functions, people, buildings and products) (18), seaport of Tanga (1), animals (2). Captions: statements explaining frames. Full captions: review (2) and summary (1).

*Tanganyika—Land and Peoples,* EG (1962). 46 frames, color, captioned, script. (*Continent of Africa: East Africa Series*—154E). $6.00.

42 photos, one map, and 3 full captions. Terrain and vegetation (11), transportation (3), animals (8), people (ethnic composition and education) (20). Captions: statements explaining frames. Full captions: review (2) and summary (1).

*(Pictures)*

*Savannah Grasslands,* PICTORIAL CHARTS EDUCATIONAL TRUST. Single sheet, color, 30" x 40". $2.00.

Economic and physical characteristics of savannah grasslands using Tanganyika as the focal point.

*(Tapes)*
*Folk Songs of Tanganyika* (#173), WTE. 10 min. $2.75.

Songs from the various tribes in brief Tanganyika with statements concerning the tribal groups. Quality of tape is fair.

*Music of Tanganyika* (#106), WTE. 20 min. $2.75.

Six musical selections. Discussion of the types of music, instruments, performers, and tribes from the various sections of Tanganyika. Major emphasis on the Haya tribe of northwest Tanganyika in which variety of music is most evident.

## Uganda

*(Written material)*
Beattie, John, *Bunyoro, An African Kingdom.* New York: Holt, Rinehart and Winston, Inc., 1960/1964. Paper. $1.50.

An historical and functional analysis of the development, government, kinship system, and principles of conflict resolution of the Nyoro of Uganda; descriptive and interpretive; brief list of suggested readings; no index. 86 pp. (Reading level: 12).

p'Bitek, Okot, *Song of Lawino.* Evanston: Northwestern University Press, 1966. Paper. $2.50.

A long satirical narrative poem about life and the personal problems of modernization in Uganda, from a woman's point of view. 216 pp.

Middleton, John, *The Lugbara of Uganda.* New York: Holt, Rinehart and Winston, 1965. Paper. $1.50.

A detailed presentation of the habitat, social structure, social customs, political institutions, and religion of the Lugbara of Uganda; includes both description and interpretation; short glos-

sary and list of suggested readings; no index. 96 pp. (Reading level: 12).

Mugahya, Yunia, *Uganda: Junior Atlas.* London: Thomas Nelson and Sons, Ltd., (distributed in U.S. by Humanities Press). 1966. Paper. $1.00.

First 11 pp. of this 8½" x 11" atlas include full color maps of Uganda's administrative districts, population density, elevation, economy, rainfall patterns, physical features and vegetation; maps of rainfall and temperature of East Africa; remainder includes maps of other regions of the world. Index. 25 pp.

*(Filmstrips)*
*Safari to Murchison Falls (Uganda),* EG (1965). 46 frames, color, captioned, script. (*Continent of Africa: East Africa—Land of Safaris Series—* 146H). $6.00.

44 photos and 2 maps. Terrain and animals of Murchison Park (30), Lake Victoria (3), dams (11). Captions: statements explaining frames.

*Uganda—Industries, Products and Cities,* EG (1962). 41 frames, color, captioned, script. (*Continent of Africa: East Africa Series—*154H). $6.00.

39 photos and 2 full captions. Agricultural products (10), mining (4), factories (4), ranching (3), cities: Kampala (9), Jinja (9). Captions: statements explaining frames. Full captions: review (1) and summary (1).

*Uganda—Land and People,* EG (1962). 46 frames, color, captioned, script. (*Continent of Africa: East Africa Series—*154G). $6.00.

42 photos, one map, and 3 full captions. Terrain and vegetation (14), transportation (5), housing and people (10). Game parks (5) and Queen Elizabeth Park (8). Captions: statements explaining frames. Full captions: review (2) and summary (1).

*(Slides)*
*The Bambouti Pygmies of the Ituri Forest in Uganda,* AMNH (n.d.). color. $6.30.

Nine color slides of Pygmies showing older adults, family group, children, young woman, a house, and different generations; may be purchased separately; description list available.

*(Tape)*
*Ghana and Uganda,* WTE (n.d.). 25 min. $2.75.

An interview with nationalists from Ghana and Uganda discussing the social, economic, and political problems facing independent Ghana and soon-to-be independent Uganda.

**Zanzibar** (see also Tanzania)

*(Filmstrips)*
*Zanzibar,* EG (1962). 45 frames, color, captioned, script. (*Continent of Africa: East Africa Series* —154I). $6.00.

42 photos, one map, and 2 full captions. History (5), people (ethnic composition, occupations) (15), resources (10), features of the city (7). Captions: statements explaining frames. Full captions: review and summary.

*Zanzibar Protectorate,* EG (1962). 46 frames, color color, captioned, script. (*Continent of Africa— Historic Cities of Africa Series*—158I). $6.00.

43 photos, one map, and 2 full captions. Location and history (4), buildings and streets (11), Arabs (6), Indians (6), Europeans (2), industries and products (14). Captions: statements explaining frames. Full captions: review and summary.


**CENTRAL AFRICA**

**GENERAL**

**Overview**

*(Written material)*
Burton, W. F. P., *The Magic Drum: Tales from Central Africa.* New York: Criterion Books, 1962. Hardcover. $3.00.

Folk tales told in the Congo (K) and handed down verbally from one generation to another; several ink drawings. No index. 127 pp. (Reading level: 6-10).

Coughlan, Robert, *Tropical Africa,* (*Life World*

*Library*). New York: Time Incorporated, 1966. Hardcover. $3.95.

A survey with many photos and maps of the land, peoples, art, history, and current problems of tropical Africa; appendix includes a list of historical dates, suggestions for further reading, and a table of information on each political unit; index. 176 pp. (Reading level: 9-12).

Kachingwe, Aubrey, *No Easy Task.* New York: Humanities Press, Inc., 1966. Paper. 233 pp. $1.50.

Story of life in a city and the political events leading up to the independence of a central African nation. It points up the nature of city life and the social, economic and political discrimination prevalent there.

*(16 mm film)*
*Central Africa,* McG-H (1967). color, narration, 20 min.

Focuses on Portuguese Africa, the revolts in Angola and the resultant refugee problems, Portuguese domination of the Africans; on Rhodesia and its racial policies; on the Congo's mineral wealth, its economic problems, its political upheavals, life along the Congo River. (ABC—Africa).

*(8 mm film loops)*
*Africa—Tropical Products,* GATEWAY, color, script. 8 mm. 4 min. $13.00.

Depicts the harvesting of eight cash crops grown in tropical Africa: tea, sisal, coffee, sugar cane, cotton, pyrethrum, pineapples, and cocoa. Mining and smelting of copper also shown.

*Herdsmen of Central Africa: Cattle Drive Across the Niger,* EALING, color, 8 mm, cartridged, super 8, 4 min. $21.50.

An abbreviated version of a Julien Bryan film on the Peul peoples, stressing the importance of community ties.

*(Filmstrips)*
*Central Africa,* EAV (n.d.). 44 frames, b/w, non-captioned, script. $3.75.

40 photos and 4 maps. Land and people: topography (3), daily activities of people (12), transportation (3), cities and ports (2), resources, production and preparation of agricultural products (15), mineral resources (5). Script provides paragraph description of each frame. Produced in England.

*Central Africa and World Affairs,* CAF (1965). 44 frames, b/w, captioned. $4.00.

27 photos, 7 maps, 4 drawings, one chart, and 5 full captions. Political turmoil and change (10), economic problems (6), political instability (6), relations with British Commonwealth (13), with United Nations (3), self-help programs (3), summary (1), and questions (1). Captions: statements explaining and supplementing frames.

*(Slides)*
*Sudan and Equatorial Africa* (Gumpert of Sweden), EAV. 31 slides, color. $10.95.

27 photos and 4 maps. General overview of the terrain (4), people (5), products (5), animals (5), buildings (3), transportation (2), economic activities (3). No script or captions to identify contents of slide or regions. Two maps not identified.

*(Transparencies)*
*Central Africa,* HAMMOND. color, script. $6.75.

Maps of Central Africa. Four transparencies: base map with rivers and political boundaries, physical features, place names. Clear plastic for writing. Used in combination only. Plastic frames provided with registration marks for alignment. Notes to teacher deal with mechanics of using transparencies.

*(Record)*
*Music of Equatorial Africa* (FE4402), FOLKWAYS. 16 bands, script. $6.79.

Side 1: 8 bands; side 2: 8 bands. Vocal and instrumental music recorded in 1946 in French Equatorial Africa. Script: introduction with notes on individual bands.

*(Tape)*
*Introduction to Central Africa,* WASHINGTON, D.C.: U.S. DEPARTMENT OF STATE (n.d.). 28 min.

The Director of the U.S. State Department Office of Central African Affairs, James O'Sullivan, presents a briefing on the peoples, resources, and problems of the nations in Central Africa.

## COUNTRIES

### Central African Republic

*(16 mm film)*
*Central African Republic (People of Africa Series),* UNITED WORLD (1967). b/w, narration, 20 min.

Concerned primarily with economic activities of country. Emphasis placed on production of raw materials, markets, and economic growth. Major products and problems of conservation included.

*(Filmstrip)*
*Central African Republic, Republic of Chad and Somali Republic,* EG (1962). 55 frames, color, b/w, captioned, script. (*Continent of Africa: Countries of Moslem Africa Series*–159B). $6.00.

49 photos, 3 maps, and 3 full-caption frames. General overview of the three countries, dealing with topography, people, agricultural and industrial activities, transportation, and urban centers. Chad (19), Central African Republic (14), Somali (16). Captions: statements explain frames. Full captions: questions.

### Chad

*(16 mm film)*
The Republic of Chad (*People of Africa* Series), UNITED WORLD (1967). b/w, narration, 20 min.

Points out the unfavorable terrain and climate of Chad. Emphasis on utilization of limited resources—cotton, cattle, salt, fishing. Economic activities of the various people and regions of Chad.

*(Filmstrip)*

*Central African Republic, Republic of Chad and Somali Republic,* EG (1962). 55 frames, color, b/w, captioned, script. (*Continent of Africa: Countries of Moslem Africa Series*–159B). $6.00.

49 photos, 3 maps and 3 full-caption frames. General overview of the three countries, dealing with topography, people, agricultural and industrial activities, transportation, and urban centers. Chad (19), Central African Republic (14), Somali (16). Captions: statements explain frames. Full captions: questions.

*(Written material)*

Turnbull, Colin, *The Lonely African.* New York: Simon and Schuster, 1962/1968. Paper. $1.95.

A series of accounts of the impact of change on various Africans, primarily peoples of the Congo Basin; points up the impact of religion, education, changing society on indigenous cultures as well as on individuals; well-written, incisive case studies. 251 pp. (Reading level: 9-12).

*(Recording)*

*Music of Chad* (FE4337), FOLKWAYS. 13 bands, script. $6.79.

Side 1: 6 bands; side 2: 7 bands. Features varieties of instrumental and dance music of the people of Chad. Script: short introduction with notes on individual bands.

**The Congo Basin**

*(16 mm film)*

*Life in Hot, Wet Lands (The Congo Basin),* CORONET (1959). b/w, narration, 10 min. $65.00.

A day in the life of a small native boy is used to illustrate the geography, society, and economy of the people of the Congo Basin. The film also suggests problems of living in hot, wet lands in other parts of the world. Teacher's guide. (Educational Collaborator: Professor W. R. McConnell).

*(Filmstrips)*

*The Congo Basin,* CG (1951) 43 frames, b/w, non-captioned, script. $4.50.

A b/w filmstrip with 3 maps, frames on Bantu (3) and Pygmy (3), life in the Congo and geography (5); economic activities (16); transportation (10). Script provides paragraph describing each frame.

*The African Village Near the Equator,* CF (1957). 29 frames, color, captioned. $6.00.

25 photos, one map, and 3 full captions: location of village (2), types of houses (5), daily activities (18). Captions: statements explaining frames. Full captions: notes to teacher, vocabulary and summary questions.

*Life Along the Congo River,* EBF (1961). 40 frames, color, captioned. $6.00.

30 photos, 3 maps, and 7 full captions. Major emphasis on village life along Congo. Village life and village farming (9), village markets (6), modern changes (6), transportation—river and land (9). Captions: statements explaining frames. Full captions: introduction and summary.

*The Copper Belt of Central Africa,* CG (1959). 27 frames, color, non-captioned, script. $8.50.

26 photos and one map. Terrain and vegetation (2), mining activities (10), types of housing and settelements (8), social services (4), transportation (2). Script provides title and paragraph on each frame.

*Living in Central Africa (Belgian Congo and Guinea Coast),* SVE. 60 frames, color, captioned. $6.00.

45 photos, 8 maps, and 7 full captions. General overview of the two regions. Congo tribes and housing (5), transportation (8), resources (4). Guinea Coast: Dakar and Accra (7), housing (2), transportation (6), economic activities (4), vegetation (4), rubber plantation (5). Captions: statements explaining frames. Full captions: questions for discussion.

*(Filmstrip/record)*

*The Congo Basin,* SVE, (1965). 65 frames, color, non-captioned, script, record. (*Africa, The Land of Developing Countries Series*–A-289-4R).

54 photos, 6 maps and 5 full captions. Record (19 min.). Location, size and physical features

(8), agriculture and industry (17), people and how they live (9), crafts (7), transportation (5), important cities (12). Script follows record. Full caption: review questions and map study exercise. (Part of a series costing $39.75.)

*(Chart)*
*Equatorial Forest Regions: Regions of the World,* PICTORIAL CHARTS. single sheet, color, 30" x 40". $2.00.

Large map of the Congo Basin. Compares primitive and advanced economies found in the forest regions; shows the seasonal work cycle of the people and the physical conditions found in forest regions.

**Democratic Republic of the Congo (K)**

*(Written material)*
Bleeker, Sonia, *The Pygmies: Africans of the Congo Forest.* New York: William Morrow & Company, 1968. Hardcover. $3.25.

A brief description of the Mbuti Pygmies of the Congo rainforest; emphasizes life in the forest, hunting, growing up, certain ceremonies, and the coming of modern influences; scattered drawings (b/w). Index. 143 pp. (Reading level: 6-9).

*(16 mm films)*
*A People of the Congo,* EBF (n.d.) b/w, narration, 11 min. $70.00.

Examines life of the Mangbetu peoples of the Congo basin, showing ivory carving, dances, housing and other activities.

*Pygmies of Africa,* EBF (1949). b/w, narration, 22 min.

Food gathering, hunting, crafts, religion, and trade of the Pygmies of the Congo River Basin; shows various activities and ceremonies. Teacher's guide.

*(Filmstrips)*
*Leopoldville–Republic of the Congo,* EG (1962). 45 frames, color, captioned, script. (*Continent of Africa: Historic Cities of Africa Series–* 158E). $6.00.

43 photos, one map, and 2 full captions. History (5), Congo River (4), population (1), modern structures (4), transportation (9), education and religion (6), port (1), recreational facilities (10), industries and commerce (3). Captions: statements explaining frames. Full captions: review (2) and summary (1).

*The Republic of the Congo: Cities,* EG (1962). 45 frames, color, captioned, script. (*Continent of Africa: Countries of the Congo Basin Series–* 155G). $6.00.

43 photos, and 2 full captions. Emphasis on key cities of the Congo dealing with major functions, buildings and surrounding area. Leopoldville (23), Elizabethville, Stanleyville, Bukavu and Luluabourg (15), and Albert National Park (5). Captions: statements explaining frames. Full captions: review and summary.

*The Republic of the Congo: The Land,* EG (1962). 45 frames, color, captioned, script. (*Continent of Africa: Countries of the Congo Basin Series–* 155E). $6.00.

44 photos, one map, and 2 full captions. Topics: history (8), terrain, vegetation, and animals (15), transportation (12), native agriculture and rural areas (9). Captions: statements explaining frames. Full captions: review (1) and summary questions (1).

*The Republic of the Congo: The People,* EG (1962). 49 frames, color, captioned, script. (*Continent of Africa: Countries of the Congo Basin Series–*155F). $6.00.

47 photos and 2 full captions. Basic tribal groups, the traditional society, and the influence of modernity. Tribal groups (3), modern influences (11), traditional society (customs, dress, markets and staple foods) (17), education and art (16). Captions: statements explaining frames. Full captions: review (1) and summary questions (1).

*Twin Cities of the Congo,* VEC. 38 frames, color, captioned. $4.00 (in color $6.00).

35 photos, one map, and 2 full captions. Brazzaville: modern buildings and industrial structures (9), and markets (5). Leopoldville: riverport fa-

cilities (2), modern structures—hotels, monuments, housing projects (11), markets (5). Captions: statements explaining frames.

*(Records)*

*Bushman Music and Pygmy Music,* PEABODY MUSEUM. 10 bands. script. $6.79.

Side 1: 6 bands; side 2: 4 bands. Bushman and Pygmy songs. Selections feature music sung by men, women, children, and mixed chorus. Script: notes on the music of Bushmen and comparison to that of the Babinga Pygmies.

*The Face of Africa* (TW91204), LONDON. script, 8 bands. $3.19.

Side 1: 6 bands; side 2: 2 bands. Presents the tribal music of the Belgian Congo. Features drums, musical instruments, selections on Congolese xylophones. Seven of the bands were recorded in Katanga Province of the Congo. Script provides notes on individual bands.

*Folk Music of the Western Congo* (FE4427), FOLKWAYS. 15 bands, script. $6.79.

Side 1: 6 bands; side 2: 9 bands. Vocal and instrumental music of the Bantu from the western part of the Congo region. Script: introduction and notes on individual bands.

*Missa Luba* (PC206M), PHILLIPS. 13 bands, script. $4.90.

Side 1: 7 bands; side 2: 6 bands. Combination of traditional Congolese songs and Christian hymns sung by the Les Troubadours du Roi Baudowin. Hymns are sung in Congolese fashion, showing a fusion of Christian hymns with native music. Script provides general introduction and comments. No notes on individual bands.

*Music of the Ituri Forest* (FE4482), FOLKWAYS. 20 bands, script. $6.79.

Side 1: 10 bands; side 2: 10 bands. Vocal and instrumental music of the BaMbuti Pygmy and more recently settle tribes of the Congo region. Songs from the BaNdaka, NaNgwara, and BaMbuti tribes included. Script: background material and notes on individual bands.

*The Pygmies of the Ituri Forest* (FE4457), FOLKWAYS. 21 bands, script. $6.79.

Side 1: 10 bands; side 2: 11 bands. Vocal and instrumental music of the BaMbuti of the Ituri Forest of the Congo Region. Script: introduction with notes on individual bands.

*The Topoke People of the Congo* (FE4477), FOLKWAYS (1959). 14 bands, script. $6.79.

Side 1: 7 bands; side 2: 7 bands. Vocal and instrumental music of the Topoke tribe of the Equatorial forest of the Congo. Script: background material with notes on individual bands.

## Gabon

*(Filmstrip)*

*Gabon Republic,* EG (1962). 46 frames, color, captioned, script. (*Continent of Africa: Countries of the Congo Basin Series*—155I). $6.00.

43 photos, one map, and 2 full captions. General overview of the country. Terrain, vegetation, and climate (8), tribal groups and education (9), natural resources and agricultural products (9), forestry (5) transportation (2). Emphasis on Libreville (people, facilities, and products) (10). Captions: statements explaining frames. Full captions: review and summary questions.

## Republic of the Congo

*(Filmstrips)*

*The Congo Republic,* EG (1962). 44 frames, color, captioned, script. (*Continent of Africa: Countries of the Congo Basin Series*—155D). $6.00.

41 photos, one map and 2 full captions. General characteristics of the country, with an emphasis on Brazzaville (14), terrain and animals (11), agriculture and agricultural products (7), transportation (5) and people (4). Brazzaville frames deal with buildings, people, and functions of the city. Captions: statements explaining frames. Full captions: review (1) and summary questions (1).

*Twin Cities of the Congo,* VEC. 38 frames, color, captioned. $4.00 (in color $6.00).

35 photos, one map, and 2 full captions. Brazzaville: buildings and industrial structures (9), and markets (5). Leopoldville: riverport facilities (2), modern structures—hotels, monuments, housing projects (11), markets (5). Captions: statements explaining frames.

# SOUTHERN AFRICA

## GENERAL

### Overview

*(16 mm film)*
*African Continent: Southern Region,* CORONET (1962). color, narration, 11 min. $130.00.

Describes the southern region of Africa, focusing on geography, history, peoples, agriculture, and mining. Social problems in South Africa are briefly covered. Teacher's guide. (Collaborator: Professor Hibberd V. B. Kline, Jr.)

*(Filmstrip/record)*
*Southern Africa,* SVE (1965). 62 frames, color, non-captioned, script, record. (*Africa: The Land of Developing Countries Series* A-289-3R).

52 photos, 6 maps and 4 full captions. Record (19 min.). Location, size, and physical features (10), agriculture and industry (16), people and how they live (13), transportation (5), important cities (12). Script follows record. Full captions: review question and map study exercise. Part of a 6-filmstrip series costing $39.75.

*(Transparencies)*
*Southern Africa,* HAMMOND. color. $6.50.

Maps of Southern Africa. Four transparencies: base map with rivers and political boundaries, physical features, place names; clear plastic for writing. Used in combination. Plastic frames provided with registration marks for alignment. Notes to teacher deal with mechanics of using transparencies.

*Southern Africa,* RAND McNALLY. $5.00.

Ranvue Relief Outline Map Series. Three transparencies in paper form: base map with rivers and political boundaries, relief map with political boundaries and rivers, place names. Used in combination. Maps of Africa south of the equator.

*(Chart)*
*New Countries and Old Problems in Africa,* NEWSWEEK MAGAZINE, November, 1966. 34" x 45".

Map of the Month for November 1966. Large wall map focusing on the problems confronting the southern part of Africa. Brief description of the nations of southern Africa and location of countries.

## COUNTRIES OF SOUTHERN AFRICA

### Portuguese Territories

*(Filmstrips)*
*Angola: Important Cities,* EG (1962). 46 frames, color, captioned, script. (*Continent of Africa: Countries of the Congo Basin Series*—155B). $6.00.

43 photos and 3 full captions. Cities: Luanda (24), Benguela and Mocamedes (8) and Nova Lisboa (2); buildings, economic activities and transportation, people of cities (9). Captions: statements explaining frames. Full captions: review (2) and summary (1).

*Angola: Land, People and Industries,* EG (1962). 42 frames, color, captioned, script. (*Continent of Africa: The Countries of the Congo Basin*—155A). $6.00.

38 photos, one map, and 3 full captions. Major emphasis on people (13), agriculture and agricultural products (11), terrain (6), resources (5), and transportation (3). Captions: statements explaining frames. Summary included.

*Lourenco Marques—Mozambique,* EG (1964). 45 frames, color, captioned, script. (*Continent of Africa: Historic Cities of Africa Series*—158F). $6.00.

41 photos, one map, and 3 full captions. City's functions (3), modern structures (11), recrea-

tion (11), education (4), industries and products (12). Captions: statements explaining frames. Full captions: review (2) and summary (1).

*Luanda–Angola,* EG (1954). 46 frames, color, captioned, script. (*Continent of Africa: Historic Cities of Africa Series*–158G). $6.00.

42 photos, one map, and 3 full captions. History (5), housing (9), role of Catholic church (4), recreation (10), industries and commerce (14). Captions: statements explaining frames. Full captions: review (2) and summary (1).

*Mozambique,* EG (1962). 44 frames, color, captioned, script. (*Continent of Africa: South Africa Series*–153I). $6.00.

40 photos, one map and 3 full captions. General overview of the country. Terrain and animals of region (9), products and industries (14), cities and ports (8), people (5), transportation (4). Captions: statements explaining frames. Full captions: review (2) and summary (1).

*(Chart)*

*Portugal and Her Overseas Territories,* PICTORIAL CHARTS. Single Sheet, color. 30" x 40". $2.00.

Map of Portuguese colonies in Africa; notes and statistics on the people, history, and products found in the colonies.

*(Tape)*

*The Portuguese in Africa* (P-126), WASHINGTON TAPES (1966). 16 min. $10.00.

History and development of Portuguese rule in Africa by the Portuguese Ambassador to the United States. Discussion of terrorist activities and Portuguese programs for social and economic progress included.

## REPUBLIC OF SOUTH AFRICA

### General

*(Written material)*

Abrahams, Peter, *Mine Boy.* New York: Humanities Press, Inc., 1966. Paper. 252 pp. $1.25.

A 1946 novel describing the life of an African who migrates to South Africa to work in the mines. It reveals the life of the Africans in their segregated section of the city, the relationships between the African miners and their white employers, and the impact of segregation.

Hopkinson, Tom, *South Africa (Life World Library).* New York: Time Incorporated, 1964. Hardcover. $3.95.

A survey of the land, history, religion, racial policies, arts, and politics of the Republic of South Africa; many photos and maps; appendix includes list of historical dates, suggestions for further readings, a list of prominent cultural figures; index. 160 pp. (Reading level: 9-12).

Paton, Alan, *The Land and People of South Africa.* Philadelphia: J. B. Lippincott Company, 1964. Hardcover. $2.93.

A survey, written like a travelogue, of the geography, history, mineral resources, peoples, and natural wonders of the Republic of South Africa; some black and white pictures; index. 162 pp. (Reading level: 9-12).

Samkange, Stanlake, *On Trial for My Country.* New York: Humanities Press, Inc., 1967. Paper. 158 pp. $1.25.

This novel, based on historic documents and letters, dramatizes the tactics used by Cecil Rhodes to deceive Chief Lobengula into assigning him control over Metebeleland (Rhodesia). It points up how the chief's ignorance of English and his misplaced trust in the white man led to the subversion of his own rule.

*(16 mm film)*

*The Republic of South Africa: Its Land and People,* EBF (1963). color, narration, 16 min.

Describes the geography, history, peoples, and customs of the Republic of South Africa; emphasis is placed on problems generated by rapid social change and apartheid. Compares ways of life of Africans, Boers; and in rural and urban areas; shows how culture of each is influenced by climate, topography, and available resources. Teacher's guide. (Collaborator: Professor Clarence W. Sorensen).

*Capetown: Republic of South Africa,* EG (1962). 48 frames, color, captioned, script. (*Continent of Africa: Historic Cities of Africa Series–* 158B). $6.00.

44 photos, one map, and 3 full captions. Buildings, surrounding region, and people are emphasized. Historic, traditional, and modern buildings (18), surrounding region and topography (8), people (ethnic and religious groups and their major economic activities) (7), city's functions (4), open markets (3), and education (4). Captions: statements explaining frames. Full captions: review (2) and summary (1).

*Johannesburg: Republic of South Africa,* EG (1962). 42 frames, color, captioned, script. (*Continent of Africa: Historic Cities of Africa Series–*158C). $6.00.

43 photos and 3 full captions. Major emphasis on industry and commerce of city: location and surrounding region (4), commerce and industry (15), population (housing, occupations, ethnic groups) (10), transportation (3), education and cultural activities (7), buildings (4). Captions: statements explaining frames. Full captions: review (2) and summary (1).

*Republic of South Africa: Important Cities,* EG (1962). 42 frames, color, captioned, script. (*Continent of Africa: South Africa Series–* 153E). $6.00.

41 photos and 3 full captions. Major emphasis on prominent buildings and modern aspects of South African cities: Johannesburg (14), Capetown (21), and Cape of Good Hope area (6). Captions: statements explaining frames. Full captions: review (2) and summary (1).

*The Republic of South Africa: Land and Communication,* EG (1962). 43 frames, color, captioned, script. (*Continent of Africa: South Africa Series–*153A). $6.00.

40 photos, one map, and 2 full captions. Terrain (20), Kruger Park (3), traditional and modern transportation (17). Captions: statements explaining frames. Full captions: review and summary.

*Republic of South Africa: Other Important Cities,* EG (1962). 45 frames, color, captioned, script. (*Continent of Africa: South Africa Series–* 153F). $6.00.

42 photos and 3 full captions. Sequel to 153E and continues coverage of South African cities, stressing prominent buildings, modern aspects of urban areas, and major functions. Pretoria (25) and Durban (17). Captions: statements explaining frames. Full captions: review (2) and summary (1).

*Southern Africa,* McG-H (1967). 40 frames, color, captioned, script. $7.00.

31 photos, 4 maps, and 5 full captions. Introduction (Why Southern Africa is the most industrialized region) (3), Europeans and economic activities (11), Indians (3), non-whites (8), industrial growth (12), conclusion: political aspects and need for racial cooperation (3). Captions: statements and questions. Part of a set of six costing $46.00.

*Southern Africa: Part II (South Africa),* EAV (n.d.). 46 frames, b/w, non-captioned, script. $3.75.

42 photos and 4 maps. Urban centers (7), methods of farming (2), activities of Coloured (11), resources, agricultural products (12), mineral products and mining (10). Script provides paragraph for each frame. Produced in England.

*(Filmstrips/tapes)*

*Southern Africa,* IMP (1969). 6 color filmstrips and 6 tapes. $75.00.

On South Africa, Rhodesia, and South West Africa. Tapes contain on-the-spot narration with accompanying background sounds, interviews, dances, music, and the sounds of Victoria Falls; filmstrips are on the following: peoples and the contrast between urban and village life; education; life of the Bantu and city life; resources and trade; Zimbabwe and music, art and dance; water and conservation. Elaborate teacher's manual and map.

*(Slides)*
*South Africa* (GUMPERT OF SWEDEN), EAV.
31 slides, color. $10.85.

28 photos and 3 maps. Overview of South
Africa: urban areas (4), terrain (6), people (11),
animals (2), economic activities (3), farming
(2); 28 photos taken in South Africa. Cities and
activities not identified. Maps not identified.

*(Charts)*
*Union of South Africa,* PICTORIAL CHARTS.
Single sheet, color. 30" x 40" $2.00.

Consists of five maps: large map of the vegetation found in South Africa, two small maps
of the rainfall and elevation, two small maps on
the crops and distribution of sheep. Notes on
the history and the people of South Africa.

*(Tapes)*
*Letters from the Cape* (#325), WTE. 15 min.
$2.75.

Recording of the letters of the wife of the First
Secretary of South Africa in 1795. Concerns the
history of the settlers, the English conquest, and
life in the South African cape region in the late
18th century.

*South Africa/South West Africa,* IMP (1969) 12
tapes. $108.00.

A series; #1 is a pre-test and introduction to
South Africa; #2-9 focus on wildlife, agriculture,
trade, mineral resources, peoples, apartheid,
Bantustans; #10-12 focus on South West Africa,
its peoples, geography, industries, farming; and
#12 concludes with a post-test. (Each tape
approx. 18 min.) Teacher's manual and 30 sets
of student folders, each with 12 activity booklets, included.

## Economic Activity

*(16 mm film)*
*Southern Africa: Industry and Agriculture,* McG-H
(1966). color, narration (15 min.).

Focuses on the sheep farms of the Veldt, Indians
of Natal, Bantu of Rhodesia, and the inhabitants
of Johannesburg. Emphasizes industrial develop-

ment and large-scale agriculture, which is not
typical of the entire region. Teacher's guide.

*(Filmstrips)*
*Republic of South Africa: Agriculture,* EG (1962).
44 frames, color, captioned, script. (*Continent
of Africa: South Africa Series*–153C). $6.00.

41 photos and 3 full captions. General characteristics of agricultural production (7), products (34), diversity of products and their importance to South Africa. Also illustrates the
importance of climate on production of varied
products. Captions: statements explaining
frames. Full captions: review (2) and summary
(1).

*Republic of South Africa: Industries,* EG (1962).
45 frames, color, captioned, script. (*Continent
of Africa: South Africa Series*–153D). $6.00.

42 photos and 3 full captions. South Africa's
industrial position in Africa (3), mining and
mineral products (22), manufacturing (14),
seaports and fishing (3). Captions: statements
explaining frames. Full captions: review (2) and
summary (1).

*South Africa: Dynamic Progress,* AVA. 54 frames,
color, captioned, script. (Produced for South
Africa Information Agency.) Free.

47 photos, 4 maps, and 3 drawings. General
overview of South Africa. History (12), cultural
activities (13), industry (8), transportation and
communication (6), military and scientific projects (6), cities (3), topography (2), racial composition (4). Script provides description of each
frame and supplements captions. Captions:
statements explaining frames.

*The South African Gold Fields,* CG (1951). 35
frames, color, non-captioned, script. $7.50.

Two maps, frames on beginnings of mining
(3), mining and processing ore (10), Johannesburg (4), area and buildings around gold fields
in Orange Free State (10), marketing gold (2).
Script has detailed description of each frame.

**118**

*(Tape)*
*Gold Mining in South Africa* (#200), WTE. 20 min. $2.75.

Description of African gold miners in South Africa. Major topics: how miners are organized, how African labor is drawn from the rural districts, how they live and work. Afrikaners' view of the benefits of working in a gold mine.

**Society**

*(Written material)*
Ford, Richard, *Tradition and Change in the Republic of South Africa.* New York: Holt, Rinehart, & Winston, Inc., 1968. Paper. $1.72.

A collection of source materials (with introductory descriptions and questions to guide the reader) that focus on the policy of apartheid, the different ethnic groups and their traditional ways of living, the Bantu and the impact of change on their way of living; maps, statistics, explanatory notes included. This is a separately bound section of Edwin Fenton's Holt Social Studies Curriculum. Index. 89 pp. (Reading level: 9-10).

Kuper, Hilda, *The Swazi: A South African Kingdom.* New York: Holt, Rinehart & Winston, 1964. Paper. $1.50.

A detailed survey of the history, habitat, selected social institutions (kinship, government, work, education, and clan organization), religion and present changes typical of the Swazi in South Africa; includes description and interpretation; brief list of suggested readings; no index. 87 pp. (Reading level: 12).

Legum, Colin and Margaret, *The Bitter Choice: Eight South Africans' Resistance to Tyranny.* Cleveland: The World Publishing Company, 1968. Hardcover. $4.98.

Biographical sketches of 8 South Africans who have been outspoken in their criticisms of and action against South Africa's racial policies; includes photos, excerpts of remarks, and life story of each man. Index. 209 pp. (Reading level: 9-12).

*(Filmstrips)*
*The Bantu in South Africa,* EBF (1961). 42 frames, color, captioned. $6.00.

32 photos, 3 maps, and 7 full captions. Examination of the conditions and activities of a Bantu village. Bantu village life–housing, dress, modern innovations, level of prosperity (17), Bantu miners (7), Bantu in urban areas–housing, economic activities (8). Captions: statements explaining frames. Full captions: introduction and summary.

*Republic of South Africa: The People,* EG (1962). 48 frames, color, captioned, script. (*Continent of Africa: South Africa Series*–153B). $6.00.

45 photos and 3 full captions. People: English and Afrikaners (11), urban Bantus (5), other Negro tribes (3), Coloured (2), and Asians (3). Apartheid (housing, education, and occupations) (21). Captions: statements explaining frames. Full captions: review (1) and summary (2).

*(Slides/tape)*
*The Colorful Amandebele,* WTE. 31 slides, color, 50 min. $5.00 for tape.

Tape and slides of a Bantu tribal group in South Africa. Emphasis on housing, style of construction, painted wall designs; also dress and decoration of women, and samples of Bantu music and speech. *Preview before showing.*

*(Slides)*
*Hottentot-Negro (K–Set 147),* AMNH (n.d.) color, $7.20.

Twelve color slides of Hottentots and Cape coloured in South Africa depicting their settlements, dress, housing, animals, and daily activities; descriptive data provided; may be purchased separately.

*River Bushmen of South Africa,* AMNH (n.d.) color. $15.00.

25 color slides of the River Bushmen of southwestern Africa showing closeups of people, their housing, fishing activities, crafts and other activities, dances, clothing; descriptive information provided; may be purchased separately.

### (Records)

*Bantu Choral Folk Music* (FW6912), FOLKWAYS. 10 bands, script. $4.15.

Side 1: 4 bands; side 2: 6 bands. Bantu folk music adapted and directed by American folk singer Pete Seeger. Sung by the Song Swappers. Script: introduction and notes on individual bands.

*The Naked Prey* (FS3854), FOLKWAYS. 15 bands, script. $5.79.

Side 1: 10 bands; side 2: 5 bands. Primarily vocal music from the movie *The Naked Prey.* Side 1 presents the traditional songs of the N'guni, Zulu, and Xhoa. Side 2 records the sounds of the villages, with the last two bands recording the animals of the regions. Notes on movie and actors. No notes on music.

### (Tapes)

*Africa Sings* (#168), WTE. 10 min. $10.00.

Narration of the music of the Bantus of South Africa. Short selections of music to illustrate points brought out by narrator. Types of music and instruments, influence of American jazz and Christian hymns discussed.

*South Africa's Racial Problem,* THE CENTER FOR THE STUDY OF DEMOCRATIC INSTITUTIONS. 60 min. $5.00.

A discussion of South Africa's racial problems by Edgar Hill, a South African newsman, and Harvey Wheeler.

*South Africa: The White Republic,* WASHINGTON TAPES, (1967). 27 min. script. $10.00.

Recorded briefing by W. B. Campbell of the State Department of the United States. Six major topics covered: overview of South Africa, doctrine of apartheid, self-government for non-whites, United States assessment of the policy of apartheid, economic sanctions, and South West Africa. (Some background noise and static on tape.)

## Rhodesia

### (Written material)

*Africa At A Glance: Rhodesia.* Pretoria, S.A.: African Institute, n.d. (distributed in U.S. by International University Booksellers, Inc.). Paper. 95¢.

A 10" x 16" data book on Rhodesia with paragraphs describing its land, people, history, and important dates (including a reprint of its 1965 Independence Proclamation), government, economy, and chief ministers. Several maps and photos (b/w). No index. (English text of 20 pp. backed by version in Afrikaans). 40 pp. (Reading level: 6-9).

### (8 mm film loops)

*Africa–City Life,* GATEWAY. (4 min.), color, script. $11.50.

First part of film depicts modern buildings, office workers, churches, and school in an African city. Second part follows an African as he enters a city, depicting such modern innovations as beauty parlors, movies, factories, worker camps, and political party activities. Ends with an aerial overview of an African city.

*Africa: Village Life,* GATEWAY. (4 min.), color, script. $12.50.

Shows the various social, economic and daily activities of life in a small rural village, Specific features include village festival, agricultural activities, food preparation, housing and people of the village. Village located in Rhodesian bush area.

### (Filmstrips)

*African Life: Rhodesia Part I,* UNITED WORLD FILMS (n.d.). 23 frames, b/w, captioned, script. $4.00.

Intensive examination of an African village in the copper belt of Rhodesia: physical layout of village (4), activities of the people (10), products (3), markets (4). Captions: statements explaining frames. Script: introduction and notes on each frame.

*African Life: Rhodesia Part II,* UNITED WORLD FILMS (n.d.). b/w, captioned, script. $4.00.

31 photos and 2 maps. Traces the life and activities of an African copper miner and his family in the copper belt of Rhodesia: mining town (5), work of miners (11), food rations and family meals (5), schools (5), leisure activities (5). Captions: statements explaining frames. Script: introduction and descriptive paragraph for each frame.

*Federation of Rhodesia and Nyasaland,* EG (1962). 44 frames, color, captioned, script. (*Continent of Africa: Countries of the Congo Basin Series* —155H). $6.00.

39 photos, 2 maps and 3 full captions. Emphasis on Southern Rhodesia and resources of the region. Salisbury (13), resources of Southern Rhodesia (9), Northern Rhodesia (7), people (7) and terrain (3). Captions: statements explaining frames. Full captions: review (2) and summary questions (1).

*Southern Africa Part I (Zambezi Area and Madagascar),* EAV (n.d.). 39 frames, b/w, non-captioned, script. $3.75.

35 photos and 4 maps. Northern Rhodesia and Nyasaland (15), Southern Rhodesia (15), Mozambique and Madagascar (5). Topics included: topography, transportation, products and urban centers. Script provides paragraph description for each frame.

*Southern Rhodesia: Scenes from the Native Reserves,* BUDEK, (1960). 44 frames, color, captioned, script. $6.00.

41 photos and 3 full captions. Concerned primarily with the government-sponsored improvements in a native reserve of Southern Rhodesia. Depicts road building (8), conservation practices (16), people and housing (14), and administration (2). Captions: statements explaining frames. Full captions: location and size of Rhodesia (2), introduction to native reserve (2). Script: introduction and descriptive paragraph for each frame.

*(Records)*
*Music from Petauke of Northern Rhodesia* (FE4201 and FE 4202), FOLKWAYS. 36 bands, scripts. $6.79.

Vol. I: Side 1: 8 bands; side 2: 9 bands; Vol. II: Side 1: 10 bands; side 2: 9 bands. Representative samples of the vocal and instrumental music from the Nsenga of Rhodesia. Scripts: background material and notes on individual bands.

*(Tapes)*
*Rhodesia,* IMP (1969). 6 tapes, teacher's manual and student folders. $54.00.

A series of 18-min. tapes recorded on the scene; #1 starts with a pre-test and introduces Rhodesia with comments on the life of Rhodesia and the city of Zimbabwe; #2-5 focus on the life of its black population, agriculture, education, natural resources; #6 discusses Rhodesia's break with Britain and ends with a post-test; teacher's manual and 30 student folders, each with 6 booklets.

*(Chart)*
*Rhodesia—Headline Focus Wall Map #7,* CES (1965).

Large 28" x 38" wall chart with brief written description of the nation and large map with pictures, drawings, diagrams, and other symbols; accompanied by brief text to describe modern features and problems of this nation.

**Southwest Africa**

*(16 mm film)*
*The Hunters,* CONTEMPORARY FILMS (n.d.). 73 min. color, narration.

Emphasizes life of the Bushman of the Kalahari, especially the search for food—digging roots, hunting a giraffe.

*Bushmen of the Kalahari,* McG-H (1967). 12 min. color, narration.

Description of life of the Bushman emphasizing social organization, family responsibilities, the process of living in a harsh environment and problems of adapting to the future. (ABC-TV *Africa*).

*(Filmstrip)*

*South-West Africa*, EG (1962). 42 frames, color, captioned, script. (*Continent of Africa: South Africa Series*–153G). $6.00.

38 photos, one map, and 3 full captions. General overview of the region. Climate and terrain (6), resources (9), people (12), cities and ports (8), transportation (3). Captions: statements explaining frames. Full captions: review (2) and summary (1).

*(Records)*

*Bushman Music and Pygmy Music,* PEABODY MUSEUM. 10 bands, script. $6.79.

Side 1: 6 bands; side 2: 4 bands. Bands consist of Bushman and Pygmy songs. Selections feature music sung by men, women, children and mixed chorus. Script: notes on the music of Bushman and comparison to that of the Babinga Pygmies.

*The Music of Kung Bushmen of the Kalahari Desert, Africa* (FE4487), FOLKWAYS. 24 bands, script. $6.79.

Side 1: 14 bands; side 2: 10 bands. Recording of instrumental music, children's songs, men and women's dancing music, and Bushmen conversations. Script consists of background material and sketches from author's trip among the Bushmen. No notes on individual bands.

*(Tapes)*

*South Africa/South West Africa.* IMP (1969). 12 tapes, teacher's manual and student folders. $108.00.

A series of 18-min. tapes; #1 is a pre-test and introduction to South Africa; #2-9 focus on wildlife, agriculture, trade, mineral resources, peoples, apartheid, Bantustans; #10-12 focus on South West Africa, its peoples, geography, industries, farming; #12 concludes with a post-test; teacher's manual and 30 sets of student folders, each with 12 activity booklets.

**Zambia**

*(Record)*

*This Is My Country: Zambia,* WILSON (1968). 1 side of 12" LP (or tape). 19 min.

Introduced with Zambian national anthem and narrated description of the location and size of Zambia; followed by interview with a Zambian briefly covering language, family organization (extended family), and life; how people make a living, education, religion, government, basic problems facing Zambia.

*(Tapes)*

*Zambia,* IMP (1969). 3 tapes, teacher's manual, student folders. $27.00.

A series of tapes opening with a pre-test and introduction to Zambia, and featuring a number of interviews; also examined are the copper industry and communications; teacher's manual and 30 student folders, each with 3 booklets.

**Other Countries**

*(Written material)*

*Africa at a Glance: Botswana.* Pretoria, S.A.: African Institute, n.d. (distributed in U.S. by International University Booksellers, Inc.). Paper. 95¢.

A 10" x 16" data book with paragraphs on Botswana's land, people, important dates, government, economy, and current president. Several photos (b/w) and maps. No index. (English text backed by identical text in Afrikaans.) 24 pp. (Reading level: 6-9).

*Africa at a Glance: Lesotho.* Pretoria, S. A.: African Institute, n.d. (distributed in U.S. by International University Booksellers, Inc.). Paper. 95¢.

A 10" x 16" fact book on Lesotho with paragraphs descriptive of its land, people, history, government, economy, and current political leaders; map and photos (b/w). (Printed in English; duplicate pages printed in Afrikaans attached.) No index. 19 pp. (Reading level: 6-9).

*Africa at a Glance: Swaziland.* Pretoria, S.A.: Africa Institute, n.d. (distributed in the U.S. by

International University Booksellers, Inc.).
Paper. 95¢.

A 10" x 16" fact book with paragraphs on
Swaziland's land, people, history, government,
economy, and leaders. Several maps and photos
(b/w). No index. (English text backed by identical text in Afrikaans.) 34 pp. (Reading
level: 6-9).

*Lesotho.* New York: British Information Service,
1967. Paper.

A brief description of the country—its land, political history, economic features, and society.
Includes reading list, map, and several photos
(b/w); no index. 31 pp.

*Botswana.* New York: British Information Service,
1967. Paper.

A brief description of the country—its lands,
political history, economic features and society.
Includes reading list, map and several photos
(b/w); no index. 31 pp.

*(Filmstrip)*
*Basutoland, Bechuanaland, and Swaziland,* EG
(1962). 46 frames, color, captioned, script.
*(Continent of Africa: South Africa Series—*
153H). $6.00.

42 photos, one map and 3 full captions. Three
areas treated separately as to their terrain, transportation, people, and major economic activity:
Basutoland (15), Bechuanaland (13), Swaziland
(14). Captions: statements explaining frames.
Full captions: review (2) and summary (1).

# SELECTED INSTRUCTIONAL MATERIALS ON
# AFRICA SOUTH OF THE SAHARA

Hundreds of materials have been examined in the course of preparing the preceding bibliography. Many of these are of questionable quality. Some, however, are outstanding in
terms of their potential for use in courses or units of study designed in accordance with the
guidelines presented in Part I of this guide. These materials have been singled out on the
basis of:

a) Scholarship and accuracy
b) Balance in presentation and emphasis
c) Technical quality
d) Currency of content
e) Cost relative to potential uses
f) Appropriateness to the guidelines suggested in Part I of this guide

They are arranged in two lists. List A includes those that should be considered for acquisition by any school that teaches about this region and its peoples in one or more of its social
studies courses. These represent a minimal set of materials to which any teacher should have
access. List B includes materials which schools teaching more than a survey-type study of
Africa might wish to consider adding to the basic materials enumerated in List A. Teachers
should preview all materials carefully before making final selections.

# LIST A

## RECOMMENDED BASIC INSTRUCTIONAL MATERIALS

*(Map)*
*Aero Raised Relief Map of Africa.* NYSTROM. $49.00.

A plastic-coated map with surface raised to scale to indicate topography of Africa; when used flat on a desk or table top students can get "eye level" views of the continent and can get a feel for its geographic assets and liabilities, for the problems involved in living and traveling there, and for the nature of this land mass; an excellent teaching aid. For content description see p. 66.

*(Filmstrips)*
*Profile of Africa.* SFS (2). $12.00.

Two uncaptioned color filmstrips with extensive teaching guide explaining each frame. A well-balanced introductory *overview.* For content description see p. 67.

*(Filmstrips/records)*
*African Art and Culture.* WSP (1968). $45.60.

A set of 3 filmstrips in color with 3 accompanying records; uses African art (masks, sculptures, rock paintings, castings, carvings) to introduce the early history of Africa south of the Sahara and to analyze the traditional and changing culture and society of the peoples of West Africa especially; excellent photos and narration; although the filmstrips are long (approximately 63 frames each) the records require only 19 min. each; an excellent use of art to gain insights into Africa past and present. For content description see p. 75.

*(Kit)*
*African Art Studies Kit.* UCLA (1969). $85.00.

An introduction to the arts of Africa (dance, music, art, sculpture, poetry) via classroom sets of three 16-page booklets specially prepared for students, two filmstrips (masks and dance), a record (drums), a folio of art, desk maps, and teaching guides; excellent color illustrations and filmstrips; good teaching guides—a fine introduction to the wide range of the arts south of the Sahara. For content description see p. 75.

*(Slides/record)*
*Emerging Africa in the Light of Its Past.* CHR (Units 1 & 2). $59.90.

A survey of the history of Africa south of the Sahara in 80 color slides (40 per unit) with recorded narrative. Excellent notes to the teacher as well as bibliography. Although the recorded narrative is quite monotonous, the slides can be used without it. Slides may be rearranged in a variety of ways for different presentations. For content description see p. 81.

*(Transparencies)*
*World History—Unit I: Sub-Saharan Africa.* K&E $39.95.

A set of 30 transparencies, each with multiple overlays. Extra large print, uncluttered content and bright colors make for easy reading from any distance. Content guide. Great potential versatility—can be used in large group lectures or in inquiry-oriented classes. May be purchased as master book from which diazo sets may be made locally ($39.95) or as individual already-made spectra transparencies varying in price from $1.75 to $10.75. For content description see p. 68.

*(Records)*
*Africa South of the Sahara* (FE 4503), FOLKWAYS. (2 records) $13.90.

A survey of African music with samples from a wide variety of peoples. Collected by Harold Courlander. Extensive notes prepared by Alan Merriam on the basic features of African music followed by analyses of each band. For content description see p. 77.

*(Art)*
*African Sculpture.* ALVA (1968). $50.00.

Authentic reproductions of nine sculptured objects, carvings and castings from West Africa, made of break-resistant ceramic; can be handled and examined by students in activities involving inquiry or exposition and can be used in the study of history and/or culture; their use secures immediate student involvement. For content description see p. 75.

*(Atlas)*

Ady, P. H. and A. Z. Hazelwood, *Oxford Regional Economic Atlas of Africa,* OXFORD UNIVERSITY PRESS. Paper. $7.00.

A collection of maps of the continent and its various regions. Statistical data on aspects of Africa's economy. At least one copy should be available for student reference. Also available in hard cover. For content description see p. 63.

*(Written material)*

Burke, Fred G., *Sub-Saharan Africa.* New York: Harcourt, Brace & World, 1968. Paper. $1.35.

A thorough study of contemporary Africa south of the Sahara and especially the politics and economics of nation-building; useful maps, charts, photos. For content description see p. 57.

Foster, Philip, *Africa South of the Sahara.* New York: The Macmillan Company, 1968. Paper. $2.20.

One of the best, most scholarly and up-to-date student paperback texts on Africa south of the Sahara; excellent map, graph, photo and chart aids; especially useful on the geography and demography of Africa but somewhat sketchy on early history; excellent study of contemporary life and problems. For content description see p. 57.

Hoff, Rhoda, *Africa: Adventures in Eyewitness History.* New York: Henry Z. Walck, Inc., 1968. Hardcover. $3.75.

A collection of primary sources (documents, diaries, travel accounts, letters, speeches, etc.) on Africa both before and after it was occupied by Europeans; excellent introductions to each source, useful as companion to a text or as a library reference. For content description see p. 60

Moore, Clark D. and Ann Dunbar, *Africa Yesterday and Today.* New York: Bantam Books, Inc., 1968. Paper. 95¢.

A collection of edited excerpts from major secondary sources on Africa—the writings of geographers, historians, political scientists, anthropologists, and so on; an excellent source for an academic study of this region and its peoples. For content description see p. 60.

Singleton, F. Seth and John Shingler, *Africa in Perspective.* New York: Hayden Book Company, Inc., 1967. Paper. $3.96.

The best available survey of Africa for the general reader or those who have never studied Africa; includes detailed studies of Africa's peoples, history and modern development; extremely lively and well-written with excellent maps, graphs and photos. For content description see p. 59.

Vlahos, Olivia, *African Beginnings.* New York: The Viking Press, 1967. Hardcover. $6.95 (also available in paper).

An exciting, informal survey of Africa's past and present with vivid descriptions of the life and culture of various African peoples today and at selected periods in history; excellent potential for use in historical or cultural studies. This is the finest single survey of Africa south of the Sahara for secondary school students. For content description see p. 80.

*(Periodical)*

*Tarikh.* HUMANITIES PRESS $2.00/yr.

An excellent journal produced especially for high school students. Libraries and classrooms should subscribe to multiple copies. See p. 64.

## List B

## RECOMMENDED ADDITIONAL INSTRUCTIONAL MATERIALS

*(Maps)*

*Wenschow Relief-Like Map of Africa,* DENOYER $29.25.

Large, conventionally colored wall map with easily read symbols and names. Shading gives three-dimensional effect. Mounted on spring roller or folded sheet for easy movement from one room to another. For content description see p. 66.

*(8 mm film loops)*

*Africa–Culture Groups,* GATEWAY. $12.00.

A color, cartridged 8 mm film loop surveying four different types of culture groups living in Africa south of the Sahara. Excellent for small group study. See p. 71.

*Africans of the River Niger,* EALING. $111.00.

Six color, cartridged 8 mm film loops on various aspects of the Bozo peoples of Mali. Excellent films for small group study. Many potential uses. See p. 92.

*Africa: Village Life,* GATEWAY. $12.50.

A color, cartridged, 8 mm film loop depicting life in a village of Southern Africa. Very good survey of major activities. Many potential uses. See p. 120.

*(Filmstrips)*

*Africa: Climate and Vegetation,* MES. $10.00.

Excellent color, detailed maps and photos of climate zones of the continent, focusing on vegetation and products of each. See p. 70.

*Africa: The Land of Developing Countries,* SVE. $39.75.

A set of six color filmstrips and three 12" LP records, each focusing on a different region of Africa—its land, peoples, and economy. Excellent maps, well-balanced surveys. Easily used in a wide variety of instructional approaches including large group presentations or independent study. See p. 67.

*Africa: Physical Features,* MES. $10.00.

Good color, detailed maps, fine photos selected to illustrate distribution of major geographic features. See p. 70.

*East Africa: People, Crops and Cattle,* CG. $7.50.

Brief but thorough color survey of various tribes and their housing and economic activities. Well organized. Many potential uses. See p. 102.

*East Africa: A Regional Survey,* CG. $7.50.

Color, non-captioned photos briefly surveying features of East African terrain, life and development. Many potential uses. Detailed script. See p. 101.

*Economic Development in Africa,* SB. $3.00.

Broad coverage of impact of modernization on various facets of African economic life. Color. Captioned. See p. 74.

*Ghana,* CG. $7.50.

Short, color survey of Ghana focusing on major sections and economic activities. Many potential uses. Detailed script. See p. 88.

*Profile of Kenya,* SFS. $6.00.

Although somewhat dated, this is still an excellent well-balanced overview—excellent color photos of various aspects of life in Kenya. Extensive teacher's guide. See p. 106.

*Profile of Nigeria,* SFS. $6.00.

Also somewhat dated, this presents a balanced overview of life in Nigeria. Focuses on all aspects of the land and peoples. Non-captioned. See p. 95.

*Tanganyika,* CG. $7.50.

Excellent color photos and maps of geographical regions, products, and peoples of Tanzania. Many potential uses. Detailed script. See p. 108.

*(Slides/records)*

*Emerging Africa In the Light of its Past: West Africa Patterns of Traditional Culture* (Unit 3). $29.95. *Patterns of Change* (Unit 4). $29.95.

These units are excellent ways to describe traditional West Africa and the impact of historical change up to the present; thorough teaching guides; although the narration gets monotonous after a few minutes, teachers can use the slides without the records. For content descriptions see pp. 83-84.

# PUBLISHERS' ADDRESSES
## PUBLISHERS OF AUDIO-VISUAL MATERIALS

AAI — *African-American Institute*
866 United Nations Plaza
New York, New York 10017

AEVAC — *AEVAC, Inc.*
500 Fifth Avenue
New York, New York 10036

AF — *African Filmstrips*
41 East 42nd Street
New York, New York 10027

ALVA — *Alva Museum Replicas, Inc.*
30-30 Northern Boulevard
Long Island City, New York 11101

AMIE — *AMIE Associates, Inc.*
123 Manhattan Avenue
New York, New York 10025

AMNH — *The American Museum of Natural History*
Slide Library
79th Street & Central Park West
New York, New York 10024

ATLANTIS — *Atlantis Productions, Inc.*
894 Sheffield Place
Thousand Oaks, California 91360

AVA — *A.V.A.*
805 Smith Street
Baldwin, New York 11510

BF — *Bailey Films, Inc.*
6509 DeLongpre Avenue
Hollywood, California 90028

BP — *Benefic Press*
103000 W. Roosevelt Road
Westchester, Illinois 60153

BUDEK — *Budek Films & Slides, Inc.*
451 Frederic Lopez Drive
Goleta, California 93017

CAF — *Current Affairs Films*
Div. of Key Productions, Inc.
527 Madison Avenue
New York, New York 10022

CAMBRIDGE — *Cambridge Book Company, Inc.*
Cambridge Building
Bronxville, New York 10708

CENTER — *The Center for the Study of Democratic Institutions*
2056 Eucalyptus Hill Road
Montecito, California 93103

CES — *Civic Education Service*
1735 K Street, N.W.
Washington, D.C. 20006

CF — *Contemporary Films—McGraw-Hill Films*
330 West 42nd Street
New York, New York 10036

CG — *Common Ground Filmstrips*
Carman Educational Assocs. Inc.
Box 205
Youngstown, New York 14174

CHR — *Cultural History Research, Inc.*
6 Purchase Street
Rye, New York 10580

CM — *Curriculum Materials Corp.*
1319 Vine Street
Philadelphia, Pennsylvania 19107

CMS — *CMS Records, Inc.*
12 Warren Street
New York, New York 10007

COLUMBIA — *Columbia Records*
Educational Dept. Orders Service
1400 Fruitridge Avenue
Terre Haute, Indiana 47805

CORONET — *Coronet Films*
488 Madison Avenue
New York, New York 10022

DENOYER — *Denoyer-Geppert*
5235 Ravenswood Avenue
Chicago, Illinois 60640

DON BOSCO   *Don Bosco Films*
148 Main Street
New Rochelle, New York 10802

EALING   *Ealing Corporation*
2225 Massachusetts Avenue
Cambridge, Mass. 02140

EAV   *Educational Audio-Visual, Inc.*
1 Claremont Avenue
Thornwood, New York 10594

EBF   *Encyclopaedia Britannica Films*
1150 Wilmette Avenue
Wilmette, Illinois 60091

EG   *Eye Gate House, Inc.*
146-01 Archer Avenue
Jamaica, New York 11435

FIDELER   *Fideler Visual Teaching, Inc.*
31 Ottawa, N.W.
Grand Rapids, Michigan 49502

FOLKWAYS   *Folkways Scholastic Records*
50 West 44th Street
New York, New York 10036

FP   *Friendship Press*
475 Riverside Drive
New York, New York 10027

GAF   *General Aniline and Film Corp.*
140 West 51st Street
New York, New York 10020

GATEWAY   *International Communication Films*
1371 Reynolds Avenue
Santa Ana, California 92705

GINN   *Ginn & Company*
Statler Building
Back Bay P.O. 191
Boston, Massachusetts 02117

HAMMOND   *Hammond, Inc.*
Education Division
515 Valley Street
Maplewood, New Jersey 07040

HAYDEN   *Hayden Book Company, Inc.*
116 West 14th Street
New York, New York 10011

HAYES   *Hayes School Publishing Company, Inc.*
Wilkinsburg, Pennsylvania 15221

HONOR   *Webster Paper and Supply Co.*
Colonie & Montgomery Streets
Albany, New York 12207

ICG   *International Communication Films*
1371 Reynolds Avenue
Santa Ana, California 92705

IFF   *International Film Foundation*
475 Fifth Avenue
New York, New York 10017

IMP   *Imperial Productions, Inc.*
247 West Court Street
Kankakee, Illinois 60901

JACKDAW   *Social Studies School Service*
4455 Lenox Avenue
Inglewood, California 90304

K&E   *Keuffel and Esser Co.*
20 Whippany Road
Morristown, New Jersey 07960

LONDON   *London Records Company, Inc.*
539 West 25th Street
New York, New York 10001

LOWIE   *Robert Lowie Museum*
103 Kroeber Hall
University of California
Berkeley, California 94720

McG-H   *McGraw-Hill Book Company*
Text Film Division
330 West 42nd Street
New York, New York 10036

MES   *Museum Extension Service*
83 Adams Street
Bedford Hills, New York 10507

MILLIKEN   *Milliken Publishing Co.*
611 Olive Street
St. Louis, Missouri 63101

MLEAT   *Museum and Laboratories of Ethnic Arts and Technology*
University of California
Los Angeles, California 90024

| | | | |
|---|---|---|---|
| MONITOR | *Monitor Records*<br>156 Fifth Avenue<br>New York, New York 10010 | RAND<br>McNALLY | *Rand McNally & Company*<br>Box 7600<br>Chicago, Illinois 60680 |
| MPA | *Museum of Primitive Art*<br>15 West 54th Street<br>New York, New York 10019 | RCA | *Radio Corporation of America*<br>RCA Educational Services<br>Camden, New Jersey 08108 |
| MPM | *Milwaukee Public Museum*<br>800 West Wells Street<br>Milwaukee, Wisconsin 53233 | SB | *Stanley Bowmar Co., Inc.*<br>4 Broadway<br>Valhalla, New York 10595 |
| NELSON | *Thomas Nelson*<br>Copewood and Davis Streets<br>Camden, New Jersey 08103 | SFS | *School Film Service*<br>549 West 123rd Street<br>New York, New York 10027 |
| NEWSWEEK | *Newsweek Education Division*<br>444 Madison Avenue<br>New York, New York 10022 | SILHOU-<br>ETTES | *Silhouettes in Courage, Inc.*<br>22 East 40th Street<br>New York, New York 10016 |
| NYSTROM | *A. J. Nystrom & Company*<br>3333 Elston Avenue<br>Chicago, Illinois 60618 | SB | *Silver Burdett Co.*<br>Park Ave. & Columbia Road<br>Morristown, New Jersey 07960 |
| NYT | *New York Times*<br>Office of Educational Services<br>229 West 43rd Street<br>New York, New York 10036 | SL | *Sounds of Learning, Inc.*<br>215 South 88th Street<br>Omaha, Nebraska 68132 |
| OCA | *Operation Crossroads Africa*<br>150 Fifth Avenue<br>New York, New York 10011 | SVE | *Society for Visual Education, Inc.*<br>1345 W. Diversey Parkway<br>Chicago, Illinois 60614 |
| OXFORD | *Oxford University Press*<br>16-00 Pollitt Drive<br>Fairlawn, New Jersey 07410 | THORNE | *Thorne Films, Inc.*<br>1229 University Avenue<br>Boulder, Colorado 80302 |
| PEABODY | *Peabody Museum*<br>Harvard University<br>Cambridge, Massachusetts 02138 | UCLA | *African Arts School Supplements*<br>*Program*<br>African Studies Center<br>University of California<br>Los Angeles, California 90024 |
| ROBECK | *Peter Robeck & Company*<br>230 Park Avenue<br>New York, New York 10017 | UM | *University Museum*<br>University of Pennsylvania<br>33rd and Spruce Street<br>Philadelphia, Pennsylvania 19104 |
| PHILIPS | *Philips Record Co.*<br>35 E. Wacker Drive<br>Chicago, Illinois 60601 | UWF | *United World Films, Inc.*<br>221 Park Avenue South<br>New York, New York 10003 |
| PICTORIAL<br>CHARTS | *Pictorial Charts Educational Trust*<br>181 Uxbridge Road<br>Hanwell, London W.7, England | VEC | *Visual Education Consultants, Inc.*<br>2840 Laura la Middleton<br>Madison, Wisconsin 53701 |

| | | | |
|---|---|---|---|
| WT | Washington Tapes, Inc.<br>Educational Systems Division<br>Doubleday & Co.<br>501 Franklin Avenue<br>Garden City., L. I., New York 11530 | WORLD<br>WIDE | World Wide Games, Inc.<br>Box 450<br>Delaware, Ohio 43015 |
| WILSON | H. Wilson Corporation<br>555 West Taft Drive<br>South Holland, Illinois 60473 | WSP | Warren Schloat Productions, Inc.<br>115 Tomkins Avenue<br>Pleasantville, New York 10570 |
| WORLD | The World Publishing Co.<br>2231 West 110th Street<br>Cleveland, Ohio 44102 | WTE | World Tapes for Education, Inc.<br>P.O. Box 15703<br>Dallas, Texas 75215 |

# PUBLISHERS OF WRITTEN MATERIALS

*Addison-Wesley Publishing Co.*
2725 Sand Hill Road
Menlo Park, California 94025

*The African-American Institute*
866 United Nations Plaza
New York, New York 10017

*African Studies Center*
University of California
Los Angeles, California 90024

*George Allen & Unwin, Ltd.*
Ruskin House
40 Museum Street
London W.C. 1, England

*Allyn and Bacon, Inc.*
470 Atlantic Avenue
Boston, Massachusetts 02210

*American Association of University Women*
2401 Virginia Ave., N.W.
Washington, D.C. 20007

*American Education Publications*
Education Center
Columbus, Ohio 43216

*American Geographical Society*
156th Street and Broadway
New York, New York 10032

*American Society of African Culture*
101 Park Avenue
New York, New York 10017

*Edward J. Arnold & Sons, Ltd.*
Butterley Street
Leed 10, England

*Atheneum Publishers*
122 East 42nd Street
New York, New York 10017

*Bantam Books*
271 Madison Avenue
New York, New York 10016

*Benefic Press*
10300 W. Roosevelt Road
Westchester, Illinois 60153

*Edward W. Blyden Press, Inc.*
P.O. Box 621
Manhattanville Station
New York, New York 10027

*Boston University*
School of Education
332 Bay State Road
Boston, Massachusetts 02115

*R. R. Bowker Company*
1180 Avenue of the Americas
New York, New York 10036

British Information Services
845 Third Avenue
New York, New York 10022

William C. Brown Company
135 South Locust Street
Dubuque, Iowa 52001

Brumley Printing Company
175 East Franklin Avenue
Gastonia, North Carolina 28052

Burgess Publishing Company
426-28 S. 6th Street
Minneapolis, Minnesota 55415

Cambridge Book Company
Cambridge Building
Bronxville, New York 10708

Cambridge University Press
32 East 57th Street
New York, New York 10022

The Canadian National Commission for UNESCO
140 Wellington
Ottawa, Canada

Christian Science Publishing Society
1 Norway Street
Boston, Massachusetts 02115

Civic Education Service, Inc.
1733 K Street, N.W.
Washington, D.C. 20006

F. E. Compton & Company
1000 N. Dearborn
Chicago, Illinois 60610

Cooperative Center for Social Science Education
College of Education
Ohio University
Athens, Ohio 45701

Cooper Square Publishers, Inc.
59 Fourth Avenue
New York, New York 10003

Council of the African-American Institute
866 United Nations Plaza
New York, New York 10017

Criterion Books, Inc.
6 West 57th Street
New York, New York 10019

Thomas Y. Crowell Company
201 Park Avenue South
New York, New York 10003

John Day Company, Inc.
62 West 45th Street
New York, New York 10019

Dell Publishing Company
750 Third Avenue
New York, New York 10017

Denoyer-Geppert Company
5235 Ravenswood Avenue
Chicago, Illinois 60640

Doubleday & Company
277 Park Avenue
New York, New York 10017

E. P. Dutton & Company, Inc.
201 Park Avenue South
New York, New York 10003

Encyclopaedia Britannica, Inc.
425 N. Michigan Avenue
Chicago, Illinois 60611

Evans Brothers, Ltd.
Montague House
Russell Square
London W.C. 1, England

Fearon Publishers
2165 Park Boulevard
Palo Alto, California 94306

The Fideler Company
31 Ottawa Avenue, N.W.
Grand Rapids, Michigan 49502

Field Enterprises Education Corp.
510 Merchandise Mart Plaza
Chicago, Illinois 60654.

Foreign Area Materials Center
University of the State of New York
State Education Department
33 West 42nd Street
New York, New York 10036

*Foreign Policy Association*
345 East 46th Street
New York, New York 10017

*Funk and Wagnalls*
380 Madison Avenue
New York, New York 10017

*Ginn & Company*
Statler Building
Back Bay P.O. 191
Boston, Massachusetts 02117

*Grade Teacher*
23 Leroy Avenue
Darien, Connecticut 06820

*Graduate School of International Studies*
University of Denver
Denver, Colorado 80210

*Greenwood Periodicals, Inc.*
211 East 43rd Street
New York, New York 10017

*Grosset & Dunlap, Inc.*
51 Madison Avenue
New York, New York 10010

*Harcourt, Brace & World, Inc.*
757 Third Avenue
New York, New York 10017

*Harper & Row, Publishers*
49 East 33rd Street
New York, New York 10016

*Hayden Book Company, Inc.*
116 West 14th Street
New York, New York 10011

*D. C. Heath and Company*
285 Columbus Avenue
Boston, Massachusetts 02116

*Hill and Wang, Inc.*
141 Fifth Avenue
New York, New York 10010

*Holt, Rinehart & Winston, Inc.*
383 Madison Avenue
New York, New York 10017

*Hoover Institution*
Publications Department
Stanford University
Stanford, California 94305

*Humanities Press, Inc.*
303 Park Avenue South
New York, New York 10010

*Indiana University Press*
10th and Morton Streets
Bloomington, Indiana 47401

*Information Center on Children's Cultures*
331 East 38th Street
New York, New York 10016

*International African Institute*
St. Dunstan's Chambers
10-11 Fetter Lane
London E.C. 4, England

*International University Booksellers, Inc.*
101 Fifth Avenue
New York, New York 10003

*M. W. Lads Publishing Company*
200 Park Avenue
New York, New York 10017

*Laidlaw Brothers, Publishers*
Thatcher & Madison Streets
River Forest, Illinois 60305

*J. B. Lippincott Company*
East Washington Square
Philadelphia, Pennsylvania 19105

*Little, Brown & Company*
34 Beacon Street
Boston, Massachusetts 02106

*Longman's Green & Company*
48 Grosvenor Street
London W. 1, England

*Longman's of Nigeria, Ltd.*
Ibadan, Nigeria

*Longman's of Nigeria, Ltd.*
Private Mail Bag 1036
Ikeja, Nigeria

*Library of Congress*
General Reference and Bibliography Division
Washington, D.C. 20540

The Macmillan Company
866 Third Avenue
New York, New York 10022

McCormick-Mathers Publishing Co., Inc.
300 Pike Street
Cincinnati, Ohio 45202

McGraw-Hill Book Company
330 West 42nd Street
New York, New York 10036

David McKay Company, Inc.
750 Third Avenue
New York, New York 10017

McKinley Publishing Company
Brooklawn, New Jersey 08030

Charles E. Merrill Books
1300 Alum Creek Drive
Columbus, Ohio 43216

William Morrow & Company, Inc.
425 Park Avenue South
New York, New York 10016

National Council for the Social Studies
1201 Sixteenth Street, N.W.
Washington, D.C. 20036

National Council of the Churches of Christ
745 Riverside Drive
New York, New York 10027

National Education Association
1201 Sixteenth Street, N.W.
Washington, D.C. 20036

National Geographic Society
17th & M Streets, N.W.
Washington, D.C. 20036

Natural History Press
American Museum of Natural History
Central Park W. at 79th Street
New York, New York 10024

Thomas Nelson & Sons, Ltd.
Copewood and Davis Streets
Camden, New Jersey 08103

New Horizons Publishers, Inc.
154 E. Erie Street
Chicago, Illinois 60611

Newsweek Education Division
444 Madison Avenue
New York, New York 10022

New York Times Book and Educational Division
229 West 43rd Street
New York, New York 10036

Northwestern University Press
1735 Benson Avenue
Evanston, Illinois 60201

Oceana Publications, Inc.
Dobbs Ferry, New York 10522

Oxford Book Company, Inc.
387 Park Avenue South
New York, New York 10016

Oxford University Press
200 Madison Avenue
New York, New York 10016

Oxford University Press
P.O. Box 12532
Nairobi, Kenya

Penguin Books, Inc.
7110 Ambassador Road
Baltimore, Maryland 21207

Pennsylvania Department of Public Instruction
Education Building
Harrisburg, Pennsylvania 17126

Frederick A. Praeger, Publisher
111 Fourth Avenue
New York, New York 10003

Prentice-Hall, Inc.
Englewood Cliffs, New Jersey 07632

Queens College of the City of New York
65-30 Kissena Avenue
Flushing, L.I., New York 11355

Rand McNally & Company
Box 7600
Chicago, Illinois 60680

Rutgers University Press
30 College Avenue
New Brunswick, New Jersey 08903

William H. Sadlier, Inc.
11 Park Place
New York, New York 10007

St. Martin's Press
175 Fifth Avenue
New York, New York 10010

Scholastic Book Services
50 West 44th Street
New York, New York 10036

Scott, Foresman & Company
1900 E. Lake Avenue
Glenview, Illinois 60025

Service Center for the Teachers of History
American Historical Association
400 A Street, S.E.
Washington, D.C. 20003

The State Education Department
Bureau of Secondary Curriculum Development
Albany, New York 12224

Sterling Publishing Company, Inc.
419 Park Avenue South
New York, New York 10016

Stryker-Post Publications
6330 Utah Avenue, N.W.
Washington, D.C. 20015

Teachers College–Bureau of Publications
Columbia University
525 West 120th Street
New York, New York 10027

Time Incorporated
Time-Life Building
New York, New York 10020

United Presbyterian Church Commission on
    Ecumenical Mission and Relations
475 Riverside Drive
New York, New York 10027

United States Committee for Unicef
331 East 38th Street
New York, New York 10016

United States Government
Superintendent of Documents
U.S. Government Printing Office
Washington, D.C. 20402

University of London Press
Warwick Square
London E.C.4, England

University of Wisconsin Press
P.O. Box 1379
Madison, Wisconsin 53701

University Tutorial Press, Ltd.
Clifton House
Euston Road
London N.W.1, England

D. Van Nostrand Company, Inc.
120 Alexander Street
Princeton, New Jersey 08540

Viking Press
625 Madison Avenue
New York, New York 10022

Vintage Books
Random House
457 Madison Avenue
New York, New York 10022

Henry Z. Walck, Inc.
19 Union Square West
New York, New York 10003

Walker & Company
720 Fifth Avenue
New York, New York 10019

Franklin Watts, Inc.
575 Lexington Avenue
New York, New York 10022

Webster Division
McGraw-Hill Book Company
Manchester Road
Manchester, Missouri 63011

World Affairs Book Center
345 East 46th Street
New York, New York 10017

World Affairs Materials
Brooklyn College
Bedford Avenue and Avenue H
Brooklyn, New York 11210

World Publishing Company
2231 West 110th Street
Cleveland, Ohio 44102

# AFRICAN
## DIPLOMATIC MISSIONS

Botswana, Embassy of
1701 New Hampshire Avenue, N.W.
Washington, D.C. 20009

Burundi, Embassy of the Republic of
1875 Connecticut Avenue, N.W. Room 1114
Washington, D.C. 20009

Cameroon, Embassy of the Federal Republic of
1705 New Hampshire Avenue, N.W.
Washington, D.C. 20009

Central African Republic, Embassy of
1618 22nd Street, N.W.
Washington, D.C. 20008

Chad, Embassy of the Republic of
1132 New Hampshire Avenue, N.W.
Washington, D.C. 20037

Congo—Brazzaville, Embassy of
5030 16th Street, N.W.
Washington, D.C. 20011

Congo—Kinshasa, Embassy of the Republic of
1800 New Hampshire Avenue, N.W.
Washington, D.C. 20009

Dahomey, Embassy of the Republic of
6600 16th Street, N.W.
Washington, D.C. 20012

Ethiopia, Consulate General of
866 United Nations Plaza
New York, New York 10017

Ethiopia, Embassy of Imperial
2134 Kalorama Road, N.W.
Washington, D.C. 20008

Gabon, Embassy of the Republic of
4900 16th Street, N.W.
Washington, D.C. 20011

Ghana, Consulate General of
565 Fifth Avenue
New York, New York 10017

Ghana, Embassy of
2460 16th Street, N.W.
Washington, D.C. 20009

Guinea, Embassy of
2112 LeRoy Place, N.W.
Washington, D.C. 20008

Ivory Coast, Embassy of
2424 Massachusetts Avenue, N.W.
Washington, D.C. 20008

Kenya, Embassy of
1875 Connecticut Avenue, N.W.
Washington, D.C. 20009

Liberia, Consulate General of
1120 Avenue of the Americas
New York, New York 10036

Liberia, Embassy of
5201 16th Street, N.W.
Washington, D.C. 20011

Malagasy, Embassy of the Republic of
2374 Massachusetts Avenue, N.W.
Washington, D.C. 20008

Malawi, Embassy of
2019 Q Street, N.W.
Washington, D.C. 20009

Mali, Embassy of the Republic of
2130 R Street, N.W.
Washington, D.C. 20008

Niger, Embassy of
2204 R Street, N.W.
Washington, D.C. 20008

Nigeria, Consulate General of
575 Lexington Avenue
New York, New York 10022

Nigeria, Embassy of
1333 16th Street, N.W.
Washington, D.C. 20036

Rwanda, Embassy of
1714 New Hampshire Avenue, N.W.
Washington, D.C. 20009

Senegal, Embassy of
2112 Wyoming Avenue, N.W.
Washington, D. C. 20008

Sierra Leone, Consulate General of
30 East 42nd Street
New York, New York 10017

Sierra Leone, Embassy of
1701 19th Street, N.W.
Washington, D.C. 20009

Somali, Embassy of the Republic of
1875 Connecticut Avenue, N.W.
Washington, D.C. 20009

South Africa, Consulate General of
655 Madison Avenue
New York, New York 10021

Sudan, Embassy of the
3421 Massachusetts Avenue, N.W.
Washington, D.C. 20007

Tanzania, Embassy of the Republic of
2721 Connecticut Avenue, N.W.
Washington, D.C. 20008

Togo, Embassy of
2208 Massachusetts Avenue, N.W.
Washington, D.C. 20008

Uganda, Embassy of
5909 16th Street, N.W.
Washington, D.C. 20011

Upper Volta, Embassy of the Republic of
5500 16th Street, N.W.
Washington, D.C. 20011

Zambia, Embassy of the Republic of
1875 Connecticut Avenue, N.W.
Washington, D.C. 20009

# AFRICAN
# MISSIONS TO THE U.N.

Botswana Mission to the U.N.
866 United Nations Plaza
New York, New York 10017

Cameroon Mission to the U.N.
866 United Nations Plaza
New York, New York 10017

Central African Republic Mission to the U.N.
386 Park Avenue S.
New York, New York 10016

Chad Mission to the U.N.
150 East 52nd Street
New York, New York 10022

Congo—Brazzaville Mission to the U.N.
444 Madison Avenue
New York, New York 10022

Congo—Kinshasa Mission to the U.N.
211 East 43rd Street
New York, New York 10017

Gabon Mission to the U.N.
866 United Nations Plaza
New York, New York 10017

Ghana Mission to the U.N.
144 East 44th Street
New York, New York 10017

Guinea Mission to the U.N.
295 Madison Avenue
New York, New York 10017

Ivory Coast Mission to the U.N.
46 East 74th Street
New York, New York 10021

Kenya Mission to the U.N.
866 United Nations Plaza
New York, New York 10017

Liberia Mission to the U.N.
235 East 42nd Street
New York, New York 10017

Malagasy Republic Mission to the U.N.
301 East 47th Street
New York, New York 10017

Malawi Mission to the U.N.
777 Third Avenue
New York, New York 10017

Mali Permanent Mission to the U.N.
111 East 69th Street
New York, New York 10021

Niger Mission to the U.N.
866 United Nations Plaza
New York, New York 10017

Nigeria Mission to the U.N.
757 Third Avenue
New York, New York 10017

Senegal Mission to the U.N.
46 East 66th Street
New York, New York 10021

Sierra Leone Mission to the U.N.
30 East 42nd Street
New York, New York 10017

Somalia Mission to the U.N.
236 East 46th Street
New York, New York 10017

South African Mission to the U.N.
300 East 42nd Street
New York, New York 10017

Sudan Mission to the U.N.
757 Third Avenue
New York, New York 10017

Tanzania Mission to the U.N.
205 East 42nd Street
New York, New York 10017

Togo Mission to the U.N.
801 Second Avenue
New York, New York 10017

Uganda Mission to the U.N.
801 Second Avenue
New York, New York 10017

Upper Volta Mission to the U.N.
236 East 46th Street
New York, New York 10017

Zambian Mission to the U.N.
641 Lexington Avenue
New York, New York 10022

## AFRICAN NATION INFORMATION SERVICES
## AND OTHER AGENCIES

Belgian Information Service
50 Rockefeller Plaza
New York, New York 10020

British Information Services
845 Third Avenue
New York, New York 10017

Ethiopian Airlines
51 East 42nd Street
New York, New York 10017

Ethiopian Trade Information Inc.
61 Broadway
New York, New York 10006

French Cultural Service
972 Fifth Avenue
New York, New York 10021

Ghana Information Service
565 Fifth Avenue
New York, New York 10017

Guinea Visa Office
295 Madison Avenue
New York, New York 10017

Ivory Coast Visa Office
521 Fifth Avenue
New York, New York 10017

Kenya Tourist Office
120 West 57th Street
New York, New York 10019

Nigeria Airways
565 Fifth Avenue
New York, New York 10017

Organization of African Unity
211 East 43rd Street
New York, New York 10017

Republic of South Africa Information Service
655 Madison Avenue
New York, New York 10021

Rhodesia National Tourist Board
535 Fifth Avenue
New York, New York 10017

South African Airways
3 East 48th Street
New York, New York 10017

South African Tourist Corporation
610 Fifth Avenue
New York, New York 10020

Zambia National Tourist Bureau
515 Madison Avenue
New York, New York 10022

# AMERICAN ORGANIZATIONS CONCERNED WITH
# AFRICA SOUTH OF THE SAHARA

Africa Department
Division of Overseas Ministries
National Council of the Churches of Christ in the
    U.S.A.
475 Riverside Drive
New York, New York 10027

African Affairs Society of America
160 Broadway
New York, New York 10038

African-American Labor Center
345 East 46th Street
New York, New York 10017

African Bibliographic Center
P.O. Box 13096
Washington, D.C. 20096

African Law Association in America
435 West 116th Street
New York, New York 10027

African Medical and Research Foundation
420 Madison Avenue
New York, New York 10017

African Student Service
11 Garden Street
Cambridge, Massachusetts

American Committee on Africa
164 Madison Avenue
New York, New York 10016

American Library Association
50 East Huron Street
Chicago, Illinois 60611

American Society of African Culture
101 Park Avenue
New York, New York 10017

Council of the African-American Institute
866 United Nations Plaza
New York, New York 10017

Operation Crossroads Africa, Inc.
150 Fifth Avenue
New York, New York 10011